HOT ZONE

HOT ZONE

Memoir of a Professional Firefighter

Christopher Teale Howes

Foreword by Cortez Lawrence

McFarland & Company, Inc., Publishers
Jefferson, North Carolina, and London

The author is donating a portion of royalties each year to the National Fallen Firefighters Foundation—firehero.org—the nonprofit group dedicated to the development and expansion of programs to honor our fallen fire heroes and assist their families and coworkers.

LIBRARY OF CONGRESS CATALOGUING-IN-PUBLICATION DATA

Howes, Christopher Teale.
   Hot zone : memoir of a professional firefighter /
Christopher Teale Howes ; foreword by Cortez Lawrence.
     p.   cm.
   Includes bibliographical references and index.

   ISBN 978-0-7864-6960-4
   softcover : acid free paper ∞

   1. Howes, Christopher Teale.   2. Fire fighters—United
States—Biography.   I. Title.
HD8039.F52U535 2012
363.37092—dc23
[B]   2012034900

BRITISH LIBRARY CATALOGUING DATA ARE AVAILABLE

On the cover: *inset* Chief Howes, formal photograph taken after
promotion to district chief (courtesy Palm Beach County Fire-
Rescue photo archive); *background image* cadre of fire officers
posing in front of a building that was used to train recruits.
Left to right: Bill Morris, Skip Moser, James Guyn, Mike Kemp,
Bruce Clark, Jim Gribble, Bruce Young, James Schaffner, John
Przybylek, Ron Beesley, Ron Lowe, Daryl Newport (courtesy
Craig Whitney); *title font* © 2012 Shutterstock

Manufactured in the United States of America

McFarland & Company, Inc., Publishers
  Box 611, Jefferson, North Carolina 28640
   www.mcfarlandpub.com

To the firefighters of Palm Beach County Fire-Rescue and to those who began their careers in the fire control districts, with a special dedication to the men and women who served with Del-Trail Fire Control District 9.—KFV-797

For Candy, who knew when it was time for me to furl the jib and reef the mainsail.

Table of Contents

Part III. Later Years: Chief Officer

Foreword by Cortez Lawrence

Chief Howes, Kit to his friends, has written a book about the fire service that captures in intimate detail what it means to work as a career firefighter. Through his memoir the reader is introduced to the hard realities, the humor, the sadness, and the emotional toll that is a firefighter's constant companion. He crafts an engaging work that will ring true with all of us who have been part of this brotherhood. He reminds us of those moments of euphoria when we have found the person trapped in a back bedroom and dragged him to safety or darkened down a fire that moments ago was rolling over our heads; and he brings clarity to those other, sadder times, when we find a victim in a late night fire that is too far gone to fight, or when our best medical interventions still leave us with a lifeless or dying patient. We feel the emotion when facing a family who has lost all their possessions and the unimaginable grief of those who have lost a loved one.

I met Kit in 1979 when I was hired by Del-Trail Fire Department. Unrest between labor and management because of a newly formed union made for an interesting work environment. And Kit, as union spokesman, was never afraid to speak his mind, which made the work environment even more interesting. I was hired as a captain and was immediately thrown into the midst of the asymmetrical warfare between Del-Trail's senior leadership and the firefighters. As a former chief and perhaps the department's most experienced operational officer, I tried to bridge the policy gaps promulgated by the chief and the board of commissioners with the implementation strategies executed by the firefighters. To the chagrin of both sides, I spoke the truth and wasn't afraid to tell folks what I knew. Today that would be called transparency. And while it did not bode well for my career prospects at Del-Trail, it did force a dialogue with the crews and even some collaboration. Ultimately, it helped build trust and the beginnings of a friendship with many of the firefighters, including Kit.

My Del-Trail career ended the following year, and I moved on to progressively more challenging jobs within the fire service, eventually joining the United States Fire Administration. Throughout those years I followed the growth and domestic disputes within Del-Trail until the merger of the Fire

1

Control Tax District departments into Palm Beach County Fire-Rescue. I followed the careers of many young firefighters as they became company officers, including some who attained the rank of chief officer. Kit's career was always one I followed, and we stayed loosely connected through those years with occasional emails, phone calls, and visits. I reconnected with Kit in a more substantive manner when he attended the National Fire Academy's Executive Fire Officer Program where I was an instructor for one of his classes. He hadn't lost a step — quick witted and still not afraid to speak his mind.

It seems our careers end too soon. When Kit announced he was retiring, I knew there would be a void within our profession. His professional demeanor and drive to always be the best fire officer possible forced me and many others to respect and admire him. I challenged him to continue contributing to the profession, thinking he might work as a fire chief for another department. What he did surprised even me: He wrote a book! When I sat down with it I realized he had written a memoir that would engage a broad audience, both civilian and firefighters, by telling the world about what we do, every day, in communities large and small. At the same time, he was also providing career insight to every young man or woman who chooses to take the oath, don the uniform and badge, and call themselves firefighter. So, on a differing path Kit has done exactly what I challenged him to do.

The firefighters in our communities, whether paid or volunteer, are our neighbors. This book is about those men and women. Although it is about one man's career as a professional firefighter, the experiences shared by Chief Howes ring true for the wider fire service community. *Hot Zone: Memoir of a Professional Firefighter* is required reading for anyone who ever wondered what it is like to leave a warm bed at three in the morning and, in the words of the author, "bring order out of chaos."

Cortez Lawrence, Ph.D., J.D., has been fire chief in LaGrange, Georgia, fire marshall for the U.S. Dept. of State, deputy director of public safety in Auburn, Alabama, national fire program director for the U.S. Fire Administration, and superintendent of the Emergency Management Institute.

Preface

This book examines the history of the fire service in Palm Beach County, Florida — specifically, the formation of Del-Trail Fire Department, one of twelve fire control districts that provided fire protection to the unincorporated areas of the county. It documents the training requirements of that era, the advent of emergency medical response, and the labor disputes that led to the first union, Local 2624 of the International Association of Fire Fighters. This book also examines the consolidation of the fire control districts to form Palm Beach County Fire-Rescue. It describes the procedures we follow when faced with fires and other types of emergencies and provides perspective on the unrelenting pace of change and the demand for excellence that is our constant. This history is told through the experiences I had during my career from rookie fireman to chief officer.

Much of the research about the early history of the district fire departments in Palm Beach County came from the tenth anniversary yearbook published by Palm Beach County Fire-Rescue. I am grateful to the yearbook staff; they spent countless hours recording oral histories and examining original fire department records, many now lost, of the different fire control districts and their contributions to emergency service. Without their efforts, much of this history would no longer be available.

Fire departments are considered semi-military in many respects, including rank structure. Palm Beach County Fire-Rescue personnel begin their careers as rookie firefighters or firefighter paramedics. They have the opportunity to move up in rank to driver engineer, then company officer, and then chief officer through competitive testing. To give the reader a sense of this progression, the book is divided into three parts, each covering a different phase of my career. The first section is a look back in time to when firefighting was a good-old-boy job, documenting my tenure as a firefighter and subsequent years as a driver engineer. The next section looks at life as a company officer, both lieutenant and captain, and the responsibilities that come with those ranks. The last section examines my later years as a district chief. At the beginning of each section is an essay that captures the experience of being first due on a job. These "On the Job" pieces are snapshots that provide a brief glimpse of the raw emotion that is an ever-present companion for those who do this work. I hope the reader comes away with a better understanding of the complexities, both emotional and technical, of the profession.

When I first joined the fire department my mother urged me to keep a journal; I didn't, and now wish I had. If some of the places and names are different than others recall, I apologize. The anecdotes are all true and as close to the real events and time frames as I can remember. The names are also real, with only a few exceptions.

Throughout the book the reader will notice I use the words "firefighter," "fireman," and "firemen" seemingly interchangeably. Purists would argue that a fireman is someone who works for the railroad. I have always used "fireman" or "firemen" in a familial sense; "firefighter" denotes the same meaning but in a more professional sense.

Firefighting is a technical business and, like many professions, has its own language. I write in the voice of the profession, and the jargon may seem confusing to the lay public. However, I make every effort to provide explanations throughout as needed. I have also provided a glossary for those who would like to know more.

Because the nature of this profession is constantly changing, some endnotes ask the reader to seek further information online. I was reluctant to resort to cite websites, but to provide the latest information on a particular subject, this is the surest way to keep pace with changes in protocol and the science of the profession. I have tried as much as possible to use websites that are part of government agencies or professional associations.

To firefighters who read this book: I hope you find it interesting and technically accurate.

Introduction

I could not have imagined how satisfying my fire service career would be when I joined Del-Trail Fire Department in 1976. It was an opportunity to participate in the shaping of a profession that has been transformed from a completely male-dominated job where the biggest criteria was a strong back to a highly skilled profession where critical thinking is essential for successful mitigation of the myriad problems faced by firefighters each day. The profession will always require strength. But now the ability to master, at a very high level, the many different disciplines is equally important. Firefighters are expected to learn and maintain proficiency in a bewildering array of technical subjects, including emergency medicine, hazardous material mitigation, building construction, all areas of technical rescue, and, of course, firefighting. Gone are the days of firemen sitting around drinking coffee while waiting for the alarm to sound. The men and women who now answer the call train for every eventuality and are among the most competent workforce in the world.

My purpose for writing this book is twofold: to share my own journey from rookie firefighter to chief officer and to dispel some of the erroneous notions people have about the fire service profession. There are many books and movies about firefighters—some are very good, but many tend to sensationalize the profession. There is no need for embellishment; the job can be sensational all on its own. This book is an unvarnished look at the fire service and what it means to be a firefighter. Thirty-one years on the job— and 112,000 calls department wide in my last year—has given me unique insight to this profession. I hope the reader comes away with a greater appreciation for what it takes to work as a professional firefighter.

There are many misconceptions about the fire service that I will try to answer. The question I field most often is why a fire engine shows up when someone is having a heart attack. Most fire departments have transitioned to a full-service concept, providing not only fire protection but also emergency medical service. This trend is moving toward everyone being cross-trained as paramedics, even those who ride the engine or the ladder. With the retirement of the old guard, that trend is now a fact in most fire departments, including Palm Beach County Fire-Rescue. So when a fire engine or a ladder truck responds to a medical emergency, the people walking up to the front door carrying all that medical equipment are highly trained firefighter paramedics doing their job, every day, with skill and compassion.

Firefighters face different challenges depending on where they work. Palm Beach County is a series of newer bedroom communities with the normal mix of light industrial facilities, mid- and some high-rise buildings, as well as significant areas of undeveloped land that contribute to large brush fires that continue to challenge firefighters. Crews responding to fires in cities and older communities face much different challenges than crews responding to house fires in the energy-efficient homes being built today. Fire behavior in new construction is far different than the fire behavior seen in older balloon construction, heavy timber, masonry, or protected steel frame.

The tactics we use in fire suppression are different as well. They are dictated by the time-temperature curve studies that reveal how quickly fire progresses from the incipient stage to a free burning stage in the tightly sealed boxes we call homes. This rapid progression contributes to a much earlier potential for flashover, an ugly phenomenon where all the combustible material within an enclosed space ignites at once; getting water on the fire as quickly as possible is the only way to win the battle. It also dictates search-and-rescue tactics. Many times, especially at house fires late at night, we employ a technique called Vent-Enter-Search. VES is rapid entry, usually through a bedroom window, where crews do a quick sweep of the room looking for victims. It's a fast, initial search by first-arriving companies that sometimes pays big dividends.

Firefighters spend one third of their lives living and working with their "other family." This book is about that other family — those who answer the alarm regardless of the time of day or night. This book also examines the changes I have witnessed during my tenure as a professional firefighter and how those changes have made the communities we live in safer. In the end, it is about the people and relationships that make the fire service such a unique calling.

There are thousands of fire departments across America, each with its own history. Although this book is about one fire department, the changing work environment we experienced mirrors what has happened in fire departments across the country.

There wasn't a day I didn't look forward to going to work. Very few people can make that claim about a career spanning three decades. My only wish is that the people doing the job now, and in the future, have the same passion for the profession that I have. I hope the reader gains a better understanding of the complexities, dangers, and emotional tolls that are constant companions for firefighters.

There are approximately one million firefighters in the American fire service, three-fourths of them volunteers. I want to thank those 750,000 men and women who volunteer their services each day; they do the same dangerous job, many times with fewer resources, but without pay. The men and women from rural communities across the country who answer the alarm are the backbone of the American fire service.

On the Job: Merry Christmas

Shift swaps are a way of life in the fire service. Working another firefighter's shift means five days off in a row or working a double, depending on which side of the swap you are on. It's great to get the time off, but payback is a bitch. We worked a three-platoon system: red, black, and green; the guys on red shift worked every holiday. The married guys with small children were always looking for a shift swap, especially around the holidays. I didn't mind helping a buddy, so when Dan asked me to work for him so he could spend Christmas Eve with his family, I said yes.

The people in Sandalfoot Cove didn't get the message about loving your fellow man at Christmas time. Station 3 was busier than usual with domestic fights, and I was happy the second half of my double shift would be at Station 5, a much slower station.

Station 5's crew had been out early, shopping for a holiday breakfast, and guys were busy cooking when I walked in. We were all looking forward to a big breakfast and a festive Christmas Eve meal with family members later in the day. After truck checks and breakfast, we set up tables in the bay to accommodate a crowd and settled in for a day of watching TV and napping, hoping we wouldn't turn a wheel.

I guess the people in Station 5's zone did get the message. We didn't run a call all day and sat down with family to a festive holiday meal at five in the afternoon. After a huge plate of turkey and sides, Lieutenant Weston, smiling and patting his stomach contentedly, announced, "Now I'm going to eat to eat." The five of us turned in early, snoring in unison in a bunkroom cold enough to hang meat.

The magic wore off around three in the morning, when we were paged for a trailer fire just down the street from the station. I climbed into the driver's seat of Engine 5, a Young Fire Truck with a 1000-GPM pump and a 500-gallon water tank. Lieutenant Weston knew the address without looking it up in the map book and directed me north on Military Trail to Cascade Trailer Park. The firefighter riding the jump seat was shrugging into his air-pack, and the two guys assigned to rescue followed us out of the bay into the cool December air. We turned off Military Trail into Cascade Park and could see the glow of the fire at the end of a dead-end street. There was a hydrant a couple of hundred feet from the address, so we dropped a line on the way in. Lieutenant Weston radioed Engine 8, second due out of Central Station, to make the connection.

This was not a typical trailer park. It was a refuge for snowbirds with well-groomed lawns and large backyards, mostly empty through the summer but full during our winter tourist season. I positioned the engine at the end of the driveway, put the pump in gear, and supplied the 150-foot pre-connect stretched by Weston and another firefighter.

Trailer fires are challenging to put out. In the early 1980s fire codes for mobile homes were not as stringent as the codes for residential frame construction. One consequence was a disproportionate number of fire-related injuries and deaths for trailer residents compared to people living in conventional housing. Lightweight framing materials, combustible wall and floor coverings, and inadequate means of egress all contributed to this problem. We had fought many trailer fires and knew that the chances of saving someone depended on very quick action.

The front of the trailer was heavily involved with fire, already venting from a window and starting to chew into the aluminum siding. The crew forced open the rear door that opened into the trailer's bedroom and took a line inside. They could see well enough with flashlights to do a proper search of the bedroom, closet, and a bathroom just down the narrow hallway. They found a dead poodle in the hallway, but no human occupant. They continued down the hall and started putting water on the fire.

I had made the connection for the supply line and Engine 8 was pumping to me. We had plenty of water to extinguish this fire and two more guys on scene to help. I continued to monitor the pump, lay out tools for the guys, and set up lighting. It seemed like we had a handle on this fire, and I was looking forward to getting off duty. Lieutenant Weston and his crew had extinguished the fire except for hot spots, and we were getting ready to overhaul. However, there was one piece missing from the puzzle. We had a dead dog and a car in the driveway, but no victim.

Weston and the rest of the crew were whipped, so he ordered me to put on an air-pack and put out hot spots and begin overhaul in the front room of the trailer. I was always happy to get on a hose line, even if it was only mopping up. Fighting fire was always something I missed from my days riding the jump seat on a fire engine. I geared up and entered through the rear door, following the hose line down the dark, smoky hallway until I found the nozzle.

The fire damage in the front room was typical: charred remains of furniture in a rectangular seating group; a fan drooping from the ceiling, its blades hanging straight down; a TV in the corner melted into the entertainment console like bad modern art; areas of the floor so weakened that I was in danger of falling through, now with most of the ceiling tiles adding to the debris on the floor. A thick haze of smoke accenting the different hues of black was slowly drifting out of the hole in the side of the trailer that used to be a picture window. I picked up the nozzle and started hitting hot spots. The room was small enough so that I didn't need to move around — water from the hose line could reach and penetrate wherever I aimed.

Most of the surreal scenes of my career happened just as the sun was coming up. I was squirting water on the still-smoldering remains inside the trailer when I found the victim we all knew was inside: I had been kneeling on her for the last 10 minutes. The light of day revealed a body charred enough to give a coroner pause. The skin on her face was mostly gone; her torso was burned so completely that I could see her ribs. She was on her back about 10 feet from the front door, one claw-like hand held up as if in supplication. I could see the depression in her pelvis where my knee had been. It was like a nightmare Escher painting with the body as the focal point, except the lines were all wrong. I shut down the hose line and stumbled out of the trailer to report my findings to the lieutenant.

I had been on the job for five years and had seen death in all of its ugly forms, including fire victims. It's something you come to expect, but it never gets any easier. I went home and took a long shower, trying to wash the smell from my body and the image from my mind. I was happy to join my girlfriend Candy and her family for Christmas, but it was a muted holiday celebration for me.

Firefighters are witnesses to events the public cannot even imagine. We see things that no one should ever have to see, all in the normal course of our employment. When Candy asked me why I was so quiet, it was difficult for me to adequately explain my feelings. I told her about the call but left out the details. It's hard to share those kinds of images with someone you love.

1—Betwixt and Between

The train sat rumbling like a monstrous ruminant dinosaur, one myopic lens peering anxiously into the foggy early morning light. The two engineers were middle-aged black men, blacker still due to the grease used to ply their trade. Unlit stubs of cigars, well chewed, were shoved into the corners of their mouths.

Every six weeks the engine would pull to a stop just south of Atlantic Avenue, and the crew would knock on the side door of Ken and Hazel's Restaurant in Delray Beach, Florida. Although it was an hour before opening, I was always happy to fix them breakfast. They were part of a work detail that traveled up and down the East Coast — they told me this restaurant was the only one close enough to the train tracks that they could stop the engine for 20 minutes and eat a hot meal.

I had moved from Arundel, Maine, in the spring of 1974 with my wife to work at the restaurant with her father and her grandparents, Ken and Hazel. Married just out of high school, and too young for that kind of commitment, our marriage was in trouble. Given the poor economy in Maine, we thought the move might help our marriage and our bottom line.

I had been bouncing from one job to another after graduating from Darrow School in 1970. With a lottery number of 50, I figured Viet Nam would be my next adventure, but a knee injury gained running wind sprints up a ski slope in my senior year of high school kept me out of the military. College would have been an easy deferment, but I swore I would never darken the doorway of another classroom. I had no idea what I wanted to do with my life.

Even though I knew nothing about the restaurant business, I was thankful for a steady job. I spent the first year learning the trade of a short-order cook, serving 150 breakfasts and almost as many lunches each day. Soon I was opening the restaurant, up at 4:30 to do prep work, light the ovens and grill, and get the fryer up to temperature. The two engineers weren't picky about what I fed them, as long as it was hot and fast. Usually six eggs over easy with toast was good enough. They would leave money on the counter and run for the engine before the next line of freight cars came through town.

My view of customers from the kitchen was through a small window in the door leading to the dining room, but I didn't have to look to know who was there; I knew my customers by what they ordered. The guy who delivered papers would come in at noon and order a garbage omelet, soft. He would solve the *New York Times* crossword puzzle, in ink, while he took a 20-minute lunch break. The woman from the bank next door would order salad, dressing on the side, and then eat a bowl of ice cream. The lady from Kings Point would order soup and slowly spoon ice from her water glass into the soup, then complain to the waitresses that it was cold.

Many of the local firefighters were regulars. Guys who worked for Delray Beach Fire Department would come in around eight in the morning and order hamburgers with fries if they had been up most of the night or eggs with hash browns if they had been lucky and slept through the night. My friend, Jay Little, who worked for Del-Trail Fire Department west of town was also a regular.

Jay and I would hang out on weekends, fishing for pompano or sailing his hobie-cat while at night we would shoot pool in local bars with friends. I was surprised one day to see Jay sitting at the counter drinking coffee at six in the morning, since we were both hung-over after a particularly creative late-night round of the local bars. I startled him enough that he spilled his coffee all over the counter when he saw me peering at him through the kitchen door window, two fried eggs slipped behind my round John Lennon glasses, yolk side out. I'm sure that for a moment he thought I was an alcohol-induced apparition.

After graduating from high school I spent several years trying out different jobs: house painting, vacuum cleaner sales, pounding nails, and even selling insurance. It was hard to meet the weekly sales quota when I spent the summer of 1973 with my buddy Jack McCullough playing the wickedly addictive card game, Spite and Malice, and watching the special prosecutor Archibald Cox preside over the Senate Watergate hearings. I know our wives weren't thrilled with this new pastime and neither was John Hancock. After several months of receiving a draw and not selling one policy, I was fired, forcing the decision to move to Florida.

I can't help wondering how different my story might be if I had not moved from Maine to Florida and become friends with Jay and other firefighters. They kept urging me to apply for a job at Delray Beach Fire Department or Del-Trail Fire Department; however, I was reluctant to give up a job with a steady income. Although I was up early six days a week, I was home by three in the afternoon. It was a schedule I enjoyed.

Firefighters work one day on and two off, and that schedule had more to do with my decision than anything else. After a bit of prodding, I applied for a job at Delray Beach Fire Department. It was a civil service process that didn't go well. They were hiring minorities, and although I got through the testing process and went on to an interview with the chief, I wasn't hired. Del-Trail was hiring part-time firefighters, so I applied and was hired there. This was fortuitous. Eight years later the State of Florida legislature mandated that Del-Trail merge with nine other tax-district departments to form Palm Beach County Fire-Rescue, now one of the largest departments in the southeast and among the most progressive in the country. The opportunities that came with working for Palm Beach County Fire-Rescue far surpassed anything that Delray Beach Fire Department could offer its employees.

I continued to work at the restaurant for the next year, squeezing in two 12-hour shifts at the fire department each week—one during the day, the other at night. Del-Trail was a combination department that relied on a cadre of volunteers as well as paid personnel. Then, as now, there was a pecking order that depended on seniority. As a new hire I cleaned bathrooms, washed dishes and trucks, swept the bay floor, mowed grass, and did anything else those more senior to me could think of.

I received some basic fire training from the full-time guys, first learning to drive and pump Brush 23, a four-wheel-drive 1974 Ford F250 that had been converted to a brush truck. It had a 300-gallon water tank and a PTO pump drive that allowed us to pump and roll on brush fires. With its beefed-up suspension to carry the extra weight of a ton and a half of water and oversized tires to carry it through the sugar sand, it was a great off-road vehicle. The one thing it didn't have was power steering; it required two hands on the wheel at all times or you were in danger of breaking a wrist. I was also trained to operate a 6 × 6 GI troop transport truck that had been converted to a brush truck. In the 1970s fire apparatus manufacturers were not building brush trucks; it was common practice for fire departments to build their own trucks and was an inexpensive way to add to the fleet.

Soon after I was hired, the department purchased another military transport 6 × 6 through Civil Defense. It was circa 1950s or even older, and in very rough shape. Mr. Mutt was the fire department mechanic, a man born to bib overalls and smelly cigars. He took the lead in converting that rusted-out troop transport vehicle into a monster of a brush truck, and after several weeks of work I was amazed at the transformation. Mr. Mutt, Chief Frye, Captain Schnabel and Larry Manley worked on the truck whenever they had a spare moment, stripping it down to the frame, grinding scabs of rust off the cab, and patching holes with bondo. They manufactured a 1000-gallon water tank out of aluminum diamond plate, sealing the inside with waterproof paint and painting the outside silver. A 500-GPM Hale pump and 200 feet of one-inch booster hose were mounted behind the cab. It was also plumbed for inch-and-a-half hose and a short length of booster line in the front. Purchasing 10 new off-road tires for the truck was one of the largest expenses; the original tires had decent tread, but the rubber was dry rotted. Lastly, the truck was painted and lettered. It took two months and several thousand dollars to convert a rusting hulk to a brush truck that was the envy of our neighboring departments.

Even though the truck had a cage on the front bumper to ride in, we would walk if Captain Schnabel was driving. He thought we could be more effective with our fire stream if we were closer to the flames. Whoever was on the line would get bumped if Schnabel thought you weren't moving fast enough. It takes a long time to pump 1000 gallons of water through a 10-foot, three-quarter-inch lead line. We prayed for that truck to run out of water. Fighting brush fires in the summer heat and humidity of South Florida quickly revealed a person's work ethic. Even though I wasn't allowed to do much beyond fighting brush fires, and had little understanding of fire science, I was beginning to enjoy the idea of being a firefighter, even while walking a fire line with Captain Schnabel driving.

Working the night shift meant sitting in the watch room answering the phone and dispatching crews to various calls. The enhanced 911 system we now take for granted would not be available in Palm Beach County until 1981,[1] so it was up to a rookie who didn't know anything about firefighting to field calls from some mighty excited people.

"Del-Trail Fire Department, what is your emergency?"

"My house is on fire!"

"Where do you live, ma'am?"

"Country Club Acres!"

"Ma'am, I need the street address."

"Hurry, my house is on fire!"

"Ma'am, I need your street address."

At this point one of the senior firefighters or the station officer would be listening to this one-sided conversation. Once they knew the development, the guys would gear up and get on Engine 8, a 1974 Ward LaFrance, and Engine 10, a 1960s-era Ford with a front-mount pump. It would be up to me to get the proper address and notify the responding crews by radio.

My job was to keep a written log of all radio transmissions from the responding crews, each time signing off with our call sign, KFV-797. It was also my job to start calling in volunteers in case we had another call. Sitting at the watch desk waiting for help to arrive, Central Station was a lonely place. I prayed the phone wouldn't ring and I wouldn't have to ask once again, "Del-Trail Fire Department, what is your emergency?"

2 — Then and Now

The early history of fire protection in rural Palm Beach County mirrors volunteer efforts throughout the United States. Concerned citizens, recognizing the need for fire protection, raised money to buy or build fire trucks and recruited volunteers to respond when the need arose. It was neighbor helping neighbor. That hasn't changed in many areas of the country; however, Palm Beach County was growing rapidly, and the fire service was forced to keep pace with that growth.

In the 1950s the western areas of Palm Beach County were comprised of large tracts of farm land supporting dairy and beef operations and huge vegetable farms. There was limited need for fire protection, and when the need did occur, cities along the eastern corridor of Palm Beach County (including the city of Delray Beach), provided fire protection for their neighbors to the west.

It's not clear what precipitated a change in policy, but Delray Beach became reluctant to provide fire protection to areas outside the city limits and eventually refused to respond to fires outside their jurisdiction. This was the catalyst for local business owners, farmers, and ranchers to start their own fire department. In 1957 they purchased a fire truck from the city of Delray Beach for one dollar and named the department Del-Trail, the name giving a nod to their eastern brethren and Military Trail, the east/west boundary between the city and the unincorporated area of the county.

The 1943 Dodge truck was housed on the northwest corner of Military Trail and Atlantic Avenue in an old mule barn owned by Rudy Blank. A siren mounted on a telephone pole outside the barn alerted local volunteers whenever there was a call. Norman Conklin, a Delray Beach police officer who lived just down the road on Conklin Drive, was elected fire chief. And so began Del-Trail Fire Department.[1]

Although the siren was effective at notifying volunteers, they hadn't figured out one of the most basic necessities of an emergency response system: an efficient means for the public to notify the fire department in the event of an emergency. The phone line to contact the fire department was manned sporadically at best, so the truck was soon moved to the southwest corner of

Atlantic Avenue and Military Trail to a Gulf Station owned by Everett Frye. During normal business hours the employees at the gas station answered the phone for fire calls. At night calls were routed to Chief Conklin's home.

In 1958 a second truck was purchased from a rural department in upstate New York. Eddie Schnabel, one of the early volunteers, drove the open cab military truck back to Florida. I can only imagine what kind of road trip that must have been. That truck was stationed at Eddie's house on Flavor Pic Road. With two trucks stationed miles apart, it was an ad-hoc system at best but sufficient for the community's needs.

As the population grew the number of fire calls also increased, and it became evident that a permanent station was needed. In 1962 Del-Trail's first station was built on Conklin Drive, north of Atlantic Avenue on the west side of Military Trail. Fire apparatus consisted of a 1953 Dodge Power Wagon and the two original trucks.

Although the infrastructure was in place, it takes money to run a fire department. Funding through donations was no longer an option. In November 1963, the Florida State Legislature passed House Bill 1293, enabling the Palm Beach County Commission to establish fire control districts. With the ability to levy taxes specifically for fire protection, a total of 12 independent fire control districts were established, all mostly staffed by volunteers with paid personnel working in key positions (see Appendix A).[2]

In 1964 the legislature appointed three fire commissioners — Leo Blair, Dick McMurray, and Joe Santee — to oversee Del-Trail Fire Department's first budget of $30,000. Paid staff consisted of Fire Chief Norman Conklin, Lieutenant Frye, and Fire Inspector Al Ulrich. The remaining staff members were volunteer firemen who were paid $50 a month. This same process was occurring at the other fire control districts within the county.

In the late 1960s the Town of Highland Beach contracted with Del-Trail Fire Department for fire protection. At this point there were enough full-time personnel to staff Highland Beach Station 2 as well as Station 1, known as Central Station. Personnel were working 24 hours on and 48 hours off and were expected to be available for calls the first 24 hours after going off duty.

The area was still mostly rural, and with personnel responding to brush fires more than structure fires, there was a need for more brush trucks. Civil Defense donated three 1952 GMC troop transports. These trucks were commonly referred to as 6 × 6s, and with tandem rear axles, they were very effective at driving off road through sugar sand and palmetto scrub, controlling brush fires that would routinely consume hundreds of acres. Del-Trail firemen provided the labor to install 1000-gallon water tanks and skid-mounted 500-GPM pumps, converting the vehicles to brush trucks.

By the early 1970s the population had increased dramatically, and plans

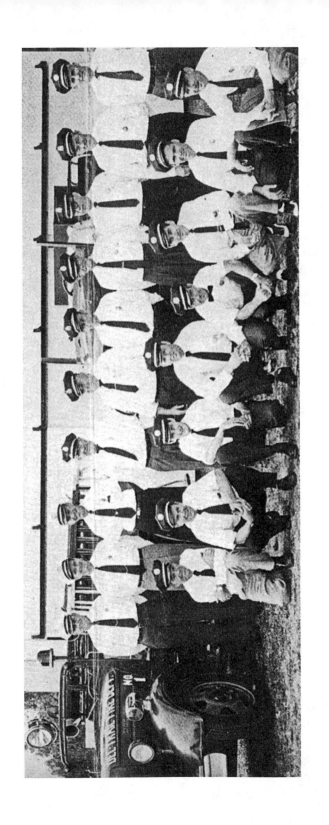

Though names are no longer available, these men were the original members of Del-Trail Fire Department (courtesy Palm Beach County Fire-Rescue photo archive).

were under way to build a station in Sandalfoot Cove, the southwestern area of Del-Trail's response zone. A mobile home was purchased as a temporary station, and it was staffed with one man and Brush 23. The permanent Station 3 was completed in early 1976, housing an engine, a rescue, and a brush truck, and staffed by five men.

Also in the early 1970s, Florida recognized the need for minimum training standards for all firefighters, including volunteers. That standard required firefighters to complete a minimum of 200 hours of training, adequate at the time but rudimentary by today's standards. Now, Florida firefighters are required to complete 398 hours of training.[3]

By now the number of structure fire responses was increasing, and the department purchased two Class A triple-combination pumpers: Engine 8, a 1974 Ward LaFrance with a 750-gallon water tank and a 1250-GPM pump, and Engine 9, a 1974 American LaFrance with a 1000-gallon water tank and 1000-GPM pump. Engine 8 was housed at Central Station and Engine 9 in Highland Beach at Station 2. These were top-of-the-line fire apparatus.

In the 1970s there was a nationwide trend toward delivery of emergency medical service. In 1975 Del-Trail purchased a used Ford Econoline van as their first rescue truck. Again, firemen provided the labor, among them Ed Hines, Terry McGowan, and Mr. Mutt. They installed cabinets and made other conversions necessary to outfit the truck with advanced life-support equipment. This was the first truck staffed with paramedics. Ambulance services, most operating from local funeral homes, would then transport the patient to the hospital. The van was soon replaced with a Ford E250 modular truck.

Fire department delivery of early paramedic service was uncharted territory. It was individual initiative on the part of firefighters seeking more advanced medical training that ushered in advanced life support in Palm Beach County. Ed Hines, Terry McGowan, Jimmy Judge, and Jim Sweat were some of the first trained by Dr. Charlie Ackes, an ER physician at Boca Raton Community Hospital. He helped train the first paramedics in the county and developed the first medical protocols that the paramedics worked under. In 1979 the State of Florida Human Resources Services took over advanced life-support training, and Del-Trail hired its first medical directors, Dr. Richard Vollrath and Dr. Fred Swartz, both general surgeons.[4]

It's interesting to note that Ed Hines was one of the first firemen from Del-Trail to be trained as a paramedic, even spending his own money to buy some of the early equipment. Despite his dedication, Ed would be treated poorly by Chief Frye after Ed's election as president of Local 2624.

It was during this period that I became a part-time paid firefighter for Del-Trail Fire Department. Although Norman Conklin was the fire chief, it was in name only; I never met the man. He lived in Okeechobee and picked up his paychecks at the post office. Everett Frye was acting chief and replaced Conklin shortly after I was hired.

Another fire station was built in 1979. Station 4 was located in an area west of Boca Raton known as Boca Del Mar. It was the first station in the county with a fire pole, and although the pole provided direct access from the upstairs bunkroom to the apparatus bay, it was rarely utilized. Sleepy firemen, rolling out of their bunks in the middle of the night, were apt to turn an ankle at the end of the 20-foot slide, so most elected to take the stairs. That station was staffed with seven people operating an engine, a 100-foot aerial platform, a brush truck, and a rescue truck.

By this time there was uncontrolled growth in the western areas of the county, and Del-Trail was making plans to build Station 5 west of Boynton Beach. That station was completed in 1982, with five people staffing an engine, a rescue, and a brush truck.

The old Central Station was now wholly inadequate as a headquarters station, so architects were busy once again. The new Central Station was located on Hagen Ranch Road, several miles west of Military Trail and a mile north of Atlantic Avenue. We always joked that this station was Frye's monument to himself, but in reality we could no longer function efficiently without it. That station was completed in 1983, just prior to consolidation.

The new Central Station had four drive-through bays and crew quarters for 15 people. It housed an engine, a ladder, two rescue trucks, and a brush truck. On the opposite side of the bays was office space for administration, including the Training Division, the Fire Prevention Bureau, and the Rescue Division. Also on the grounds was a maintenance facility to service all of the fire apparatus. The old Central Station was sold to Tire Kingdom, an inglorious end for a fire station that was part of the early fire service history in Palm Beach County.

The last station Del-Trail planned to build prior to consolidation was Station 6, west of Boca Raton. Consolidation of the fire control districts occurred before the station was built, but construction was completed shortly thereafter. This station is located five miles south of Atlantic Avenue on State Road 441 and houses an engine, a rescue, and a brush truck. The initial staff consisted of five personnel.

In 1984 the Florida State Legislature once again acted in the public interest, dissolving the tax districts. This forced the merger of the remaining 10 fire control districts into Palm Beach County Fire-Rescue. Included in this merger was the Department of Airports, which provides fire and rescue protection for Palm Beach International Airport.

Palm Beach County Ordinance #83–23 finalized this process, allowing the consolidation to go forward. At the same time, Florida Statute Chapter

Patches are important historical symbols for fire departments. These are the patches for the 12 original fire control districts, plus the new Palm Beach County Fire-Rescue patch (courtesy Palm Beach County Fire-Rescue photo archive).

125.01 created a new funding mechanism known as a Municipal Service Taxing Unit (MSTU). These MSTUs were divided into four geographical areas. Some people were happy, and some angry, depending on whether their taxes for fire protection went up or down with the advent of the MSTUs. The passage of this new funding mechanism effectively circumvented the public's ability to vote on the measure.[5]

Rumors of consolidation had been circulating among the districts since 1979, the same period when Del-Trail firemen were forming a union. Unrest between Chief Frye and the men was documented in the papers on a regular basis, and the county commissioners were not happy with the labor management unrest.

County Commissioner Norman Gregory first broached the idea of consolidation to the Palm Beach County Commission during budget hearings in late 1979. In an inter-office communication dated November 14, 1979, Palm Beach County Commissioner Dennis Koehler wrote to Commissioner Norman Gregory expressing his appreciation for Gregory's suggestion of consolidation as a way out of the Del-Trail crisis and as a means to fund the fire districts equitably (see Appendix B). In 1979 there was a huge disparity in the level of service among the fire districts. Del-Trail was the wealthiest district and, as a result, provided better fire and paramedic service to the residents; however, pay and benefits were still far below those of city departments. This, and Frye's unwillingness to recognize the union and bargain in good faith, caused tremendous bitterness within the ranks. I'm sure this served as part of the catalyst for the Palm Beach County Commission to begin talks that would lead to consolidation of the fire control districts.

In 1984 there was a much different political climate at Del-Trail. We were in the second year of our second contract and were making as much money as, if not more than, other area fire departments. We were also getting ready to phase in Blue Cross Blue Shield medical coverage for members and their families, a benefit that would have been paid at 100 percent by Del-Trail. The other fire control districts welcomed the consolidation initiative, but Del-Trail was the big kid on the block with better pay and benefits, as well as better staffing and equipment. We felt it would be a step back for us, and it was, but only for a short while.

Del-Trail firemen weren't the only ones opposed to consolidation. The people we served were adamantly opposed to the idea, mainly because of the

Station 4's crew expresses their sentiments about consolidation of the district fire departments. Shown left to right: Skip Moser, unidentified fireman, John Tiersch, Mark Anderson (courtesy Ed DeVries).

way the MSTU funding was structured and the impact it would have on their taxes. A public forum on the issue of consolidation was held at the courthouse in West Palm Beach on February 1, 1983. Six hundred South County residents were present to oppose the measure, citing concern that the level of service would go down and their taxes would go up. They were supported by off-duty firemen from Del-Trail.[6]

This was a valid concern. The legislative task force guiding the consolidation initiative finally agreed to additional safeguards that would address these concerns. Their recommendation to the Florida State Legislature included a 3-mill cap, down from 10 mills, on taxes. Additionally, tax money collected within each MSTU could only be spent within that taxing district. This change in language gained support for consolidation from many influential people in the South County area.[7]

Just prior to consolidation, Del-Trail Fire Department employed 136 people with a budget of $7.2 million. At the beginning of consolidation in October 1984, with the incorporation of the other fire control districts and the Department of Airports, Palm Beach County Fire-Rescue employed 458 people with a budget of $19.9 million. The newly formed department served a population of 295,000 people living in a service area of 538 square miles. The department operated out of 23 fire stations, providing fire protection, emergency medical response, hazardous material mitigation, public education, and fire prevention service to half the population of Palm Beach County.[8]

As of 2010, Palm Beach County Fire-Rescue has grown to 1500 personnel operating out of 49 fire stations with a service area that covers 75 percent of Palm Beach County. The annual budget in 2010 was $325 million. Expansion of the service area continues to occur, with smaller communities merging into Palm Beach County Fire-Rescue's system. The ultimate goal is a regional fire rescue delivery system within Palm Beach County, something that larger cities continue to oppose. County-wide consolidation of the emergency 911 system is already in place, with a push to have the closest unit respond to an emergency, regardless of jurisdiction.[9]

The days of parochial thinking with regard to fire department jurisdiction should be something from another era. Unfortunately, there continues to be resistance to a regional fire department. As a firefighter, I understand why. The cities along the coast— Boca Raton, Delray Beach, Boynton Beach, West Palm Beach, and Riviera Beach — have a long, proud fire service history and they don't want to lose their autonomy. However, the citizens who pay taxes for emergency services would be better served by a regional fire department. Economy of scale is a valid theory when the cost of fire department service is examined. When I first became a firefighter, the cities were the big kids on the block. They used to call us "stump jumpers," because all we did was put out brush fires. Now, if you fly down the coast at night, Palm Beach County is a sea of lights from north to south and west to the Everglades, with a population approaching one and a half million people. It may be a series of different communities, but in reality it is one large metropolitan area.

There is an old saying in the fire service about 150 years of tradition unimpeded by progress. It's time to amend that saying and put the citizens' best interests above tradition. Del-Trail firemen didn't want to give up their history and tradition, but approaching 30 years of new traditions with Palm Beach County Fire-Rescue, the citizens within our response zones are safer and have a more cost-effective fire department that is among the best in the nation. It is now time for a regional fire-rescue delivery system

One of the biggest accomplishments that Palm Beach County Fire-Rescue achieved is accreditation through the Commission on Fire Accreditation International, Inc. This status was attained August 10, 2005, after a rigorous multi-year review process. Becoming accredited through CFAI forces continual self-assessment by asking three questions: Is the organization effective? Are the goals, objectives, and mission of the department being achieved? What are the reasons for the success of the organization? Accreditation usually takes three to five years and is not guaranteed. Palm Beach County Fire Rescue is one of only 114 departments worldwide to have achieved this status, and to retain accreditation it must continue to meet self-assessment goals that are reviewed by CFAI.[10]

The year 1984 was one of change and tremendous turmoil. Imagine 10 separate departments, each with a fire chief with his own idea about how things should be done — thinking their way is the best way to serve the citizens of Palm Beach County. These were only a few of the leadership and management challenges facing the new fire-rescue administrator, Herman Brice. Chief Brice had recently retired as chief of department with 31 years of experience in the fire service. With a participatory management style, he was the perfect fit to lead 10 disparate fire departments with 10 different corporate cultures into becoming what is now one of the most progressive departments in the country.

Part of the deal going into consolidation was that no one would lose their job, but finding the right jobs for 10 fire chiefs was not an easy task. Each chief had enjoyed total autonomy in his old department; now they were being asked to take on a lesser leadership role. Many did not have the people skills to cope in this new and threatening environment and were eventually placed in slots where their lack of interpersonal skills would not impede the growth of a new culture. Others did well and became the new leaders within the department. And through their mentoring, the firefighters and lieutenants of 1984 are now the leaders of Palm Beach County Fire-Rescue in 2010.

The first five years for Palm Beach County Fire-Rescue were tremendously challenging. There was parochial infighting between men and women from the old district departments, but eventually there was a slow transition from the us-against-them mentality that eventually led to a grudging respect for how others could do the job. Large egos gave way to a spirit of cooperation, sometimes even outright cooperation. Experts in interpersonal dynamics were brought in for in-house training of all personnel, and company officers received training in management and leadership with an emphasis on understanding small group dynamics. These training sessions were helpful, but time and working together saving lives was the ultimate healer. In the end, we respected each other as firefighters.

The name Herman Brice is instantly recognized within the international fire service community. He

Fire-Rescue administrator Herman Brice, with 56 years in the fire service, came to work each day with a smile on his face and the energy of someone half his age. Enjoy your retirement, Chief! (courtesy Palm Beach County Fire-Rescue photo archive).

served as chairman of the board of the National Fire Protection Association and as president for both the Florida Fire Chief Association and the International Fire Chief Association. He was Palm Beach County Fire-Rescue's fire chief for 25 years, a leader in every respect, and his comments about the consolidation process capture the essence of what it means to serve a community as a firefighter: "I remember the early years as a time of great accomplishment. Reflecting back, I realize, with all our differences, these accomplishments were possible because there was a silent but common bond among us—we were people who had a calling to serve our community, and we had the skill and knowledge to aid persons in time of an emergency. We were proud to be part of the fire service and we had the notion that things should and could be better."[11]

3—Early Training: Fire and EMT School

Chief Everett Frye's outlook on life wasn't too far removed from that of a plantation owner of an earlier generation. He expected us to work hard, without complaint, from seven in the morning until five in the evening. If running calls interrupted a work detail, we would have to finish the work even if it meant working beyond the normal quitting time. I was hired full time by Del-Trail Fire Department in November 1976, and was beginning to wonder if quitting the restaurant was a good idea.

Soon after being hired, I attended South Technical Center in Boynton Beach, Florida, to begin learning the science of fighting fire. It was a small class of around 20 newly hired guys from city departments and other tax district departments, including several of us from Del-Trail. It was almost like boot camp in the military, very regimented, with physical training each morning and instructors who loved to yell at us.

Five days a week we reported to class, studying fire behavior, hydraulics, ropes and knots, ladders, self-contained breathing apparatus (SCBA), ventilation and the minutiae in between that tie the science of fighting fire together. I learned how heat is transferred through conduction, convection, radiation and direct flame contact. I learned about the fire triangle — that it takes heat, oxygen, and fuel to create and sustain fire, and if you take away any one of those components, the fire will go out. And I learned a great deal about my own character. I soon began to realize that this was the beginning of a profession that I could embrace.

We studied ropes and knots until we could do it blindfolded, tying bowlines, clove hitches, becket bends, half-hitches, sheep shanks, figure eights, and what we termed the rescue knot (two loops for the legs and a quick wrap around the chest). The instructors reminded us that a rope and the right knot could be a lifeline out of a burning building. We believed them, and I can tie those knots even now.

We learned about fire pumps and hydraulics, the science of moving water through hoses, nozzles, and appliances. We rolled and unrolled hose; practiced advancing hose lines into buildings, up stairways, and up ladders; and learned what seemed like a bewildering array of ways to pack hose in the bed of a fire truck: accordion loads, horseshoe loads, flat loads, and skid loads. We also learned how to check each length of hose for gaskets. After spending a half hour or more loading 1500 feet of hose into the bed of a fire truck, and then being quizzed by an instructor about a missing gasket he would be twirling on his finger, we learned to check for gaskets. It only took us a few times of loading hose and admiring our work, only to have to pull it all off, uncouple it, look for a gasket that might or might not be missing, and once again line up the couplings, using the higbee cut as an indicator that the coupling was lined up correctly, to learn it was the little things in this business that make a difference. We quickly learned to pay attention to the smallest details, a habit that has seen many a firefighter through a dangerous situation. And the instructors were quick to reinforce a lesson by rapping on our helmets with a spanner wrench, their subtle way of telling us to pay attention.

We learned how to handle different types of ladders and the importance of teamwork when handling some of the bigger ladders. We studied the nomenclature associated with ladders: dogs, rails, rungs, tip, heel, bed, fly, halyard, rope, and pulley. We practiced different techniques for ventilating a building to remove heat and smoke. As part of this training, we were introduced to chainsaws and the K12 circular saw. We used chainsaws to open up roofs, first learning how to sound a roof with an axe so we didn't cut through rafters before using the saw to remove roof decking. We used the K12 saw to cut through metal roof decking or to gain access through the side of a metal-clad building.

We all had fun rappelling, though it took a bit of a nudge the first time. In 1976 we were using hemp rope and ladder belts, equipment that belongs in a museum now. We would climb the stairs in the training tower to the fourth floor, run the rope through the hook on the ladder belt, verify that a safety man was holding the end of the rope that trailed to the ground, and ease ourselves out the window. My first experience of rappelling was a leap of faith. I remember the instructor had to almost kick me out the window, but after my first descent I didn't want the training to end. We begged the instructors to let us rappel whenever there was a free moment.

And we learned how to use a Scott air-pack. In fact, we lived in air-packs whenever we were performing hands-on skills. Wearing an air-pack can be a debilitating experience. The Scott pack weighed close to 40 pounds, and the straps didn't have any padding. Our shoulders were raw after weeks of wearing the damn thing. Beyond wearing the packs for routine training such as ladder and hose work, we spent long hours in wet gear crawling through mazes inside the tower, learning how to use them for their intended

Author rappelling off Platform 55 using hemp rope and a ladder belt, the same equipment used during the initial fire training. This picture was taken in the mid–1980s. We had been lobbying for better equipment, and the department purchased rope and hardware that was designed for rappelling soon after this picture was taken (courtesy Lee Tenney).

purpose: safely operating in a hazardous environment. The instructors would stoke a barrel full of hay until smoke filled the bottom two levels of the tower, and then we would be required to find our way through the maze without running out of air.

The maze consisted of plywood partitions that formed a narrow tunnel, complete with roof. There were dead-end corridors; areas of the roof that sloped down until you had to remove your air-pack to wriggle through; debris, including old bed springs that snagged equipment and hands and feet; and the constant din of instructors pounding on the partitions while yelling, "Hurry up! You're gonna die!" I never had much trouble with this, but some guys decided that being a fireman wasn't a good career choice, and they quit. After several days of this training my skin and hair was permeated with smoke. It took weeks to get rid of the smell and almost as long to stop picking black snot out of my nose.

We had done a lot of training with various kinds of ladders and we all felt pretty cocky about our abilities, until we were introduced to the church raise. Everyone was nervous about this stage, and the instructors were good at heightening the anticipation. We knew if we failed to complete this part of the ladder training, we would not pass the class. The church raise involved hoisting a Bangor Ladder (a huge 50-foot, three-section ladder with stabilizing poles) to a vertical position in the middle of a parking lot. Four ropes tied at the top of the ladder, held taut by four men on the ground, stabilized the ladder. Two more men held the stabilizing poles. One at a time, we were required to climb the ladder all the way up, swing over the top and then climb down the other side. The purpose behind this stunt is to give firefighter trainees confidence in their equipment and in their buddies holding the ropes. That theory was lost on me; it scared me witless. Peer pressure, and the thought of failing the class, got all of us up and over.[1]

After that ordeal it was easy to scale the side of the training tower with a Pompier Ladder. That ladder is nothing more than a 10-foot aluminum pole with a hook at the top and tiny rungs welded to the pole at two-foot intervals. We would place the hook over the sill of a window and then climb to the window, hook a leg over the sill and then pull the ladder up and repeat the process until we were at the top of the four-story tower. We didn't carry Bangor or Pompier ladders on our trucks, and I never climbed one after leaving the fire academy.[2]

While at the academy, we knew we were becoming members of a brotherhood. Daryl Newport and Tom Phillips worked for different tax district departments. Although we didn't know it then, we would all be working for Palm Beach County Fire-Rescue in eight years, and the friendships formed during that early training would last throughout our careers. We would all go to lunch together and then play flag football for 20 minutes before returning to school. I usually lined up across from Tom. He had me by six inches and 50 pounds, and it only took me one block to figure out I had better take him low. It was a rough game, and we had more bruises from football than from physical training or humping hose.

At the end of the five weeks we took a written and hands-on test administered by the State of Florida Fire Academy. We were all nervous because we didn't know what to expect from the state instructors. We knew they would be tough on us, but our instructors had trained us well. After a grueling day, both mentally and physically, we all passed and were certified as Florida State Firefighters. That was one of the proudest days of my fire service career.

This was only the beginning of thousands of hours of technical training that I would receive during my fire service career. Now firefighters receive a minimum of 398 hours before becoming a state-certified firefighter. People on the job now are amazed at the rudimentary training we received. Although it seemed the learning would never end, I soon came to realize that when you stop learning in this business, you become a liability rather than an asset, something I would preach to my crews when I became a company officer and later as a chief officer.

Then, as now, becoming certified as a firefighter only gives you license to ride to the fire; it doesn't give you the skills necessary to stay alive on the fire ground. Mentoring and experience gained from observing fire behavior over many years, coupled with ongoing training, is what produces a competent firefighter. That, and the camaraderie you find in every fire house in the world, is why this is such a unique calling. It's why we greet other firefighters as "Brother" or "Sister."

After becoming a certified firefighter, I attended emergency medical technician school, again at South Technical Institute, now Palm Beach State College. The fire service in Florida was just beginning to provide emergency medical response, and after 16 weeks of medical training I was certified as an EMT and assigned to ride on one of the first advanced life-support rescue trucks operating in South Florida.

I will always remember responding to a medical call around three in the morning on January 17, 1977. When I opened the bay door the apron in front of the station was covered with an inch of snow. My partner on the rescue truck had never seen snow and thought I was crazy as I did slow, four-wheel drifts around the corners on the way to our call. I assured him that I knew what I was doing, having spent more than a few winters doing the same while living in Maine.

Even now, many departments rely on private companies to provide paramedic service. Del-Trail and several other departments in the area were beginning to offer paramedic service in the mid–1970s. Now a fire department isn't considered full service unless they cross-train their firefighters as paramedics.

On my days off I worked for AA Ambulance Company, one of the largest providers of ambulance service in Palm Beach County, where I received further on-the-job training by observing post mortems at the local hospital. The pathologist would call us whenever he was conducting an autopsy, first just to watch, but eventually he let us assist. We had learned a lot about the human anatomy during EMT school, but nothing could replace the experience we gained from actually putting our hands inside the human body. I learned about the Y incision that exposes the internal organs, allowing the pathologist to remove each organ for weighing and further examination. I can still hear the high-pitched whine of the Stryker saw and smell the burnt odor caused by the saw as the pathologist cut through the skull to expose the brain.

Tom Croft was the owner of AA Ambulance and there will never be another like him. He was bottom-line driven and had no tolerance for EMTs or paramedics who thought they could play doctor on the way to the hospital. He wanted us to drive the ambulance to the call, pick up the patient, deliver the patient to the hospital as quickly as possible, and then be ready to do it all again. His profit margin was directly related to the number of patients transported, and I can still hear his raspy voice calling us on the radio: "52, you've got a call holding. Don't let any grass grow under your wheels."

I was working for AA in the winter of 1979, transporting a patient in respiratory arrest to Bethesda Memorial Hospital in Boynton Beach. A medic from Delray Beach Fire was in the back along with my partner. Despite Tom's mandate that we not play doctor, the medic and my partner were doing their best to keep this patient alive.

It was an early Sunday morning, and I was driving north on Federal Highway in Delray Beach. I braked to a full stop at Atlantic Avenue and looked to verify that traffic had stopped before proceeding through the intersection against a red light. However, people were impatient, and a car drove around a truck that had stopped for me, striking the front bumper of the ambulance. The bumper absorbed the hit pretty well, but the guys in the back didn't fare so well. My partner had been bagging the patient through an EOA tube. After the collision, he was straddling the engine mount looking at me, with the ambu-bag and EOA in his hand. The EOA (esophageal obturator airway) is an airway adjunct device placed in the patient's esophagus. It's basically a large plastic tube with holes in it with an inflatable cuff at the end of the tube. When the cuff is inflated, air forced down the tube is rerouted into the trachea and then into the lungs. The cuff is supposed to be deflated before extubating. I don't suppose the patient minded too much because he was almost dead, but the docs frowned on us violating that protocol. The efficacy of the EOA was always in question, and medical protocols soon changed, allowing medics to intubate with an endotrachial tube.[3] In addition, the IV the medic had started was ripped out of the patient's arm, and the floor of the ambulance was littered with medical equipment and blood. It took about 30 seconds to see that the occupant of the car that had hit me was not hurt, so I continued to the hospital as I reluctantly radioed AA's dispatch about the accident.

I figured Tom would be waiting at the hospital with a gun in his hand but was notified by our dispatch to drive to his house after dropping off the patient, who was now truly dead. Tom was sitting by the pool with a Bloody Mary in his hand. His wife was fixing breakfast and invited us to stay. Tom put his arm around my shoulder and said not to worry about it, that he had done worse.

I found out later that wasn't the first time one of his rigs had been in a wreck. Tom and his partner Bob often worked the night shift, and they had managed to tear the rear bumper off an ambulance responding to a call late one night. The police had set up a road block for something unrelated to the call Tom and Bob were running. Two police cruisers were nosed toward each other, with just enough room to drive between them. However, there wasn't enough room for the ambulance to squeeze through going about 50 miles an hour — they left the rear bumper of the ambulance in the road and some really pissed-off cops cursing their receding tail-lights.

Most of the guys who worked for Tom were firefighters moonlighting for extra money. We enjoyed each other's company and took every opportunity to have fun, usually at someone else's expense. Mickey was my partner one day when we were dispatched to a traffic accident with minor injuries. It was a single vehicle accident, and the driver was dead drunk. Delray Beach Fire Department was on scene and, after checking the guy out, told us to take him to Boca Hospital. Mickey decided he was going to have fun with the guy and loaded him feet first and face down on the stretcher, after removing the mattress. We strapped him down and shoved him in the back of the rig, his head a foot from the door. Mickey climbed in the back with the patient, and I hopped in the front, turned up the volume on my favorite rock-and-roll station, and drove south on I-95.

I guess the music was too loud to hear Mickey screaming at me to stop. When I pulled into the hospital and walked around to the back of the ambulance to unload the patient, I was more than a little surprised to see the stretcher already halfway out of the rig. Mickey was hanging on to the end of the stretcher, arms trembling with exertion, and his feet braced against the lock in the floor of the ambulance that is supposed to secure the stretcher.

The patient seemed to have sobered up. He was still lying face down on the stretcher, strapped in tight, now staring bug-eyed at the ground. Mickey thought it would be fun to open the back doors as we were traveling down I-95, which he did. Then he thought it would be even more fun to ease the stretcher out just enough so the patient was staring at the road going by at 85 miles per hour. This wouldn't have been too much of a problem, except he eased it out too far and the wheels dropped onto the rear bumper, giving the patient an interesting perspective of the road surface from about a foot away. I told Mickey that was the new cure for drunk driving.

4 — Captain Schnabel

Wake-up call would come at 0600 by way of five-gallon plastic water jugs bowled down the hallway into the bunkroom, bouncing off beds and sleeping bodies. Sometimes the captain would feel particularly inspired and would march down the hall into the bunkroom using the lids off large steel garbage cans as cymbals, banging away like a crazed one-man Prussian marching band. If you weren't on your feet in what he thought was a timely manner, which was immediately, Captain Schnabel would simply turn bunks over two at a time, spilling bodies onto the floor. At six two and on the north side of 300 pounds, he was larger than life and the first officer I worked for when I joined Del-Trail Fire Department in 1976.

Captain Schnabel is the strongest man I have ever met, and the stories are legion and true about his feats of strength. One of the first calls I ever went on where I was witness to his incredible strength was a brush fire. We didn't have a lot of resources back then, and it was Cap and me responding in Brush 23. We could see smoke long before we arrived, and Captain Schnabel commented that it was a grass fire. I didn't say a word — Schnabel wasn't the kind of man who invited conversation — but I was impressed. That early in my career, I didn't know enough to understand that smoke color is a tip-off for different types of burning fuels. Reading smoke is basic fire knowledge, something that is routinely taught to firefighters now. Upon arrival we could see a slow-moving grass fire burning on the other side of a canal. There was no way to get around the canal without driving for several miles, so Captain Schnabel ordered me to wade across. Being a rookie firefighter, I wasn't about to argue with him and dutifully waded across, water up to my waist and filling my boots. Meanwhile, Schnabel had pulled about 100 feet of booster line off the reel, coiled it up, and threw it effortlessly across 30 feet of canal. A booster line is like a garden hose on steroids: one-inch-diameter heavy gauge rubber, big around as a man's wrist. I would wager that 100 feet of hose probably weighs at least 250 pounds. I had all I could do to stretch it out to its fullest extent to reach the fire.

Every firefighter remembers their first structure fire. Mine occurred a month after I was on shift. It was a rainy Sunday afternoon when the call came in for a house fire on Dixie Highway at the C-15 canal, at least a 15-minute response east of the station. I rode on the tailboard of Engine 10 and was soaked through and cold by the time we arrived. The house was an old Florida Cracker home sided with Dade County pine, apparently abandoned, with light smoke coming from an open front door. The guys went to work trying to locate the fire while I observed. I had not been through fire training, so Schnabel wouldn't let me do much except fight brush fires. A smoldering fire was finally located under the crawl space, and Schnabel told me to crawl under with a booster line and put the fire out. He also told me to whistle if I found more fire. I didn't have the nerve to tell him I couldn't whistle loud enough for anyone to hear.

As I look back over three decades, that first fire certainly wasn't exciting. But in the winter of 1976, I felt as though I had joined the brotherhood. More exciting, and a call that occurred just a week later, was a cross burning by the Ku Klux Klan on the front lawn of Temple Emeth. Schnabel ordered me to take Brush 23 and put the fire out. It was midnight, with no one around except me and a very vivid imagination, squirting water on a blazing cross that stood 15 feet tall. I could already see the headline in the morning paper: "Rookie fireman shot by Klan." That call is forever etched in my memory.

We had been talking about putting up a basketball net behind the station and persuaded the local power company to drop off an old telephone pole so we could fasten the hoop to it. They drilled the hole for us but didn't set the pole. Four of us tried for an hour to wrestle the pole upright into the hole. Schnabel had been watching us and finally came over, picked the pole off the ground at one end, walked it up like he was raising a ladder, put his arms around it when it was vertical, picked it completely off the ground, and dropped it into the hole. He never said a word, just kind of grunted and walked back into the station. We watched in amazement, knowing we had just witnessed a superhuman feat of strength.

Captain Schnabel's hands were as hard as bricks. He was changing out florescent lights in the truck bay one Saturday afternoon and disposing of them in a rather unusual manner inside a 55-gallon garbage can. He would hold each tube at one end and drive the other end into the can, shattering the glass within a foot of his hand so that an eight-foot tube would neatly fit into a four-foot garbage can. He also amazed us by cupping wasps in his bare hands and then holding them between his thumb and forefinger. They would try to sting him, but his skin was so tough the stinger couldn't penetrate that thick hide.

Captain Schnabel was a big kid at heart and loved to keep us guessing about what he would do next. We had a regulation-size pool table in the day-room that received a lot of use. Sometimes he would pick up one end of the table and chase some poor soul around the room until they were pinned in a corner. Whoever was pinned would have to crawl over the table to get out. It would take the rest of the crew to wrestle the table back to the center of the room.

He also loved to play practical jokes that sometimes got out of hand. One of his favorite jokes was to order a firefighter to get a tool out of a side compartment on one of the trucks. Earlier in the shift he would have placed a possum or sometimes a rat snake in the compartment and then would wait for the reaction of the unfortunate fellow sent to fetch the tool. The chief eventually put a stop to Schnabel's pranks when he carried it a little too far by placing a boar raccoon in the side compartment of Engine 9. The raccoon had been foraging for food in the station's dumpster, and Schnabel calmly grabbed it by the scruff of the neck and threw it into the compartment. When that raccoon finally saw the light of day, it was highly pissed. Why the fireman who opened the compartment door wasn't eaten alive remains a mystery.

Schnabel grew up with the Everglades as his playground. When he was in high school, he and his brother would camp in the Everglades during the summer for weeks at a time, building shelters on hardwood hammocks. They would live off the land, eating fish, frogs, snakes, gators and swamp cabbage. He was absolutely attuned to the natural environment and would sit for hours in the watch room, gazing out the window at the fields and woods beyond the station. It wasn't unusual for him to point out an animal that only he noticed and then lecture us on how it fit into the environment, how important each creature was in the grand scheme; however, he certainly wasn't averse to sustaining himself on what the land offered. One day he jumped up from the desk and ran into the field, returning with a large rattlesnake. He gathered us around to show off his prize and informed us that we would be dining on snake that evening. Nobody dared object to this culinary delight, and we were pleasantly surprised to learn that, though a bit bony, rattlesnake was pretty tasty.

Captain Schnabel was also a collector, mostly of what we thought was junk. He had barrels and barrels of various kinds of metals at his house and was proud to show off what he had collected. When I learned that the majority of metal in those barrels was copper, and the price of copper was 60 cents a pound, I didn't think of it as junk anymore — at the height of his scrounging he probably had close to three tons of copper. The problem lay in how he collected the copper. We ran a lot of fire calls on abandoned structures, and he would crawl under the house, hack saw in hand, removing copper water pipes while we were attempting to extinguish the fire. It was a wonderful incentive for us to quickly extinguish the fire so our fearless leader didn't die an ignominious death. He also collected bread and donuts and fruit out of dumpsters and would kindly contribute his haul to the station. We always checked expiration dates on anything he left in the kitchen.

Captain Schnabel was well aware of his incredible strength and would sometimes employ his strength in rather questionable ways. One day during morning station chores, Schnabel picked a firefighter straight out of a recliner by grabbing a handful of the poor guy's belly. Evidently he wasn't moving fast enough to suit Captain Schnabel when the order was given to clean the station. Schnabel believed in teamwork, especially when it came to station duties, and if you weren't working along with everyone else, he would get pretty excited.

No one dared cross him, and every once in a while he would resort to what he euphemistically termed "the claw," his way of reminding us that he was the boss.

Despite his rough ways, Eddie Schnabel was a changed man whenever his wife Elsie would come by the station for a visit in the evening. His whole demeanor would soften, even toward us. Elsie was diminutive, standing maybe five feet tall to Eddie's six feet plus, but her tiny stature was every bit a match for her husband. She was like a house mother to us, and we never worried about checking expiration dates on the wonderful desserts she would bring to the station.

Eddie had a soft spot for children, and his gentle demeanor was on display at Christmas when he would play Santa for the children of migrant farm workers. Rural Palm Beach County is home to hundreds of migrant workers and their families. They

A young Edward Schnabel standing in front of Central Station (courtesy Edward DeVries).

live in squalid conditions, and the children suffer the most.[1] We would collect toys for children of various ages, and on the day before Christmas Captain Schnabel would make the rounds of all the labor camps in our response zone. We could see the joy in the eyes of those children when Captain Schnabel, dressed as jolly old Saint Nick, stepped down from the fire truck with a sack full of toys over his broad shoulder, shouting, "Ho, ho, ho, Merry Christmas!" As we distributed toys to the children we could see mothers with tears in their eyes and fathers standing off to the side, a mixture of pride and sadness on their faces. We didn't speak Spanish and they didn't speak English, but that day it did not matter; we all spoke a universal language. We learned much more than firefighting from Captain Schnabel.

5—Driver Engineer

In the late 1970s it wasn't unusual to use the expression "tailboard fire-fighter." I rode the tailboard as a rookie firefighter, a dangerous position if you didn't have your wits about you, especially when bouncing down a rough road. We wore ladder belts around our waists, which clipped into the rail that ran across the back of the hose bed. If you weren't hanging on to that rail with both hands, chances were good that you might finish your ride to the fire dangling from the hook. Thankfully, those days were soon gone. The back step of a fire engine is designed for access to the hose bed and equipment mounted on the rear of the truck; it was never intended as a place to ride to the fire. With the addition of engines with jump seats, though still open cab, firefighters were able to ride seated and safely belted in. Now, engines are fully enclosed and firefighters ride in air-conditioned comfort, wearing a radio headset so they can communicate with the officer.

Regardless of how I rode to the fire, I loved everything about fire-fighting: the adrenaline rush when the alarm sounded—we prayed for the blare of three bells that meant a structure fire—the satisfaction of donning my bunker gear, then climbing into the jump seat and putting my arms through the straps of the air-pack and hanging the mask around my neck; the ride to the fire, trying to quell my nervousness as I listened to the siren and air horn; and finally arriving at the fire, seeing the smoke pushing out of the building and knowing I was about to go into that building with a hose line. I did that for three years before sitting for the driver engineer's test. As I moved up in rank I looked forward to the new challenges that awaited me, but I will always miss being the first guy through the door on a hose line.

When notice of the driver's exam was posted, I immediately began studying. There was an overwhelming amount of material that had to be memorized for the written portion of the exam: the size and type of pump and water tank capacity on Engines 8, 9, 10, and 11 as well as on the four brush trucks; the amount of supply hose, pre-connects, and booster line on each engine and brush truck; and all the tools and equipment and their location on each piece of apparatus. We studied friction loss formulas, hydrant locations, street names, and development names and locations; we had to know all the developments with a hydrant system, what size mains fed the hydrants and how much water each hydrant would supply, as well as what developments didn't have hydrants and the location of alternative water sources. There was also a practical portion of the test that involved driving and pumping various apparatus.

I scored an 89 on the test and was promoted to driver engineer in November 1979, and subsequently assigned to Central Station. The frontline engine at that station was Engine 8, the 1974 Ward LaFrance with a 1250-GPM Hale pump and 750-gallon water tank. It had an automatic transmission and an air horn that would wake the dead. I loved driving that truck.

My new supervisor was Captain Henry Cusell, a by-the-book man with little sense of humor, or so I thought at the time. He had no tolerance for people who didn't know their job. I had worked for Captain Cusell as a firefighter on shift swaps and was prepared for his very tough but fair management style. I knew that if I did my job well, I wouldn't have any problems.

Fire stations the world over can be a breeding ground for petty feuds between shifts. Central Station wasn't immune to this phenomenon, especially when Captain Cusell and Captain Kemp were at odds about dirty dishes and pots and pans left in the sink. Captain Kemp relieved us, and many times he would refuse to accept the station at shift change. Kemp was a stickler for cleanliness, especially in kitchens and bathrooms. Sal Salcito found this out as a rookie firefighter when he informed Captain Kemp, "I don't do bathrooms, Shorty." Sal cleaned both bathrooms, every shift, for two years, scrubbing grout lines in the showers with a toothbrush. It was fun to watch the dynamics between Kemp and Cusell, even though it was juvenile behavior. Kemp would walk into the kitchen and start throwing pots and pans on the floor that he perceived as dirty. Of course we would wash them again, even though they were spotless.

Henry Cusell was born in Cuba and immigrated to the United States at the age of 10. English was never his first language; he would slip into Spanish when he was excited. I wasn't on duty at the time, but the story of this fire call has become part of the lore of those early years. Central Station responded to a storage facility fire where incendiary smoke bombs had ignited. The smoke was so bad at the entrance to the facility that the firefighter on Engine 8 had to walk in front of the engine to find the way into the fire. Henry was on the radio advising dispatch that they had a working fire and to send another engine; however, he was speaking in Spanish. Rick Hodges was the officer on the next due engine and had been monitoring radio traffic, knowing they would probably be called. When Henry requested assistance in Spanish, Rick turned to Al Sierra, who speaks fluent Spanish, and said, "What the hell was that?"

Captain Henry Cusell taking a siesta in the dayroom at Central Station (courtesy Bob Briley).

Ed DeVries was Henry's driver that day. When Henry continued, in Spanish, to give orders to his crew, Ed said, "That's good, Cap, now give it to us in English so we know what to do."

But Henry wasn't through yet. When the second engine arrived, Henry announced, "Half of you go this way! Half of you go that way! The rest of you, follow me!"[1]

Captain Cusell didn't give the impression that he had a sense of humor, but we soon learned otherwise. To test the preparedness of a new dispatcher, Henry called in a rather serious, but phony, hazardous materials incident on the inland waterway. Everyone was in on this, except the dispatcher, and she did an outstanding job. When the Coast Guard called, inquiring if we needed their assistance, Henry realized he might have gone too far. He knew he had gone too far when Chief Frye found out. He kept his captain's badge, barely.

My duties as a driver were much different from those of a firefighter. I was responsible for ensuring the truck was ready to respond no matter the hour, safely driving the truck to the fire, pumping water, laying out tools, setting up the Hurst Tool on wrecks, and a hundred other ways of supporting the firefighting effort. In the morning, instead of cleaning the station, I was checking and cleaning Engine 8. Checking a fire truck is routine, boring work that is an essential part of the job, and I was always very methodical when checking the truck and the equipment. There was a sense of duty and a work ethic that had been instilled in me by the veteran firefighters I worked with when I first came into the fire service. I didn't want to find that the Hurst Tool wouldn't start on a bad wreck or the truck wouldn't go into pump gear on a fire. I was proud of my job as a driver engineer and determined that an equipment malfunction due to a cursory inspection wasn't going to happen on my watch.

Each apparatus has a checklist fastened to a clipboard that lists every tool and piece of equipment carried on the truck. A box next to each tool or piece of equipment on the checklist allowed me to make a check mark, ensuring an accurate inventory. I started my truck check at the engineer's compartment located on the left side behind the driver's door. Inside the compartment was a large tool box with an assortment of small hand tools, including wrenches, screwdrivers, channel lock pliers, a hammer, duct tape and electrician's tape, wire nuts and various sized gaskets for fire hose, barway wrenches for connecting booster hose, sprinkler heads, and a bar of soap used to stop small leaks on car gas tanks. I would inventory the contents on each shift because it would be on my head if something was missing. Usually there was nothing wrong, but sometimes a firefighter would "borrow" a tool and not return it. Also stored within that compartment were a five-pound sledgehammer, a hydrant gate valve, a gated wye and a siamese, and, mounted on the inside of the door, a hydrant wrench and two spanner wrenches.

Attached to the running board next to that compartment were reducers, two-and-a-half inch double males and double females, and a six-inch strainer for hard suction hose. The next compartment, behind the wheel well, contained a compressor for the Hurst Tool, a spreader and cutter and 50 feet of hydraulic hose. This equipment was mounted on a slide-out tray for easier access. We also carried electrical cord for portable lighting, and a small generator to power the lights.

Above the left-side compartments hung two trays, each with a 10-foot section of six-inch hard suction hose. We used this hose to draft water from ponds, canals, and swimming pools when there were no hydrants available. Mounted above the suction hose was a folding attic ladder. Mounted underneath the left-side chassis were short and long handled shovels. The left-side jump seat held an air-pack mounted in a bracket behind the seat that allowed a firefighter to slip into the straps of the air-pack while riding to the fire. A flat-head axe and halligan were mounted on the left side of the engine cover.

At the rear of the engine was a large step that gave access to the hose bed. On the step was a water-can fire extinguisher, a dry chemical extinguisher, and two-and-a-half-inch fog and smooth bore nozzles. In the hose bed we carried a split load of 1500 feet of two-and-a-half-inch supply hose, 750 feet on each side with a divider between. This hose was packed in a flat load set up for a forward lay, meaning that the engine would lay in from the water supply to the fire. Engine hose lays can be configured in different ways, depending on availability of water. In a rural area with no hydrants, a hose bed is typically set up for a reverse lay. This means the engine would stop at the fire and lay out to a pond or canal. Engine 10 was set up for a reverse lay with a horseshoe load of two-and-a-half-inch supply hose and a skid load of one-and-a-half-inch pre-connects on a piece of plywood, a configuration we called a Ciscoe load. The plywood would be jerked off at the fire and the female coupling of supply hose, with a double male attached, would be connected to the gated wye that supplied the two pre-connects. This set-up allowed firefighters to stretch lines to fight fire with a continuous supply of water from an engine at draft.

Single or double lines can be laid, depending on the distance to the water supply and depending on the amount of water needed to fight the fire. On a long lay the engine dropping supply line would lay a single line of 1000 or more feet out to a water source where it would pump from draft, and then another engine would lay another 1000 feet from the supplying engine back to the fire ground, thereby doubling the flow of water. The engine laying back to the fire would receive water from the two lines and pump to the attack lines. A two-and-a-half-inch supply line can deliver approximately 300 gallons of water per minute, although this is dependent on friction loss, which is a function of the distance that water travels through a hose line, the diameter of the hose, and the pressure applied to pump the water.

I would continue my inspection of equipment on the right side of the truck at the compartment just behind the wheel well. We carried two five-gallon containers of Aqueous Film Forming Foam (or A-Triple-F) and a foam inductor. The inductor is a pick-up tube that is connected to a pre-connected hose line. The tube is placed into the foam bucket and foam is then entrained into the water stream at a predetermined setting, usually between 3 and 6 percent. Foam is generally used for flammable liquid fires, and we could flow foam for five to ten minutes using tank water, depending on how the inductor was set up. Now, engines have built-in foam reservoirs, enabling the driver to send a preset concentration of foam to a pre-connect by activating a control valve at the pump panel.

The next compartment, forward of the rear wheel well, contained medical equipment. We carried what we called a 747 box, a large plastic box that was hinged at the top and organized with trays holding a basic complement of medical equipment that included bandages, multi-trauma dressings, stethoscope and BP cuff, OB kit, adult and pediatric oxygen masks and an esophageal obturator airway. Also in the compartment were an oxygen cylinder, various splints for long bone fractures, and a traction splint for femur fractures.

Above the two right-side compartments hung a 24-foot extension ladder, a 12-foot roof ladder, and a 10-foot pike pole. The right-side jump seat mirrored the left with an axe, halligan, and air-pack. We carried Survive-Air breathing apparatus in the jump seats, state of the art at the time, but wearing it wasn't mandatory back then. Many guys refused to wear one, but I always had mine on. Thirty-plus years later I'm glad I did. A lot of firefighters who started in the mid–1970s and earlier have chronic respiratory problems, or worse, from breathing smoke on the fire ground. Even now, firefighters sometimes have to be reminded to stay on air during the overhaul stage of the fire. These days routine testing for carbon monoxide levels helps remind everyone on a fire scene that an atmosphere can still be dangerous even hours after the fire has been extinguished.[2]

The next area I examined was the cross lays. Fire engines carry pre-connected hose for immediate deployment at a fire, and Engine 8 carried this hose in two large trays running parallel to the hose bed. Each tray contained 150 feet of inch-and-a-half hose with a variable flow nozzle that could be set for different patterns, from a wide fog stream to straight stream. A straight stream is used for penetration and a fog is used in a confined area to generate steam to suppress fire or for hydraulic ventilation. Now, most fire departments carry one-and-three-quarter-inch attack lines, which provide much more water. Mounted forward of the hose bed was a deluge gun. This is a portable device that can flow a thousand gallons of water per minute, and that could also be dismounted from the truck and used on large fires. Also mounted in that area were two Circle D lights we used for portable lighting and extra SCBA bottles.

The last items checked were found in the cab: map books, reference books for identifying hazardous materials, and binoculars. I would also turn on all the lights and do a walk-around to check warning lights, turn signals, brake lights, and headlights. I would thump tires and drain any condensation out of the air brake tank reservoirs during this walk-around.

After this daily check, which lasted an hour, I would drive the truck onto the apron in front of the bay and exercise the pump. This involved moving a pump select switch located in the cab from road to pump drive, then shifting the truck into drive gear. The truck transmission would power the 1250-gallon-per-minute pump. After putting the truck into pump drive, I would climb out of the cab, stand at the pump panel, and open the tank-to-pump valve, allowing water to flow from the tank to the pump. Then I would place the booster line into the top of the tank, completing a circuit of continuously flowing water so the pump wouldn't overheat. There was a throttle at the pump panel that enabled me to set pump pressure, and I would circulate water at idle speed. If the truck needed washing, I would do that while completing this last part of the truck check.

Attaining the rank of driver engineer meant a new badge and a certain amount of authority over men in the firefighter ranks. Captain Cusell would give me areas of responsibility that involved limited supervision of other people, such as cleaning the bay floors or waxing trucks. It was my first experience supervising others, and though I didn't realize it at the time, my management skills and leadership style was being shaped by those early experiences.

I worked as a driver at Central Station, Station 2 in Highland Beach, Station 3 in Sandalfoot Cove, and Station 4 in Boca Del-Mar. This tour of different areas forced me to become familiar with all areas of Del-Trail's response zones, something that would serve me well in later years as a lieutenant and captain.

When Station 4 opened in Boca Del-Mar, the department bought an engine and a ladder truck for the new station, both made by Pierce. Although the ladder truck's chassis was made by Pierce, the ladder itself was manufactured by LTI. It was a 100-foot aerial platform with a permanent waterway supplied by a 1500-GPM pump. It had a bucket at the end of the ladder that extended over the front of the cab, thus resulting in the designation "aerial platform." A weekly check of this truck involved setting the out-riggers and raising the ladder to its fullest extension. There were dual controls for the ladder, one set in the bucket and one on the turn-table. I usually operated

This picture was taken in the late 1970s at the Central Station. I was on a different shift and would relieve John Tiersch as the driver on Engine 8. Left to right: Dennis Peek, John Tiersch, Brad Murphy, Doug Watson, John Boike, Sal Salcito, Ed DeVries (courtesy Edward DeVries).

the ladder from the bucket, but it gave me the willies if there were clouds scudding across the sky. I knew better, but it seemed as though the truck was tipping over with the perspective of the clouds moving against the stable backdrop of the truck. It was an impressive piece of equipment that got a lot of looks going down the road.

Usually a ladder wouldn't be housed in a residential area, but we had mid-rise buildings (some light commercial) and a large number of single family homes that were huge, several exceeding 15,000 square feet. Politics and money always have the last say, and a lot of influential people had lobbied for a fire station in that area, with shiny new equipment.

Senior drivers were given the opportunity to bid on a slot at Station 4, so I bid on the ladder. A representative from LTI spent a week training us on ladder operations and the various systems on the truck. The ladder portion of the truck was complicated, and safe operation came only after long hours of training. Driving the truck was also a challenge, much different from driving an engine. The platform was a straight-axle truck, 55 feet long, 10 feet high, and 8 feet wide. With the addition of the bucket extending five feet in front of the cab, the driver had to always be cognizant of obstructions when making a turn. The first time I drove the truck, the rep from LTI was riding with me. I was negotiating a secondary road that was not designed for fire apparatus and managed to thread my way between two cars parked opposite each other, leaving only a very narrow lane to drive the truck through. I was traveling around 30 miles per hour and never slowed down; I knew I could make it, but the rep wasn't so sure. He almost had a heart attack when I drove the truck between the cars with a foot to spare on each side. I always found it incongruous that I would drive to work in a VW Bug and then climb into the cab of that huge truck.

To my recollection, the ladder's elevated waterway was only used a few times. I think the first time we used the ladder pipe was on a fire at a clubhouse, and by the time the truck was set up and we had an adequate water supply for the two-inch, 2000-GPM nozzle, most of the building was on the ground. I don't recall ever using the truck for rescue purposes. A ladder truck is designed for 20 years of service, so I'm sure there were instances after I moved on from Station 4 in which it was used for rescue as well as for an elevated master stream.

The general public doesn't have a clue how to share the road with large vehicles, even giant red fire apparatus with lights flashing and sirens and air horns blaring. I know that most of my grey hair came from driving fire apparatus on those congested roads, dodging people who didn't understand that it was polite and proper, not to mention the law, to yield to a fire apparatus that was responding code three. West Boca is a wealthy area, and it's not unusual to see BMWs and other expensive cars being driven by self-absorbed people. One day opportunity presented itself in the form of a white Mercedes convertible driven by a middle-aged woman who had been weaving in and out of traffic and had managed, twice, to force me hard on the brakes. I pulled to a stop at a red light at Power Line and Glades, and the woman in the Mercedes pulled to a stop on my right side, just opposite the ladder truck's exhaust port. I thought to myself, "Yes, there is a God in heaven." A diesel engine produces a huge amount of black, sooty exhaust if the engine is fed too much fuel too fast. When the light turned green, I stomped on the accelerator. The Mercedes disappeared in a black fog of diesel smoke. Certainly not something I'm proud of doing, but it was sweet revenge nonetheless.

Lieutenant Abell looked at me and said, "Now, Kit, why did you do that?"

6—Labor Relations

The wife of one of the commissioners roared into the parking lot at the Central Station, jumped out of her car, and set up a card table on the sidewalk outside Chief Frye's office. She placed a pair of cowboy boots on the table and yelled through the window at Frye, "Here's your walking boots!"

There were three commissioners for each fire control district, each appointed by the governor of Florida. They were the ruling authority for the tax district fire departments in Palm Beach County, with budget oversight responsibility and the authority to hire and fire personnel. Labor relations had deteriorated to a level where there was talk of a strike, even though it was illegal for public safety employees to take such a job action. To have the wife of a commissioner support us in such a public and dramatic fashion tells the story of how far relations between labor and management had deteriorated.

January 27, 1978, was the tipping point in our relationship with Chief Frye and the commissioners when 28 men signed applications for membership in the International Association of Fire Fighters (IAFF). On February 28, 1978, a check in the amount of $148.76 was sent to the IAFF from the Del-Trail Fireman's Association, starting a process that would eventually designate us as Local 2624.[1]

Labor relations in 1978 were at an all-time low, but with support from the public and the news media, including editorials written in support of our efforts to win better pay, working conditions, and benefits, we thought our problems would soon be resolved. We quickly learned how stubborn Chief Frye could be and that no amount of public empathy would facilitate this process. An editorial opinion from the *Boca Raton News* confirmed our fear that our fight had only just begun.

Thirty-five years brings a clearer perspective of Chief Frye's animosity toward firefighters who had the audacity to unionize, but this is an important part of the history of Del-Trail and glossing over the difficult times we went through in attempting to establish a legitimate bargaining unit would not be fair to the old guard who finally stood up for their rights. Granted, Chief Frye was one of the early members of the department from the 1960s, when it was an altruistic avocation to serve the community as a volunteer firefighter. This may explain, in part, the anger and vindictive behavior he directed toward firefighters when we began the process of unionization.

A large part of the problem was Frye's reluctance to spend money unless it was absolutely necessary. Perhaps lack of a funding mechanism in those early days, other than fund-raising efforts, explains his resistance, but it doesn't explain his reluctance to spend money on normal business expenditures or his use of money as a tool to punish employees. This parochial attitude was evident when he refused to pay the city of Boca Raton $18,000 for the use of fire hydrants in the unincorporated areas west of the city, even though all the other fire departments in the county budgeted to pay an annual fee to municipal water utilities for fire hydrant maintenance and water usage — it was simply a part of doing business.[2] In July 1977, Boca Raton filed suit against Del-Trail in circuit court. The suit was heard by Judge Kapner, who ordered Del-Trail to deposit $22,312.50 into an escrow account until the dispute could be resolved.[3] Del-Trail eventually paid the bill, but this is a good example of how stubborn Frye could be.

Lieutenant Ed Hines was among the original signatories for Local 2624, and he was also our second union president, after Ray Smuda resigned. Frye demonstrated how vindictive he could be when he decided that Ed would make a good fire inspector, even though Ed had no training, or interest, in the job. That didn't matter to Frye or the commissioners, who voted unanimously to support Frye's decision. Fire Commissioner C.R. Stanley stated, "We're not in the position of second guessing the chief and we're not going to."[4] Although Ed's salary remained the same, he was assigned to days, ending his ability to work a part-time job, something we were all forced to do because we couldn't make it on fireman's pay alone. This resulted in a $3000 loss in yearly income, significant even by today's standards. Hines said he knew that "it was all cut and dried before the meeting. I have no plans to resign, but the day that Chief Frye retires I'll be holding the door."[5]

A month later Frye again demonstrated that he was the boss. Driver Engineer James Grady was a reserve member of the United States Coast Guard and was denied his pay during his annual two-week drill. In 1977, when Grady first joined the Coast Guard Reserve, Frye refused to pay him or give him time off, clearly a violation of federal law. Grady complained to the U.S. attorney in Miami, Ralph Person. Their Office of Civil Liberties agreed that Grady should be paid, and Person sent a letter to Frye, informing him that Grady was eligible for 17 days off each year without loss of pay, time, or seniority. Grady was finally compensated $376 when Frye was advised by the U.S. attorney that he would lose the case if it went to court.[6] All these events occurred after we voted to unionize. It was obvious we were in for a protracted fight. It was also painfully clear at this point that no matter how much bad press

Chief Frye and the fire commissioners received, public sentiment in favor of our cause was not going to help.

When Frye and the commissioners refused to acknowledge Local 2624 as the legitimate collective bargaining unit, we turned to Florida's Public Employee Relations Commission (PERC). A secret ballot election was conducted between November 13 and November 29, 1978. Those eligible to vote for unionization included the positions of firefighter, firefighter paramedic, driver engineer, lieutenant, and fire inspector. Those positions ineligible to vote included fire chief, chief executive officer, executive officer, assistant executive officer, fire marshal, chief engineer, training officer, rescue officer, captain, secretary, and dispatcher. Of the 38 people eligible to vote, 33 voted. The vote to unionize carried, 32 in favor and 1 opposed. Local 2624 members were certified by PERC on December 12, 1978, with a certification case number of 442 (see Appendix C).

The PERC vote came only after we were able to prove unfair labor practices, something that was occurring each day and was self-evident to us. The IAFF petitioned PERC to intervene on our behalf once official depositions were recorded, including one I wrote dated May 19, 1978 (see Appendix D). The working conditions cited in my deposition are only a small part of the story and, taken alone, don't seem that onerous. But it's hard to consider yourself a professional firefighter when most of the day is spent mowing grass, cleaning out drainage ditches, painting fire stations, and even cleaning out septic tanks. I'm sure we were asked to do these things to save money but they were also used as a tool to punish us. This left little or no time to train, a necessary part of staying current in the firefighting profession.

In addition to days filled with manual labor that had nothing to do with the fire service profession, Frye passed over for promotion men who were active in the union and promoted people less qualified who were not in the union, even if it meant skipping an intermediate rank. Also during this period, Frye granted a 5 percent pay raise to himself and his executive officers. No consideration for a raise was given to the men. He may have been bound legally not to give us raises because of the bargaining unit, but his timing was meant to send a message. He was quick to point out that he didn't recognize the union, even though our unionization efforts had been in the news for a year.

This ongoing harassment continued, even after certification of Local 2624 by PERC. Frye certainly tried to intimidate us leading up to that vote, and when the vote was overwhelmingly in favor of unionizing, the harassment got even worse. This was the tipping point for more direct action. Men depended on a decent wage to feed their families, impossible on a base salary of $9500 per year. In fact, many of the guys were on food stamps to make ends meet. Firefighters, including firemen from other departments, began informational picketing in front of fire stations. When asked why he was supporting Del-Trail firefighters, a paramedic from the Delray Beach Fire Department responded, "These guys start out making $1500.00 more than the national poverty line. How can you support a family on $9500.00? Chief Frye is a dictator. I thought dictatorship went out when Hitler was killed."[7]

The people we were sworn to protect were becoming increasingly concerned about the ability of the fire department to retain trained personnel and respond with adequate resources to fires and emergency medical calls. Firemen were resigning en masse (including our first union president, Ray Smuda) and more were threatening to quit; 11 men had resigned in the past year. Del-Trail was losing experienced men to area departments that were paying $6000 more per year. Of the 51-man combat force, 14 percent had a year or less on the job. By now the papers were calling for updates on a daily basis.

Several firefighters, including myself, and the press attended a Fire Commission meeting in January 1979. When Frye informed the commissioners that several firemen were resigning, we asked the commissioners why they felt the department was losing people. Leo Blair, chairman of the commission, responded, "That's what makes a great America. I think it's great that any man can come and go and do any job he wants. If they have a better opportunity, I'm in favor of letting them move on." Frye said that he was "unaware" of any dispute between labor and management. When asked about working conditions at the department, he refused to comment.[8]

Frustration mounted as Frye continually refused to recognize Local 2624 as the legitimate bargaining unit for the men, finally forcing a blue flu. We knew we were on dangerous ground; it was illegal to take any action that jeopardized public safety. Frye certainly thought it was a coordinated union move when reporters were calling the station 10 minutes after shift change. The reporters knew about it because I called them. It was hard for me to keep a straight face when I told Frye that I was simply concerned about our ability to respond with adequate resources to emergency calls with only four guys showing up for work and that it never occurred to me it might be a union ploy. I was dead in his sights the next day when a front-page article in the *Sun-Sentinel* questioned Del-Trail's ability to respond to emergencies with such reduced staffing. As union spokesman, I took a lot of heat.

This job action could have hurt our cause, as an editorial by the *Sun Sentinel* dated August 14, 1979, states: "Union officials claim the increased absenteeism is not a ploy by the firefighters to win sympathy for their wage demands. The Del-Trail fire chief and the fire commission, however, must closely monitor the situation. Work slowdowns can jeopardize the safety of the community, and if high absenteeism persists the commission must take swift and decisive action to discipline employees." The editorial goes on to say, "A wage freeze has been in effect for two years. The firefighters want a 20 percent wage boost, but the fire district officials are offering only a 5 percent increase during a time when inflation is running at 13 percent annually."[9] After examining Del-Trail's budget, an editorial by the *Miami Herald* dated November 11, 1979, points out that Del-Trail could more than afford to give raises: "We are shocked that professional firefighters and paramedics are paid so little." This editorial was also the first to start voicing the idea of consolidating the tax district departments: "A settlement is vital. And county officials must use any legal means possible to take control of the fire district and begin a process of consolidating the 11 independent fire districts. Meanwhile, Governor Bob Graham should use his appointment powers to replace the three men on Del-Trail's Board of Supervisors."[10] With that sentiment expressed by the *Miami Herald's* editorial board, we knew it would only be a matter of time before there would be resolution to our protracted bargaining issues.

In late March 1979 labor and management finally met at the negotiating table. After the first round of talks, the administration canceled the next three negotiating sessions, and it wasn't until the end of May that a second session was held. Firemen continued to complain of bad faith and stall tactics on the part of the administration.[11] In late July 1979 the two sides met for the seventh time, to no avail. James Crossland, attorney for Del-Trail's administration, rejected the union's bare-bones request for a 10 percent wage increase, down from the original 15 percent increase. We were also asking for a 10 percent cost of living increase because of high inflation. Charles Kossuth, attorney for Local 2624, stated, "We made an attempt in this proposal to offer what we could live with. It appears that your position has not changed on the important issues to us. I don't think it would be productive or helpful to continue meeting along those lines." Kossuth then suggested asking PERC for a mediator.[12]

Meanwhile, Del-Trail's budget proposal had been approved by the county commission. At $1.9 million, it was the largest of the 11 tax district budgets, even though the tax rate had gone down. The growth in population and the increase in assessed property value had lowered the millage rate from 1.9 mills to 1.65 mills, resulting in more than enough money to pay for raises.[13]

The next round of talks occurred in August. Armed with information about the department's budget, the union asked for a 20 percent raise phased in with 5 percent increments every four months beginning in October. Surprisingly, this offer was not rejected out of hand, with Crossland and Frye asking for time to review the offer.[14]

Another sticking point during this negotiation session was the promotional policy. The union wanted promotions to come from within, but Frye refused. It was clear, at least to us, that he was trying to put pro-management people in officer positions. Frye did hire from the outside, bringing in Edward Sarpy, Richard Hodges, Patrick Murphy, and Cortez Lawrence. Chief Frye hoped they would support his management policies, thereby weakening the union. We did our due diligence on the new hires and were especially impressed with Cortez Lawrence. He had gone through the Florida Smoke Diver School in the mid–1970s, so we knew his skills as a firefighter were vetted. Hodges was brought in as a lieutenant, and he told me he had no idea he had just walked into a war zone.[15] Cortez had worked as a fire chief in LaGrange, Georgia, and Frye figured he would be pro-management. However, Cortez was not someone who could be intimidated or molded to conform to Frye's management philosophy. Cortez's hiring interview focused on Frye's concern about the reliability of his current supervisors; he felt that because of their union sentiments, they couldn't be trusted to carry out his policies. I asked Cortez whether Frye ever brought up the subject of union busting, and he said it was never discussed. Cortez was dismissed at the end of his one-year probationary period, largely because Frye was threatened by Cortez's stature with the men. Frye would not tolerate anyone who usurped his authority.[16] The fact that Cortez supported our union efforts didn't help his cause. Sarpy stayed on for several years before retiring, Hodges stayed on after consolidation, and Pat Murphy finished out his career with the department.

At the suggestion of the union's attorney, a federal mediator was now involved in bargaining talks. Commissioner Robert C. Leitner of the Federal Mediation and Conciliation Service was trying to find common ground between the two sides. Having an impartial third party removed some of the emotion from the bargaining process, and this was the breakthrough we needed.[17] Several more negotiating sessions were held, and a tentative agreement was reached in October 1979. A one-year contract was signed on December 3, 1979, retroactive to October 1, 1979. Although this contract was heavily weighted on the side of management, including prohibition against picketing, we did receive a 20 percent pay raise (see Appendix E).

Although we had finally ratified a contract, working conditions didn't improve. In fact, they continued to deteriorate. And men assigned to Central Station were in the spotlight, especially me as union spokesman. To give the reader a sense of how angry we were at the administration, and Frye in particular, a story about Cookie is appropriate. Cookie was a mixed terrier that accompanied Frye wherever he went. When Cookie died there was serious discussion among the more radical element within the union of exhuming the body and having it stuffed. They wanted to mount Cookie on a skateboard and roll him down the hallway past Chief Frye's office, thinking this might put Frye over the edge.

Immediately after ratification of the first contract, Local 2624 started preparing for next year's contract negotiations, gathering data from area fire departments on wages, benefits, and working conditions. Ed DeVries, assigned as the lieutenant at Station 3, worked on contract language while on duty. He could have been terminated if caught, so lookouts were posted. He would hide his work above the ceiling tiles in his bunkroom whenever Frye came by the station. Guys assigned to Central Station did their part by paying close attention to the strategy sessions Frye held with the commissioners and his executive staff. Although Florida had a Sunshine Law that required an open-door policy for public meetings, this rule was routinely disregarded. Snippets of conversation could be heard through the closed door of Frye's office and by listening at the outside wall of his office with a stethoscope. All of this information was funneled to the union. We would continue negotiating one-year contracts until the fire control districts were consolidated. The process didn't get any easier, though much of the wrangling now was about benefits and not salary.[18]

The specter of consolidation did more to improve labor relations than anything else. None of us thought it would be a benefit, including the administration and the public we served, so it became one area of common ground. We can thank the Palm Beach County Commission and the Florida State Legislature for having the courage and foresight to force the fire control districts to merge. Disparate levels of staffing, training, equipment, salary, and benefits all contributed to that decision. The long public battle between Local 2624 and Del-Trail's administration also forced commissioners to work toward consolidation.[19]

People have strong opinions about labor unions, but these early labor battles set the stage for better salaries, benefits, and working conditions for all firefighters. The International Association of Fire Fighters was formed in 1918 to improve safety, wages, and working conditions for our nation's fire-fighters. And it is only recently that firefighting has been considered a professional occupation, rather than a job comprised of an unskilled labor force. Now, the IAFF gives a voice to thousands of local unions across the United States and Canada, ensuring better education, safety, wages, and benefits to the men and women who protect our communities. I am proud of my small part in bringing Local 2624 from an idea formed in John Tiersch's living room and the apparatus bay of Del-Trail's Central Station to a reality that dramatically improved our wages, benefits, and working conditions.

7—Country Jams and Unions

The year 1979 was tumultuous, to say the least. Labor-management issues were at a head and our newly formed union, Local 2624, needed money to pay for attorney's fees in our fight for better working conditions, salary, and benefits. It was a time for union members to stand strong, but that wasn't going to happen without a lot more money flowing into our union bank account. A lot of ideas were floated on how to raise money, but we kept returning to the idea of a barbecue. We figured people would pay to eat chicken, drink beer, and listen to music. The problem was where to hold the proposed gathering. The union didn't own property and what we envisioned would require a big piece of land with proper infrastructure.

Nick Knott was one of our many volunteers, and though not involved with the union, he was very supportive of our efforts and offered his property as a place to hold the cookout. Nick was one of the last holdouts in an area that was slowly giving way to housing developments and huge gated communities. A conservative family man, Nick dressed in blue jeans and denim work shirts, and was rail thin from hours spent working his land and raising his family. He lived on 10 acres west of town, and his property was perfect: far enough out so we wouldn't disturb the neighbors, complete with a covered area with power for the band to set up, a homemade cinderblock grill big enough to cook several hundred chickens, and a big field to park cars. The only amenity he lacked was toilets.

I was one of several men on the organizing committee for this party, and a suggestion was made to "borrow" portable toilets from the Kings Point construction site, now one of the largest Jewish retirement communities in South Florida. In 1979 it was hundreds of acres of cow pasture dotted with scrub pine and palmetto with survey stakes snaking throughout to denote future roads. And there were portable toilets everywhere. Several of us were tasked with requisitioning toilets, and we were able to procure three that didn't have much in their holding tanks, a priority when tipping the toilet into the bed of a pick-up truck. We posted signs on the three toilets: "women only — men out back!" Returning them was easier. Nick had a tractor with a loader, so it was a simple job to load them onto the trucks and then tip them off back at the construction site, albeit somewhat used.

Tickets went on sale in early March with a date of April 8, 1978, set for the big bash. We billed it as Local 2624's Country Jam, and little did we know how successful it would be or how many Country Jams would be in our future (see Appendix F). Ticket sales were brisk, especially to brother firefighters from neighboring departments, nurses from the local hospitals, and local law enforcement personnel. We charged five dollars for a chicken dinner and a soda, and sold beer on the side — any restaurant or bar will tell you that is where the money is made. I think we cleared six or seven hundred dollars — not as much as we had hoped, but it was our first venture into the entertainment business and proved that the food, beer, and music formula worked. Future Country Jams would clear tens of thousands of dollars.

Music was provided by Hot Lanta Band, a group my buddy, Bill Rogers, started in the early 1970s. They covered all the songs of the Southern rock genre, and many that Billy wrote. I can still hear Bill belting out "Free Bird" as he played the keyboard like a madman at the Gipper Lounge in Delray Beach, Florida. I will always remember those gigs, because I helped him move his ancient Wurlitzer organ. We would bust a gut loading it in the back of my pick-up truck; it had to weigh 400 pounds.

We held the Country Jam at Nick's place two years running, and Nick and Roger Hackle did the cooking. Roger was a driver engineer at the Central Station where I worked and a wonderful cook. For me, the fire department was a finishing school for cooking. Roger taught me many things, including how to cut up chicken (a vanishing skill and something the supermarkets have taken advantage of with a higher price per pound for quartered chicken over whole chickens; after cutting up 150 chickens for the barbecue, a process that took about 20 seconds per bird, I have never bought anything but whole chickens). He also taught me how to sharpen knives, a skill that goes hand in hand with cutting meat.

Roger was a master at Southern barbecue. I remember a party he threw at his house that was billed as the "Beast Feast." He used a huge smoker to prepare venison, wild hog, alligator, possum, armadillo, and raccoon, then cut the meat into indistinguishable chunks glazed with sauce. I had no idea what I was eating, but everything was delicious. I live in Tennessee now, but the rednecks here don't have anything on those Florida boys, including making moonshine. After a day of cooking and staying hydrated with beer and shine, Roger fired up his airboat and did a couple of laps around the house, blowing pine needles everywhere. His wife was not amused.

In addition to good food and cold beer, we had a concession stand where we sold T-shirts with a screen-printed logo advertising Local 2624's first

John Tiersch, shown standing in front of Engine 10, was a leader in efforts to unionize. John was also one of the first to be cross-trained as a paramedic. He is wearing medical gloves and was checking the rescue truck parked to the left of Engine 10 (courtesy Edward DeVries).

annual Country Jam. Besides being a skilled musician, Bill Rogers was a talented artist and designed the graphics for the first and all subsequent T-shirts we sold at other Country Jams. Billy's signature work was a cartoon of a short, dumpy fireman with a helmet pulled down over his eyes so that just a large nose stuck out. He would use this caricature in many ways, even painting it on the side of Rick Hodges' personal pick-up truck. Hodges had dared him to do it, not thinking he would. That cartoon depicted a fireman saluting an upside-down American flag, the universal sign of distress, with a hand-lettered caption below it declaring, "Hodges' Heroes." I still have some of those original cartoons, satirizing various non-union staff during the troubles; they would often mysteriously appear on station bulletin boards and, though quickly torn down by the chief, would reappear as soon as he went home. I wish they could be displayed on these pages, but they are probably best left in my filing cabinet, to be pulled out when old retired firemen come to visit and it's time to open a bottle and reminisce.

If memory serves, we held five jams. I chaired most of them and the most memorable was the last, held off Clint Moore Road at the South Florida Polo Grounds in Boca Raton. By then, organizing the event was almost a full-

Though this photograph was taken long after the Country Jams, it is one of the only photographs of Nick Knott shown with other Del-Trail firemen. Left to right: Mutt Gaylord, Lenny Volpe, Bill Rogers, Henry Cusell, Nick Knott, Larry Manley. Kneeling: Lee Tenney and Roger Hackle (courtesy Lee Tenney).

time job, and we enlisted corporate help from Budweiser and Cisco Food. In addition to food, beer, and music — still Hot Lanta Band — we had dunk tanks and clowns for the kids. I'm not sure there was ever an official tally at the gate, but the press reported attendance at close to 1,200 people. It had grown far beyond a small party for emergency service personnel. I remember changing out taps on the two Budweiser trucks that were set up as our beer station. I'm certain that selling 50 kegs of beer qualifies as a party. By then it was a serious money-maker, and we continued to have a serious need for money.

Although the Country Jams started as a way to raise money for bargaining rights, we were now in a larger fight. In 1984 the tax districts merged to form Palm Beach County Fire-Rescue. The different local unions merged as well, recertified as Local 2928. Now the push was to woo county and state politicians. We were becoming better organized and understood that involvement in local and state politics would play a major role in the success of both the union and the fire department. At this point the office of union president was a full-time position, and through bargaining the president was able to maintain his rank and department benefits.

In the late 1990s union and fire department relations were still rocky. At one point there was a vote of no confidence in the fire chief after stalled contract talks, a vote I never agreed with. A billboard proclaiming the same was prominently positioned across the street from fire rescue headquarters at Military Trail and Southern Boulevard. Firefighters didn't realize Chief Brice was building a fire department from the ground up; dealing with the union was not an immediate priority. However rocky the marriage was, it was a marriage neither side could afford to walk away from and differences were put aside. The union wanted better pay and benefits; the administration wanted better funding levels from the county. Uncontrolled growth meant building new fire stations, hiring additional personnel, and buying more fire apparatus, a hugely expensive proposition and something the Palm Beach County administrators and fire rescue weren't always in agreement on. But growth wasn't slowing down. The union was able to get out the vote for politicians who favored fire rescue, so, with give and take from both sides, relations improved. Ultimately, it was a process that brought both sides together in a working relationship that benefited everyone.

As the years went by, more men and women from other departments decided to join our union. Now, Palm Beach Gardens, Lake Worth, North Palm Beach, Palm Beach, Riviera Beach, Delray Beach, and Tequesta are all under the umbrella of Local 2928, increasing our membership to approximately 2000 people.[1] This increase in membership broadened our influence in local politics, the life blood of unions across the country. Now, when someone wants to run for office, they know that union support is critical. Politicians know the value of being able to count on 100 or so firefighters holding campaign signs, especially during a close race.

We were also becoming more active at the state level. When Rick Scott was elected governor of Florida in 2011, Local 2928's two legislative vice presidents lived in Tallahassee, spending their time conferring with state representatives in an attempt to blunt some of the governor's more egregious initiatives. The union wasn't completely successful in its efforts, but at least Florida firefighters didn't lose ground the way firefighters from other states lost benefits, especially retirement benefits.

There are many partnerships between the local union and the department that benefit everyone. One that means a great deal to operations personnel is a partnership that helps families cope with hurricanes. The nature of our work means we are on duty when everyone else is at home protecting their families and property from the storms that visit us each hurricane season. Imagine boarding up your house and kissing your family goodbye, hoping, but never knowing, that they will be safe as you go to work for 48 or 72 hours. This partnership between the union and the department allows personnel to work outside the normal scope of their duty, visiting any family whose husband or wife is on duty and needs assistance. If a family needs gas for a generator, ice for a cooler, or a tarp to patch a leaking roof, union members make sure these needs are met. If a firefighter on duty can't reach a family member by phone, someone from this team will go to the person's home and report back. These team members give the men and women on duty assurance that their families are safe, which allows the people on duty during the storm to complete their mission without unnecessary worry.

Another successful partnership between the local and the department is our annual fund-raising effort for the Muscular Dystrophy Association. In 2011, firefighters across the country raised $27.2 million for MDA in their fill-the-boot campaign, more than any other single organization. Over the past several years, Local 2928 has collected close to $100,000. All the money goes to local organizations within the community that help families care for loved ones who suffer from muscular dystrophy. Many of our firefighters also participate in camps that benefit children who live with muscular dystrophy.

Unions will remain controversial, especially if your views lean toward management rights. And even though labor and management frequently work toward common goals, the union will always place its membership's interests first. Labor organized for a reason; in the case of firefighters, it was an effort to improve safety on the fire ground. The IAFF continues to lobby Congress for health care reform, economic security, and safety for all union members. They are also directly involved in many programs that address safety issues. One program, called the Near-Miss Reporting System, allows crews to formally report situations that almost caused injury or death. It is hoped that by sharing these experiences, other crews can learn from them and not repeat the same mistakes. My last year on the job, my crews had a near-miss experience that I reported through this system.[2] Approximately 100 firefighters die each year and tens of thousands are injured. Firefighting is inherently dangerous work; I doubt that will ever change. Thankfully, the IAFF continues to lobby for new legislative initiatives designed to improve firefighter health and safety.

One of the biggest threats to emergency service personnel is inadequate staffing levels. In fact, there is a direct correlation between inadequate staffing and increases in injuries and death on emergency scenes. The Federal Emergency Management Agency (FEMA) provides grant money through a program called Staffing for Adequate Fire and Emergency Response (SAFER) to help fire and police agencies maintain safe staffing levels.[3] Again, this initiative is supported through the IAFF.

There have been a lot of changes since our clandestine union meetings in John Tiersch's living room, where we plotted our next move against Frye and his administration. Every fireman who worked for Del-Trail during that period describes those early years the same way: rough times in which we all had a sense of purpose. We were pioneers in the nascent push for better working conditions, salary, benefits, and firefighter safety. The Country Jams helped raise money for our cause and brought us together as brothers. The bond Del-Trail firemen formed in those early years is as strong now as it was then.

8—Banished to the Beach

Ray Abell would pick me up at my house every duty day at a quarter to six. I would be dressed in my Class A uniform, shirt starched and ironed, pants creased, and shoes shined, ready for another day of R & R at Station 2 in Highland Beach. Ray was the lieutenant, and I was the driver on Engine 9. We averaged four calls a month, most of them medical, and spent the rest of the time playing ping-pong or swimming.

I was transferred to Highland Beach during the winter of 1981 after Chief Frye decided I was being too vocal about my union views. As the union spokesman, I was an easy target for Frye's anger. Ray was assigned as the lieutenant because Frye couldn't send just me. Ray and I were good friends, and my year at the beach was one of the best of my career.

The station was in the middle of a four-mile strip of A1A, lined on the beach side by towering sand dunes studded with Australian pines and palmetto scrub and on the intra-coastal side with beautiful older homes that were slowly giving way to high-rise buildings and condominiums. With only a few side streets, we could be at any address within three or four minutes.

We always stopped at the Clock Restaurant in Delray Beach for breakfast before reporting for duty. They served wonderful coffee, and we both looked forward to breakfast and relaxing conversation before going to work. We talked about many things, but the conversation would usually come back to Ray's nursery business. He owned two acres west of town and sold ornamental plants and small trees. He would discuss his business plans, telling me how he was going to expand. Abell's Nursery is now one of the largest growers of ornamental plants in South Florida, encompassing over 65 acres with annual sales averaging millions of dollars. Most firefighters work on their days off; few were as successful as Ray.

Our daily routine never varied much. After relieving the off-going crew we would both change into jump suits and start our morning chores. Ray would clean the station, and I would check the equipment on Engine 9. Even though the engine rarely turned a wheel on calls, I was always methodical about the truck check. The last piece of equipment checked was the most important: binoculars. I always walked across the street to the beach to check for focus. There were a lot of Canadian women who vacationed in the area, and they liked to sunbathe topless or even in the nude.

Morning chores completed, I would talk to Ray about dinner, a popular topic in any firehouse. We were both good cooks and would take turns in the kitchen preparing wonderful meals. Some of our favorites included Rock Cornish game hens with rice pilaf and stir-fried green beans with garlic and roasted peppers, or lasagna with a sausage meat sauce and homemade garlic bread, or skirt steak with chimichurri sauce and roasted sweet potatoes with thyme.

Meal planning out of the way, we would get on with the real business of the day: playing ping-pong or swimming. I usually elected to swim first and would wear my bathing suit under my jumpsuit, grab a portable radio and walk across to the beach. We termed this "physical training" in case anyone asked why a fireman was swimming on duty. If I was lucky, there would be a girl sunbathing who would monitor the radio. If I was real lucky, she would be topless.

My marriage had ended amicably, and I was dating Candy. Occasionally, she would walk to the station for lunch. After eating we would walk across to the beach and sit on the driftwood bench, talking about our plans for the future. When she was ready to leave, I would give her a ride in the engine to the end of our response zone, lessening the distance of her walk from five miles to three. Any gal who would walk that distance in the heat of a South Florida summer was tops in my book. We were married in 1984 and remain happily married.

Ray and I would play competitive ping-pong for hours. The table was set up in the bay, and we would strip down to shorts and T-shirts to play. He was much better than me, and after an hour of play and only winning three or four games out of 15 or 20, I would slam my paddle on the table and quit. I'd be back at the table the next shift, always thinking that I would improve. It never happened. Ray reminded me of that fact years later at my retirement party with the gift of a ping-pong paddle.

Occasionally we had to run a call. With an average of four calls per month, which is less than one call every other shift, the only two calls I remember with clarity were a fire in an old beach house and the birth of a baby. We were paged for the fire call around 3 A.M., a time of the morning that invariably meant a working fire. The second due engine was coming from Central Station on Military Trail, a long 20 minutes away. Knowing we were on our own for that length of time was scary and tends to focus your attention. In 1981 there were no rules governing how many firefighters had to be on scene before fire operations could begin. The National Fire Protection Association and the Occupational Safety and Health Association finally addressed this issue by mandating that at least four firefighters be on scene before interior operations can begin. Although the language is directed at Industrial Fire Brigade members, the standard has been adopted by most states, including Florida. Essentially, it requires that two members with adequate training be stationed outside a structure before two other members may initiate operations inside a structure.[1]

The two of us arrived at a small beach house within five minutes of the page and found black smoke pouring out the front door. An old man, disoriented from the smoke, was standing in the doorway, making no attempt to move the few more steps that would have taken him away from danger. I put the truck into pump gear and pulled a pre-connect while Ray moved the old man out of the way. We both donned our Survive-Air breathing apparatus and made our way into the house. We found a mattress on fire in the bedroom and quickly hauled it out to the parking lot. Ray did a sweep to make sure there wasn't anyone else inside or further fire extension, while I attended to the man. The second due engine arrived about the time the old man was getting his bearings, thanks to a little oxygen therapy. Captain Kemp was the officer on the incoming engine, and he was pissed that we put the fire out so quickly; he was hoping to play. You have to be a firefighter to understand that kind of thinking.

The medical call was one of the most bizarre I ever responded to. The information from dispatch was muddled; they weren't sure if the woman was in labor or had already delivered. Ray was a first responder, not an EMT, so it would be up to me to take the lead in providing medical assistance. This would be the first of three OB calls in my career, and I was frantically trying to recall all the steps I would have to take to help with a delivery. We pulled into the driveway of a mid-rise and parked behind a Highland Beach police cruiser. I grabbed the 747 med-box and Ray grabbed the oxygen. We rode the elevator to the fifth floor in nervous silence, wondering what we would find.

We were met by a surreal scene as we walked into the apartment. It was 11 o'clock at night, not a light on anywhere; the only illumination was candlelight. A nude woman lay on the living room floor with a baby between her legs, umbilical cord still attached. The coppery smell of blood was overpowering. The woman was surrounded by lighted candles, wax pooling into the carpet. Her husband sat in a chair smoking a cigarette, a somewhat late postcoital smoke. I tried to shake off what I was seeing and began medical care for the baby and mother. I clamped and cut the cord, wrapped the baby in a multi-trauma dressing to preserve his body heat, and placed him on his mother's belly, while Ray administered oxygen to both mother and child. She had lost a lot of blood and was in shock, and the baby was cyanotic.

The ambulance arrived, and we loaded mother and baby in the back and turned the scene over to the police. One of the frustrating things about our business is the lack of closure on medical calls. We never did learn why the father was sitting there casually smoking a cigarette while his wife struggled with a newborn amid a circle of burning candles.

My year at the beach came to an end when Chief Frye found out how much I was enjoying my exile. I was transferred to Station 3 in Sandalfoot Cove, the southwestern-most station in Del-Trail's response area. It was a station that would be my home off and on over the coming years, both as a fire-

Del-Trail Fire Department Patch (courtesy Cindy Smith).

fighter and as an officer; this station would also feature prominently in the on-the-job training that is such an essential part of transforming young firemen into students of the profession. I guess Frye hadn't figured out that it didn't matter where he sent me; I was always going to have fun. Ray was assigned as the lieutenant, and we went from four or five calls a month to four or five a shift. Ask any firefighter and they will tell you it's better to be busy, especially when you get to fight fire every day.

Part II. Middle Years:
Lieutenant and Captain

On the Job: Little Blue Dress

I was promoted to captain in 1986 and assigned to Station 42, headquarters station for Battalion Four. The first significant call I ran as a newly minted captain was a traffic accident on the Florida Turnpike that ranks as one of the worst calls I have ever seen. I spent 31 years working in some of the busiest stations and have seen my share of the dark side. This was a truly horrific call, and even now, writing about this accident is a difficult process. Images long buried in that special place in the brain that keep most firefighters sane have once again been brought to the forefront, as disturbing today as they were then.

I supervised 11 people, staffing an engine, a ladder, two rescue trucks, and a brush truck. We averaged 18 calls in a 24-hour shift; sleep was something we dreamed about but rarely achieved. Beyond the call volume, headquarters stations are always busy. There were administrative offices for the battalion chief and my immediate supervisor, District Chief Glen Kimberly, as well as the recruit-training academy. It was a place where a new captain was apt to be observed pretty carefully.

Maybe because Chief Kimberly and I shared the same building, although we had different offices, he thought it was his duty to help me manage the day-to-day operations of my shift, despite also being the supervisor of six lieutenants at six other stations within the battalion. We spoke on a daily basis, behind closed doors, about his unique management style until he finally relented and let me manage affairs at my own station.

One of my duties each morning was to balance staffing among the stations within the battalion. Station 46 at the south end of the county usually had an extra person, so it was my responsibility to call the lieutenant, Al Sierra, and tell him to shift his extra person to a station that was short staffed. Nobody liked to give up personnel, and Al always complained bitterly that I was "robbing" him. I would curtly inform him to "just do it" and hang up. Getting staffing adjusted as soon as possible is a critical priority, and this wasn't the time for debate. After repeated mornings of the same scenario, with Al complaining and me telling him to just do it and then hanging up, he started calling me Captain Happy. The nickname stuck, and when I made chief several years later, my nickname changed to Chief Cheerful.

It's funny how different sayings that are attributed to a person can stick with you throughout a career. I enjoyed cooking and used to make supper for the crew as often as possible. It was something I had done as a lieutenant and I found that it helped build crew morale. When you work with other people on a 24-hour shift, they become a second family. After working hard all day it was relaxing to sit down with the shift and discuss the day's events, review how various calls went, catch up on the latest rumors, and field any problems that might need my follow up. I always charged three dollars, regardless of the cost of the meal. Sometimes it was more, sometimes less, but the cost averaged three dollars. Excess money would go into the kitty, or I would take money out as necessary. Inevitably, someone would ask, "What's for dinner?" I never knew what I was going to cook until I went to the store and could see what looked good and would work within that three dollar budget, so I always said, "Three bucks, damn good meal!" If someone didn't feel like eating and paying the three dollars, I would tell them, "No problem, you're still doing the dishes." Like family, everyone ate together.

I still meet people, usually guys who were on my shift, who greet me with, "Three bucks, damn good meal!"

I had been a lieutenant on an engine company running my own station for the past three years, but taking the step up to captain was a real paradigm shift. The workload was double what it had been, and even though the nature of emergency calls stayed pretty much the same, my responsibilities as incident commander changed. I was in command of more complex incidents and given the latitude by the district chiefs to run the scene, even though they always had the option of assuming command. I was about to learn that command of an incident sometimes comes at a terrible price.

Station 42 received the page for a traffic accident on the turnpike at 0330 hours, the type of call we routinely run with one engine and one rescue. The accident was just south of the interchange, and I could see a glow in the sky that told me it might be more than a traffic accident. I told my firefighter to gear up for a fire and radioed dispatch with an update and asked if there was further information.

They replied, "Negative."

We arrived about a minute later to find a tractor-trailer truck with the cab completely engulfed in fire, including the saddle tanks that were loaded with 100 gallons of diesel fuel. Seventy-five yards beyond the semi was a pick-up truck partially involved in fire and 50 feet from the pick-up was a car that was fully involved. There were five people lying on the road, all with third-degree burns, and a man with third-degree burns standing over them. I still have a clear image of that man, flesh charred black on his arms, chest, and face, his hair and eyebrows burned off, trying to speak to me as he gestured toward the pick-up and car. His lungs and larynx were severely compromised from the burns, so it was difficult for him to speak, but he managed to tell me that he was the driver of the semi and had hit the pick-up and the car. He was the one who pulled the five people out of the burning car.

There was also a man dressed in a turban and robe, uninjured, standing with his arms folded, a look of detachment, even disdain, on his face as he observed us trying to bring order out of chaos. He looked like a character from a late-night movie that had shown up on the wrong set, but I was too busy to question him. I radioed an arrival report to dispatch; ordered another engine, a tanker, four more rescue trucks, helicopter transport, and a district chief; and established command.

Our first priority was patient care, and it was a long 10 minutes before adequate help started to arrive. As we assisted the paramedics with triage and treatment, I was watching the fires grow larger. Chief Kimberly was first to arrive; I briefed him on what we had and transferred command to him.

Additional help soon started to arrive, allowing us to suppress the vehicle fires and package and transport the burn patients. The next engine in was assigned to extinguish the pick-up truck and the car. The tanker arrived and supported my engine in putting out the tractor-trailer fire. The rescues came in and started dealing with patients. After what seemed like hours but in reality was only about 30 minutes, the fires were out and the patients had been transported to area hospitals, the most critical going by helicopter. It was time to gear down, get some water into us and start to figure out what had happened — it was time to talk with the man in the turban.

The Florida Highway Patrol covers the turnpike, and they were starting their investigation to try and determine the sequence of events that had caused such a horrific accident. A traffic homicide investigator was now on scene because it was almost certain that one or more people would die from injuries sustained as a result of the accident. He began by questioning the man dressed in the turban and robe. What we learned enraged us to the point that some of my guys had to be restrained.

The man being questioned was a member of the Yahweh, a fringe religious sect. All of the people involved in the accident were being recruited into the sect and were caravanning in the pick-up and car, on their way to Miami for indoctrination, when the car quit running. Rather than pull into the break-down lane, they simply stopped in the right-hand travel lane to hook up a tow-rope from the pick-up to the car and continue their journey. That's when the driver of the tractor-trailer hit the car and the truck. He estimated his speed at 75 miles per hour and stated to the trooper that he never touched his brakes because he simply did not see the vehicles.

As the sun started to come up, the light of day showed the true horror of the scene. The car was a charred hulk, the tractor-trailer cab was burned down to the frame and the front of the trailer was melted, revealing a cargo of appliances that would never reach their destination. The pick-up bed was burned down to the rails, but the cab was still intact. The familiar stench that accompanies vehicle fires permeated the air.

I walked over and peered into the cab of the pick-up and was sickened to discover a small girl in a blue dress curled in a fetal position on the passenger-side floorboard. She was dead, looking as if she had just fallen asleep. The coroner's report showed that she died from smoke inhalation. I'm still haunted by the image of that little girl, and I will always wonder whether she may have been alive when we first arrived.

I assumed command responsibilities at this accident. And even though command was transferred to Chief Kimberly early on, it was my job to thoroughly assess the scene. Would the outcome have been different for that little girl if I had done a more thorough job assessing the scene? I second-guess myself, even now.

If only the man dressed in the robe and turban had said something. If only I had taken the time to question him. There was no doubt now that it would be a traffic homicide investigation with him as the main focus.

9—Promotional Process

Competitive examinations are a way of life in the fire service, and it has been interesting for me to witness the evolution of testing from my early days with Del-Trail Fire Department, when it was a loosely defined competitive process, to Palm Beach County Fire-Rescue, where testing is a structured process that is part of the collective bargaining agreement and administered by an outside agency. I always acquitted myself well in the classroom and was good at taking examinations, something that served me well when testing for driver engineer, lieutenant, and captain.

I briefly described the testing process for driver engineer in a previous chapter; that promotional examination fell into the "loosely defined competitive process" category. I don't think there were any irregularities, but it certainly would have been easy for the administration to promote the person of their choice, regardless of test scores. Testing for lieutenant occurred in 1983 while I was still working for Del-Trail, and this was a more structured process. Like the driver exam, it was a two-part test, written and practical, with a large number of books and manuals that covered fire behavior, management principles, and building construction. The practical portion of the exam was administered by fire officers from other fire departments in the area.

I breezed through the written portion but knew this part of the exam only accounted for 40 percent of the overall score. The practical part of the test was administered in a classroom setting using slides that depicted an escalating apartment complex fire. Looking back, it doesn't seem like such a difficult fire, but as a soon-to-be new lieutenant, it was a daunting scenario. There were 12 of us who had made the cut from the written portion of the exam, allowing us to move on to the practical. We had no idea what the scenario would entail, only that it would be a fire and we were expected to use the same resources normally available. We were sequestered in a room down the hall from where the scenario was being run, each of us nervous but trying not to show it.

When it was my turn, I was given a portable radio and an index card that told me I was the officer on the first engine to arrive at a two-story apartment complex with one second-floor apartment on fire. When I walked through the door into the classroom, I was confronted with a large screen with a slide depicting a two-story apartment building, the middle apartment on the second floor showing fire and heavy smoke. I noticed four fire officers sitting at a table toward the back of the room with notepads and pencils in front of them. They were the guys who would determine whether my performance warranted a gold badge.

My first action was to speak into the portable radio and notify dispatch about present conditions. I described the building as a concrete structure with a common open balcony running the length of the building with a stairway at both ends. I stated that there was a hydrant in front of the building and my driver was doing a hook-up. I announced that my company was stretching a line to the apartment on fire, requested a second alarm, and ordered the second due engine to ladder the back of the building for a second means of egress.

As the scenario played out, additional index cards, each with another problem, were placed in front of me and different slides were shown. If a candidate was making the right decisions, the fire would start to go out. If a candidate was making poor decisions, the slides showed more fire and the index cards kept coming. None of us put the fire out — that was how the scenario was designed — but toward the end of that long 10 minutes I had white smoke coming from the apartment.

It was a week before we were notified of our standing, and I was surprised to learn that I had scored number one. However, the department used the rule of three, which meant they could pass over the two highest-scoring candidates and choose the number three man. Because I had been union spokesman, and at constant odds with Chief Frye, I was worried they might do just that. However, they went right down the line, and I received a gold lieutenant's badge with bugles to match on December 1, 1983.[1]

I had begun to develop my own management style while working as a driver engineer, partly by emulating officers I had worked for since coming into the fire department and partly from my own beliefs about how things should be done. Being in charge of a couple of firemen who are cleaning a bay floor or waxing a truck is far different from being in charge of a station. Leading individuals who didn't feel the same passion I felt toward the job was the most difficult part of the transition process. I will never understand, or have any respect for, firefighters who come to work with a lousy attitude and are not willing to train every day.

A firefighter's position at the bottom of the rank structure is an easy position to be in. All you have to say is "yes, sir," and do your job. As a driver engineer I had officers above me who told me what to do, but I also had firefighters below me over whose actions and job duties I had limited responsibility. As lieutenant, I still had officers above me directing my actions, but now I had a station full of firefighters who were very good at pushing the envelope, challenging my decisions at every turn. This is a vetting process that every officer goes through when they receive their gold badge. I'm sure the reader can recall how they acted in high school whenever there was a substitute teacher in the classroom.

Mike Sedgewick was a person you loved to hate; he knew how to push my buttons. Tenacious, with a truly acerbic personality, he was skillful at always being on the edge of insubordination but never falling off the wire; he knew just how far he could push me. We worked it out over time, a battle of wills through which we both learned valuable lessons about small group dynamics. I became a better fire officer and he became a better firefighter, eventually replying, "yes, sir," but never with any deference. Deference has to be earned, something that doesn't come easily (and for some officers, not at all). Taking care of your people, demonstrating skillful management, and utilizing a leadership style that is fair and consistent is the foundation that will lead to respect and, if you stay the course, maybe deference.

I was promoted to captain on September 13, 1986, two years after consolidation. The testing was conducted through an outside agency, and again I scored number one, this time among a much larger pool of applicants (according to official correspondence from Palm Beach County personnel department). At this point I was comfortable managing people, but moving to the rank of captain was a transition process that required exceptional time-management skills. Because there weren't a lot of captains, the rank came with more authority, more responsibility, and much more administrative work that tied us to a desk for hours at a time.

The next step up the promotional ladder was district chief, and I was promoted to that rank on December 18, 1999, and assigned to Battalion Two.[2] This was the second time I had taken the district chief's exam. I didn't place high enough to be promoted on the first examination, a bitter pill to swallow, but I had no one to blame but myself. The testing process for district chief was similar to the captain's exam, but the amount of study material had tripled. Twelve different texts were used, and we could be tested on any portion. It was a bitch of an examination.

All organizations have people in positions of authority that make you scratch your head and wonder how they made it to that level. Fire departments are no different, and the Peter Principle (indicating those who have risen to their highest level of incompetence) was alive and well at both Del-Trail and Palm Beach County Fire-Rescue. Most of the folks who held this coveted title weren't on shift running calls but higher in the chain of command, pulling the strings for the rest of us. Not surprisingly, most had never taken a competitive exam. There is no need to be more specific; that wouldn't serve any purpose. But it is interesting to note how these folks forced the rest of us to become innovative. We became very adept at doing an end-run around policies that didn't make any sense at all. Dealing with these folks can wear you down or make you stronger. It made most of us stronger, and over time we were able to prevail against policies that inhibited our ability to provide the best emergency service to the public.

Randy Pausch was a professor at Carnegie Mellon University who was dying from cancer and wanted to leave a legacy for his children. He accomplished this through a series of lectures that were presented to students and faculty at Carnegie Mellon. In his last lecture, "Really Achieving Your Childhood Dreams," Professor Pausch speaks about those in positions of authority who are always saying no. He describes this as running into a brick wall, something that is all too common in many organizations. But he goes on to say that the wall is only there for those other people, the ones who give up too easily. He went over, around, or through the wall, doing whatever was necessary to get the job done — in his case, teaching in the most innovative way possible. In his lecture, he speaks at length about innovation, and how easy it is for people to throw stones at the innovators.[3]

Innovation is something firefighters do well. Telling a firefighter it's against policy or there is no money in the budget is a red flag; it only makes that person work harder. One example is a discussion about new technology associated with our radio and dispatch system. Chief Jim Gribble and I were asked to represent field personnel in deciding what system would be most beneficial to the people running the calls. We were a lonely voice in the wilderness. Others on the committee had more bugles and more authority over the budget process. When Jim and I kept arguing for a particular feature that would have made our job in the field easier and safer, they kept saying that it wasn't technically possible.

After several hours of circular argument, I finally asked if anyone was familiar with the expansion theory posed by Mark McCutcheon, a Canadian-born electrical engineer. Of course I received blank looks, so I gave them an overview of the theory, which posits that electrons have a constant subatomic expansion rather than an endless charge. McCutcheon's theory unites the four fundamental forces of nature: gravity, electromagnetism, and both strong and weak nuclear forces.[4] I was fairly worked up and came to the point by saying that if this guy could develop a theory that had mainstream scientists reexamining decades-old theories about the expansion of the universe, surely we could figure out a way to install a radio system that would be beneficial to the folks putting their butts on the line every day. When I threatened to start drawing equations on the walls, they finally relented and agreed to incorporate the changes we were asking for.

You might ask what this has to do with promotions, and I will once again refer you to the Peter Principle. A lot of mid-level folks, and even many department heads, never took a competitive exam to gain that position; they were appointed. I guess they were born on third base and thought they had hit a triple. Many did a good job, but there seemed to be more than a few who had just enough power to keep throwing up those brick walls, forcing the rest of us to come to work each day with more resolve.

It's gratifying to see the people I supervised early in my career stepping into upper-management positions in different areas of the department. Although there isn't a testing process for moving from district chief to battalion chief and above, it is a process where candidates are vetted before being appointed to the position. Most of the people recently appointed are excelling in their new positions. The department has reached a point where the old guard has been replaced with people who had to take competitive examinations throughout their careers to attain higher rank. The result is a high level of competence, inclusive management, and a better understanding of how their roles in the organization support fire department operations. All the functions of a fire department ultimately support Operations, the division that provides emergency service. Fire departments are forever evolving, sometimes getting better, sometimes not. Palm Beach County Fire-Rescue continues to evolve as an organization, providing cost-effective service to its constituents through an ongoing commitment to excellence that is rarely compromised, in large part because the people running the department now remember where they came from.

10—Sandalfoot Cove

Station 3 in Sandalfoot Cove played a pivotal role in my early years as a firefighter and later as a driver engineer and station officer. I worked at that station first as a rookie firefighter under Lieutenant Ed Hines, later as a driver under Lieutenant Ray Abell, and finally as the station officer. I worked with crews who were exceptional at their job, and we ran some of the toughest calls of my career while working at Station 3. It is those types of calls that harden firefighters to the reality of the work. And it is those types of calls that provide the experiences and training that give fire officers the ability to quickly evaluate a situation and make good decisions on the best way to mitigate an emergency, regardless of the nature of the call.

When I was assigned to Station 3 as a lieutenant, Sandalfoot Cove was a rural, unincorporated area in the southwestern portion of Palm Beach County. Bordered by the Everglades to the west and thousand-acre farms to the east and north raising vegetables for markets throughout the country, it was old Florida. Huge areas of pasture and scrub grazing land for dairy and beef cattle supported brush fires that would burn for days. Migrant farm workers living in squalor kept us busy with trauma-related medical calls; their trailers and shacks that passed for housing burned on a regular basis. It also seemed as though our station was a magnet for every kind of vagrant passing through. It was an exciting place for me to work as a young officer, and I was blessed with a crew of guys who were hard-core firefighters, staffing an engine, a rescue, and a brush. We waited a long time for any kind of help from second due companies. That suited us just fine.

John Larkin was my driver, and at six foot two, 245 pounds, he was a calming presence when the natives were restless. Bobby Perrault was my firefighter, a little shorter than Larkin, but around the same weight and inhumanly strong. He would work out with 85-pound dumbbells, doing 50 reps at a time. Perrault was my forcible entry guy on fires. Usually a shoulder into a door would do the trick; he was always a little embarrassed if he had to resort to a sledgehammer. Larry Esteban and Bruce Chelton were my paramedics and equally competent as firefighters. Larry was a gun nut, and I had to repeatedly dissuade him from carrying a shotgun on the rescue truck. He argued that because we worked in such a tough area, and sheriff's deputies were spread pretty thin, it was prudent to have a shotgun racked in a side compartment to get us by until law enforcement arrived. He had a good argument, but I could only bend the rules so far. We weren't supposed to have weapons in the station. Most station officers looked the other way concerning that rule, but carrying a shotgun on a rescue was pushing the envelope a bit too far. Chelton had his own demons. We called him "Sybil" because we were never sure whether good Bruce or bad Bruce would show up for work; it depended on his love life. Regardless of his mood, he was always squared away on calls.

We ran a lot of calls to the migrant camps that provided the stoop labor for harvesting tomatoes, peppers, celery, and lettuce. Whole families lived in one-room shacks, and it wasn't unusual for the men to get into fights on Saturday nights after drinking all day. It wasn't so bad if it was just a fist fight, but they all carried machetes. When they started carving each other up, it got ugly. We practiced battlefield medicine and became very good at treating traumatic injuries. All of us were trained as EMTs, at a minimum, so the engine always responded with the rescue to provide an extra set of hands for the paramedics. Local deputies responded as well. Even with law enforcement watching our backs, Larkin and Perrault would come off the engine with a halligan or an axe in case someone needed extra persuasion to back off.

It was already a busy Saturday night when we were paged for a fight with injuries at Jones Labor Camp, located five miles north of the station on State Road 441. We rolled out into a humid Florida night and were happy to see blue lights ahead of us. When we pulled in, I knew right away it was going to be a bad call. About 20 people were trying to crowd into a 10-by-10 shack that served as housing for a family of eight. Women were wailing in Spanish. We grabbed our equipment and followed the deputies inside. I could smell the familiar, coppery odor of blood even before we were through the door. There was a man lying on the floor with loops of intestine glistening through a five-inch slice in his stomach, where someone had eviscerated him with a machete. His right hand had three partially severed fingers, probably from defensive wounds.

Emergency medicine is never pretty, especially when it's practiced on a dirt floor in a labor camp at 11 o'clock at night. None of the shacks had more than one bare 60-watt bulb keeping the cockroaches at bay. Dim lighting and unwashed bodies sweating in 95-degree heat pressing in for a better look, clouds of mosquitoes and flies vying for blood, tense deputies trying to clear people out so we could treat the patient, rounds out the picture. Chelton and Esteban went to work, sticking the guy in the jugular vein with a 14-gauge needle. His peripheral veins had collapsed from blood loss, so the jugular was the only place to get a line started. Perrault was setting up bags of ringers that I would hold as the fluid flowed into the patient's vein. Larkin placed a mask with high-flow oxygen over the patient's nose and mouth and started handing multi-trauma dressings to the medics so they could cover the intestines that were looped outside his body and wrap his hand to keep his partially severed fingers in place. The guy was losing so much blood that he was bleeding clear after one bag of ringers.

I needed to see about setting up an LZ so we could fly the patient out. There weren't any more hands available to hold the bag of ringers, so I handed the bag to one of the migrant workers still in the room watching us work. I pantomimed holding the bag up high. He shook his head yes, and though he was a bit wide-eyed, I figured he understood. When I walked back in, he was gone, and the bag was impaled in a door frame with a six-inch knife — so much for a sterile environment. I gave the cops a WTF look, but they just shook their heads and said they didn't know where the guy went.

Treating a trauma patient is a race against time. Our job was to stabilize the patient and try to keep him alive until we could get him to the hospital. If he was going to live much beyond that golden hour, he needed blood and a surgeon. He didn't need us holding his hand on scene. The patient was soon loaded aboard our Bell 412 helicopter and flying to the trauma center that was five minutes away by air. We learned later that he survived and was back working in the fields toward the end of the summer.

I know it sounds like a cliché, but we had a Dalmatian as a mascot. Tucker was a big male and very confused about his role in the station. With so many different masters, I didn't blame him. Over time he developed a mean streak toward the world in general and toward strangers in particular. You had to watch him pretty closely during shift change in the morning; he'd get kind of anxious about who was going to be in charge. We tolerated his behavior because he was a good watchdog and took the job seriously. Not a bad thing, considering the neighborhood.

One Sunday afternoon the five of us were eating lunch —chili and grilled cheese sandwiches— enjoying a few minutes of down time. Bobby was in his usual position at the end of the table, guarding his food. He sort of reminded me of Tucker, right down to eating his chili out of a bowl that looked suspiciously like Tucker's dog food bowl, when we got banged out on a trailer fire. The bay doors operate on automatic timers, and Tucker was always spooked by the doors coming down without any human assistance. He would slink behind the hose rack until the doors were down and he was sure they weren't going to move again. Shortly after we left, an old man on a bicycle rode into the bay looking for directions, just as the bay doors were coming down. I guess Tucker took offense, because he had the guy pinned in a corner, teeth bared and continually lunging at the poor man, until we returned to the station after fighting fire for about three hours. That was the last straw in a series of escalating events involving Tucker. The week before, he had chased a guy riding a bicycle past the station and knocked him off the bike (I'm sure he was pleased to have finally caught someone on a bicycle). Chief Frye told us to get rid of the dog. It took a while, but we found a good home for Tucker just down the road from the station at Bowman's Dairy Farm.

It wasn't unusual for us to get late-night visitors at the station. Usually it was someone looking for directions, but sometimes a passerby would notify us of a wreck or a fire or maybe a car in a canal. I had my own room at the front of the station, so it was up to me to answer the door. I heard the doorbell ringing and glanced at the clock on my way to answer the door, wondering who was out and about at three in the morning. I opened the door to find a guy covered in blood from his scalp to his sneakers, his clothes in shreds. I got on the station's PA system, notifying my crew that we had a walk-in medical and then called our dispatch center, requesting a deputy. Turns out the guy was trying to break into the Sandalfoot Bar and Grill. He obviously wasn't a local, or he would have been better prepared for the German Shepherd that lived there after hours. He was lucky to get out alive.

Early morning calls, no matter the type, were the ones I dreaded most. My early morning routine includes a bathroom stop, above all else, and getting banged out on a call just when nature is calling is not a comfortable feeling. One morning, right when I was about to step into the bathroom, we caught a trailer fire. Adrenaline is not your friend at a time like this, and I really had to go by the time we pulled up to a trailer that had a lot of smoke pushing out the front door. The resident was standing in the driveway and told us he had set the kitchen on fire. I ordered my crew to take a line in and put the fire out, impressing on them not to let the fire come down the hallway because I was headed to the bathroom. There I was, struggling out of my bunker coat, air-pack on my lap with the mask over my face so I could breathe air from the tank, bunker pants around my ankles and smoke down to the floor, sitting on this guy's toilet while praying my guys were putting the fire out.

Though I wasn't on duty when this occurred, one of the most bizarre scenes imaginable greeted crews returning from a late-night fire call. Their first indication that something wasn't quite right was glass and blood on the bay floor. The window in the door leading from the bay into the dayroom was broken, and puddles of blood on the floor, the walls, and even the ceiling led them into the back bunkroom and then into the bathroom, where they found a young woman barely alive, lying unconscious in a shower stall. We learned later that she had run to the station looking for help, trying to get away from her boyfriend. She must have run into the bay just after crews left on a call and was trapped inside with her enraged boyfriend wielding a baseball bat when the bay doors came down.

Perhaps the strangest event crews experienced at that station was the theft of Brush 24. Guys were sitting in the dayroom when they heard the truck crank up and thought for a minute it might be a mechanic doing a check, until the truck pulled out of the bay and headed south on State Road 441 towards Broward County. The guys on duty called the law, and a slow police chase ensued. A brush truck isn't designed for speed, but it has other attributes, including a stout front bumper. The cops figured out after three dented cruisers that getting in front of the truck and trying to stop it wasn't going to work. Broward County deputies eventually resorted to shooting the tires out. We were proud to claim the rights to the only brush truck in the department that had been stolen and still bore bullet holes in the fenders.

It takes a long time to mold a crew to your way of doing things. On fire calls especially, it is invaluable to work with guys who know what needs to be done and can anticipate orders. This type of crew cohesiveness requires long hours of training and a large measure of trust in each other, but all good things must come to an end. After several years of working with the same people, I was reassigned. During my tenure at Station 3 I learned valuable lessons about leadership and managing emergency scenes. It was on-the-job training of the highest order, refining my skills as a fire officer for work yet to come.

11—Second Chance

It was 6 A.M. on an unusually cold 28-degree morning in early January 1985. We were returning from a fire alarm call at the Holiday Inn on Glades Road in Boca Raton, and the timing of this alarm would play a significant role in the miraculous rescue of a woman trapped in a watery grave. I was the lieutenant on Engine 56, and my good friend Bill Rogers was the lead medic on Rescue 56. With another hour and a half on duty before the end of the shift, my mind was on a strong cup of coffee, certainly not on a call that would test us all and become a defining moment in my life. A firefighter's career is a series of routine calls that we come to take for granted, but occasionally there are calls that test our training and serve as a reminder that complacency can never be part of our thought process. Working in this business is always challenging; the call on that cold January morning left images in my mind that are as fresh today as they were then.

We were westbound on Glades Road, ready to turn south on 441 and go back to the station, when we were paged for a car in a canal at the intersection of 441 and Clint Moore Road. We hit the lights and siren and turned north instead of south, rolling toward Clint Moore a short three miles down the road.

The western areas of South Florida border the Everglades, and they are interlaced with canals that farmers use for crop irrigation. There is a big feeder canal on the east side of State Road 441 that provides water for smaller irrigation canals, and one of those smaller canals flows east parallel to Clint Moore Road. The first thing I noticed when we turned onto Clint Moore was the ice condition on the bridge. The second thing I noticed was tire tracks slewing across the bridge into the narrow canal, leading to a car that was upside down in the water. The only portion of the car that was visible above the water line was the four tires and the undercarriage. I remember thinking there was no way anyone would be alive inside that car.

As we came to a stop I radioed a quick arrival report to dispatch, ordering a tow truck and a sheriff's deputy to respond to our location. As I climbed out of the engine to assess the scene, my mind was still fixed on body recovery, until I heard a woman screaming, "Get me out of here!"

Talk about a motivator. I ordered a roof ladder placed from the bank of the canal to the car and shouted at the woman to tell me where she was located in the car. She told me she was in the backseat and screamed at me again: "Get me out of here!"

Normally it would have been a matter of breaking a side window to gain access to the interior of the car, except this canal wasn't that deep and the Cadillac was upside down and completely wedged between the banks. We couldn't even see the side windows of the car, and I wasn't about to put one of my guys in the water to try and break the front or rear windows. Doing that would have involved diving under either the trunk or the hood of the car. An officer's job is to always weigh risk versus benefit. I wasn't going to risk the lives of my guys until all other options were exhausted.

Normally extrication from a car is pretty straightforward, and we have a wide range of tools at our disposal to do the work, including Hurst Tools, reciprocating saws, and air chisels, to name just a few. But none of us had ever attempted to breach the undercarriage of a car to gain entry, and I wasn't sure we had the right tool to solve this problem. After a quick conference with my crew, I ordered my driver to set up the air chisel. I was confident we could cut through the bottom of the car, but I wasn't confident the woman would survive our attempt; we would have to be damn lucky to make this work. If you can picture a woman trapped in the backseat of an upside-down car, head tilted up with her nose barely above water breathing from a tiny pocket of air, you quickly realize that options are extremely limited. I knew that as soon as we started cutting with an air chisel, that pocket of air was going to disappear and she would drown.

The last time I had used an air chisel was during a training session. The bit kept coming off or else it would skate across the metal surface without biting in, so that it took forever to make a cut. With only 90-PSI operating force, it was never our first choice as an extrication tool.[1] I knew if we had those kinds of issues, this woman was going to die. I also knew I couldn't delegate this job; I was the one who would make the cut.

I spoke to the woman in a calm voice and told her what we were going to do and that we would get her out of that car. I asked her to try and describe exactly where she was in the backseat so I could pinpoint where to make my cut. I knew if I was off by just a little bit, and cut through the bottom of the car where the seat was, she would drown. I had to look at the bottom of that car and visualize where the backseat was and where you would normally put your feet. That two-foot-by-two-foot area was my target.

I stepped down the ladder onto the car with the air chisel in my hand, and she really started screaming. My added weight on the car pushed it down into the mud just enough that she was losing her air pocket. I tried to block out her screams and concentrated on making the best cut I had ever made with an air chisel. As I started my cut, it was almost like someone else was guiding my hand. The chisel worked perfectly, and I was able to cut a large oval in less than 20 seconds. What I couldn't do was remove that oval piece of metal. Billy was standing at the top of the ladder, and he came charging down and ripped the cut metal upward. As soon as he did that, the woman punched her fist through the carpeting on the floorboard. Billy grabbed her wrist and pulled her through the opening. She really wanted out of there. She was hypothermic from being immersed in 40-degree canal water, so the medics bundled her into the back of the rescue truck and transported her to Delray Community Hospital.

We soon learned who the lucky lady was. Bernadette Quilter was a nurse that many of the medics knew, and she was on her way to work at Delray Community Hospital when the accident occurred. Her husband met her at the hospital emergency room, and she checked herself out against medical advice 20 minutes after being admitted. Five minutes after she walked out of the hospital, an out-of-control car came through the wall of the emergency room and destroyed the bed she had been lying in. Was it divine intervention? I don't know. That is a larger question that I'm sure we all ponder. I do know it wasn't her day to die.

The next shift her husband, Sean Quilter, came by the station and invited all of us, as his guests, to his Irish pub in Fort Lauderdale. Sean was also professor of religious philosophy at Florida International University, and we had a wonderful conversation over more than a few beers about life and death and the role serendipity plays in the grand scheme of things. Bernadette told me that when she slid off the bridge into that cold water her father, long dead, appeared in the windshield and spoke to her, telling her to go to the backseat, where she would be all right. She spent a long 15 minutes watching turtles and fish peering in at her, in wonderment of her father's advice, before we cut her out of that car. If we had been at the station rather than returning from a fire alarm at the Holiday Inn, she probably would

Palm Beach County Fire-Rescue Patch (courtesy Cindy Smith).

have died. Our location shaved at least five minutes off the normal travel time from the station.

Because canals in the western area of the county are so ubiquitous, the call volume for vehicles in canals is fairly high. Sometimes we would have a witness who could point out exactly where the car entered the water. Sometimes the occupants of the vehicle were sitting on the bank, soaked and scared. But many times when we arrived there would be no one on scene, and we would have to play detective. We would look for an oil slick on the water's surface, skid marks on the road, or tire tracks across the embankment before locating the point where the vehicle entered the water. Once we found an area that looked promising, we would weigh the risk of putting divers in the water. If it didn't seem credible, we might poke around with a pike pole, but usually we put a swimmer in the water.

There were many times in my career when, after an extensive search, nothing would be found. Early one morning in the early 1980s, dispatch received a call stating that a van had gone into the Boca Rio canal that parallels the Florida Turnpike. The caller was shouting in Spanish, so it was difficult for the dispatcher to capture the exact location. Back then we didn't have bilingual dispatchers as we do now. It was four in the morning, dark enough that we could see the Milky Way arching across the sky, and after searching for at least a half-hour up and down a mile of roadway, we were unable to find any signs of a vehicle entering the water. This canal is a major waterway, very deep and 70 feet wide; it could easily swallow a bus without leaving any sign after the ripples vanished. At shift change, we turned the information over to the oncoming crew, and they went out and looked but found nothing. Five years later sheriff's divers working a recovery in the area found a van with five skeletons entombed within. We will never be sure this was the same van, but the circumstances point in that direction.[2] This is the nature of our work. Never pretty, many times with no closure, and sometimes with closure no one wants.

I lost touch with Sean and Bernadette until we were reunited through a mutual friend. It was a glorious reunion that occurred just before I retired from the fire service, and I invited them to my retirement party. At the end of the evening I asked Bernadette to join me on stage, where I told the story of her rescue. I was trying to capture the meaning of what it was like to serve as a firefighter through her story. I ended the evening, and the story, by putting my arms around her and hugging her, and then turning back to the audience to say, "That's what it means to be a firefighter and why I am so proud to have been a part of such a noble profession."

12—Just Another Fire Alarm

"Engine 55, Ladder 55, Rescue 55, Engine 56, District 5, EMS 5, fire alarm, 2255 Persimmon Circle, 0310." Station 55 is one of the busiest stations in the county, and this was our fifth fire alarm and our 16th call for what was becoming a long 24-hour shift. I wondered how the dispatcher could sound so damn cheerful, especially at this hour of the morning, as I staggered out to the engine, cursing the lack of sleep in general and fire alarms in particular. We have an ongoing debate in our department about the necessity of dispatching a full assignment on a fire alarm. Responding with two engines, a ladder, a rescue, an EMS supervisor and a chief on a call that is almost certainly a false alarm is, in my mind, a monumental waste of resources, not to mention dangerous. Any time fire apparatus are on the road, there is risk to the crews and to the public. You never know how someone is going to react to 20 tons of fire engine, lights flashing and sirens and air horn blaring, trying to navigate a busy intersection. This time I would be glad there was a full assignment.

I had been working as a captain for a number of years, first at our headquarters station in western Delray Beach and then, after consolidation, at Station 55. I had been blessed with great crews at both stations, but the guys at Station 55 were a cut above the rest. Sometimes it's a function of chemistry between people, sometimes it's the luck of the draw, but I like to think it was partly due to the way I managed the crew. I would hold a shift meeting each morning and lay out the day's activities. We would discuss training, inspections, ongoing projects, and the all-important dinner menu, and I would tell the guys that once the work was done, their time was their own. This meant a lot to them because some old-school company officers thought that a busy crew was a happy crew. I was considered old school, but my management and leadership practices had improved dramatically over the years.

One of the projects that involved all three shifts was a quick routing index. Station 55's zone was a complicated area. When the area was platted the planners weren't thinking about emergency responders. There wasn't a straight road in the zone, and with hundreds of subdivisions it was almost impossible to learn the area. We didn't have GPS and relied almost exclusively on hand-drawn maps. But even with the maps it still took too much time figuring out the best route to follow to get to the correct subdivision. We would sometimes have to study a map to determine whether to turn left or right out of the station, so we developed a routing index that directed us by the quickest route to each subdivision.[1]

My driver, Dave Farwick, had already cranked the engine and my fire-fighter, Perry Lindberg, was shrugging into his air-pack as I climbed into the right seat of the engine. I didn't need to consult a map for this run; the development was just down the street from the station. Perry, better known as Tilt, has a tendency to list to one side. It might have had something to do with his recreational activities off duty, but on duty he was the best fireman I ever worked with. Tilt, as usual, had all his turn-out gear on, even though he knew it was probably just another false alarm. I never had to tell him to gear up; he was always ready to work and would come off the engine with tools in his hand. A lot of other companies were a little more relaxed about wearing their turn-outs on fire alarms, but we were old school and dressed for the party, every time. Even though it was three in the morning and my gear was wet and smelled of smoke from working a car fire in the rain earlier in the shift, there was always a sense of satisfaction each time I climbed into the right seat of the engine, cinched down the straps of my SCBA and hung the mask around my neck. As we rolled out of the bay into the warm Florida night, my mind kept going back to a fragmented dream I couldn't quite recall. Even though dispatch paged this as a fire alarm, I cleared my mind and started thinking about actions that would need to be taken if it wasn't just another fire alarm and there was smoke showing.

Persimmon Circle was around the corner from the station, and we were first on scene. When the engine turned into the cul-de-sac I could see black smoke coming from the back of a single-story, four-unit apartment building. People were milling around in the street, pointing to the back of the building, and mothers were corralling kids in pajamas who were watching us with wide eyes as our parade of fire apparatus rolled in. Going from sound sleep to arriving at a working fire, all in less than five minutes, can't be good for you, especially when you factor in the adrenaline that is coursing through your blood. But training took over, and I was immediately on the radio advising the remaining assignment to step it up to code three: we had a working fire. According to the people in the street, everyone was out of the building, so at least we didn't have an immediate rescue problem.

Chief Cosby arrived just behind us and established command. We had a hydrant off the corner of the building where Dave positioned the engine for a large sleeve hook-up, leaving the front of the building for the ladder. I did a quick recon and reported to command that as far as I could tell we had a room and contents fire, probably a bedroom, on the back side of the building in the corner apartment. By this time the rest of the assignment had arrived and standard operating procedures were starting to kick in. A quick sweep of the uninvolved apartments confirmed no fire extension and everyone was out.

Fighting fires is about prioritizing resources, and on the initial attack there are usually never enough resources to quickly accomplish everything that needs to be done, forcing the incident commander to make decisions based first on life safety, then incident stabilization and lastly property conservation. Even though we were assured that everyone was out of the building, we still did a search of the apartment that was on fire. Ladder 55 was assigned to do a left-hand search while Tilt and I took a line in to extinguish the fire in the bedroom. Engine 56 pulled a back-up line to the front door, feeding us our line as we made our way in. Dave positioned a fan for positive pressure ventilation, set up lights and pumped the engine. Rescue 55 was assigned as outside vent and a back-up in case anyone got lost or hurt in the building (what we would now call a Rapid Intervention Team). EMS 5 was assigned as a safety officer.

Every once in a while everything goes according to the script, and this was one of those times. Rescue 55 vented the bedroom window as we moved in, creating positive pressure ventilation from the fan, which quickly lifted the smoke condition. Tilt and I hit the fire hard and it darkened down immediately, even though it was starting to roll out of the bedroom and across the ceiling into the hallway. Ladder 55 reported all clear on their search and having Rescue 55 standing by in the event of a problem gave everyone working on the inside a sense of security. Having a crew whose only assignment is watching your back is now a routine part of incident management, but in the late 1980s it was one of life's great luxuries. After Tilt and I put the fire out, Engine 56's crew came in and started overhauling, a process of opening up door and window casings and any other areas where fire could be smoldering. It's poor form to come back on a rekindle, so guys are always very methodical during this process.

I shook my head in amazement as I walked back to the engine to gear down and start picking up. My driver had every one of those wide-eyed, pajama-clad kids outfitted in toy plastic fire helmets, kneeling with each child in turn, helping them squirt water from the booster line. A driver's job is pretty hectic on a working fire: pumping the engine at the correct pressure for the size and number of lines in operation, setting up lighting and laying out tools, and doing anything else that qualifies as an ancillary job on a fire scene. Dave was all that and more. To coordinate all that he had to do to support our fire suppression efforts and still see through a child's eyes and make their dream of being a fireman come true is a testament to him and to the profession. As a captain on a busy engine company, it was not only a luxury to have such a good crew, it was also a privilege.

I was blessed throughout most of my career with good crews and very competent drivers. Dave was one of the best, along with Doug Watson, Ken Donechie, Brian Clough, Tim Monaghan, Alan Sulewski, Jeff McCord, Jimmy Johnson, and John Larkin. A driver can make or break an officer; like sergeants in the military, they keep an officer from doing dumb things. And believe me, officers aren't immune to doing stupid things.

I spoke of the need for innovation in an earlier chapter, and the drivers were the ones who were always a step ahead on the innovation curve. They made it happen, at least in my stations. If we needed more cribbing, or a special piece of equipment, or more basic hand tools, or another lounge chair for the dayroom, it was the drivers who went around, over, or through any existing brick walls to make sure their captains got what was needed. Here's to the drivers—past, present, and future.

13—Rescuing the Rescuers

Frank would wake in the middle of the night, screaming for his crew to take cover. He was a veteran, not long discharged from active duty in Viet Nam, where he had served as a medic in the U.S. Army. His skills as a paramedic and a firefighter were exceptional, but he was still traumatized from combat. The guys would gently wake him, reassuring him until he stopped shaking. In the early 1980s we didn't know much about post-traumatic stress disorder, but we were about to learn. The call we would soon run gave us a glimpse of the horror that Frank lived in his nightmare each night.

It was just after 11 P.M., and I was ready for bed when we were paged to a traffic accident in the 1200 block of Federal Highway in Boynton Beach. I knew it was a divided highway with a posted speed limit of 45 miles per hour, so I wasn't expecting much. As we rolled east, dispatch advised me that Boynton Fire was responding as well. That portion of Federal Highway in Boynton Beach is a county pocket and a long way from Station 42. Whenever we had a call in that area, Boynton Beach Fire Department would provide mutual aid.

I had been working for the fire department over 10 years and considered myself a veteran, working in some of the busiest stations, but, with the exception of Frank, I had a young crew. Randy, recently promoted to driver, had five years on the job. My firefighter was just out of rookie school, and Frank's partner on rescue was a green medic, still trying to get his feet on the ground.

We pulled up as Boynton Fire's rescue truck was leaving for the hospital. I walked up to the captain of Boynton's engine and asked him what he needed done. He looked at me and said, "This is a county pocket, this is your scene, we're out of here." He turned around, got on his engine, and left without another word.

I was left with one of the eeriest scenes I had ever seen. A car had run into the back of a tractor-trailer moving van. The rig was parked in the breakdown lane, and it was obvious the car had been moving at a high rate of speed when it hit the van. There was no need for patient treatment: Boynton had transported three people to the hospital, and the two remaining were dead.

We had all been on traffic accidents involving fatalities, but what we were looking at was truly bizarre. The front-seat passenger was strapped in and sitting upright, except his head was missing. The rear passenger was half out of the vehicle, his torso on the pavement and his legs and buttocks still sprawled across the backseat. The front passenger's head was resting in his lap. The man lying on the ground had his eyes open, and the head's eyes were also open. They were staring at each other, seemingly in disbelief. Traffic homicide investigators theorized that blunt-force trauma from the decapitated head killed the man in the backseat.

I had known the captain of Boynton's engine since my initial fire training. He was the lead instructor at South Tech's fire academy, and I couldn't imagine why he had acted so abruptly. Surveying the scene, I was beginning to understand.

Police had arrived at the same time as Boynton Fire, and there had been a lot of banter between the cops about the guy lying on the ground getting a little head. That stopped when they discovered a pistol strapped to the ankle of the front-seat passenger. Someone finally dug the victim's wallet out of his back pocket; a badge and identification revealed he was a reserve police officer with the sheriff's office. That information stopped the banter.

It was a macabre scene. We didn't want to look away, yet we couldn't wait to leave. When the coroner asked me to put the head in an evidence bag, I knew it was time to go. I told him rather emphatically, "No," and we left.

Firefighters see things that the general public can't even imagine, and if you are in this business long enough, you get to see the dark side of the human experience. Sometimes we may only peer over the edge; other times we are thrown headlong into a stygian pit of carnage and human emotion where it is difficult to claw your way out. The public looks on us as heroes. The reality is that we are working men and women who see things that no one should ever have to see; we experience the same range of emotions as everyone else, yet we have a job to do. And we must do that job dispassionately and professionally, regardless of the emotional circumstances.

Sometimes these experiences leave scars, and writing about them, even years later, is a difficult process. Recalling past events that your mind has successfully buried can sometimes be cathartic, but usually it's just painful. It is impossible to erase the image of a baby with its flesh burned black and its skull split open from heat, lying dead amid the rubble of what used to be a bedroom. It is equally impossible to erase the image of the baby's mother lying in a fetal position in front of the still-smoking trailer, moaning and crying for her child.

We were fortunate to have a Critical Incident Stress Management team that provided skillful intervention when emergency service workers were in crisis. I had never requested the team before, but I knew from the looks in the eyes of my crew that this might be a good time to find out what it was all about. I advised dispatch that our assignment was complete and requested the crisis team. We got back to the station around one in the morning, and three team members were sitting at the kitchen table. There was a fresh pot of coffee brewing. None of us knew what to expect.

The team consisted of a clinician and two peers, and they used what is known as the "Mitchell Model" to defuse or debrief emergency responders who are trying to cope with the psychological trauma of a bad call. It's a deceptively simple process that involves a structured conversation, leading people in crisis to a clearer reality where they are able to face more directly, and cope with more appropriately, their mental demons.

Even though this occurred years ago, I cannot speak about the debriefing because of confidentiality issues that are a necessary part of this process. No one is allowed to sit in on any type of crisis intervention unless they were on scene, and the first question asked at a debriefing addresses whether only the principals are in attendance.

Jeffery Mitchell, PhD, developed the Critical Incident Stress Management[1] process after his brother, a Baltimore police officer, experienced a traumatic event involving the decapitation of a child. Doctor Mitchell reasoned that the only people who could understand what someone was going through would be other emergency responders in the same profession. Even though they might not have experienced the same event, they still did the same job and had gone through similar experiences. This concept of peer support works very well, and the debriefing helped all of us move on from a very dark place.

I was thankful for the support that we gained from the intervention, and subsequently attended a training session and became a peer. Several years later the team was going through a leadership transition, and I became involved in the management aspects of running the team, eventually becoming the team's administrator.

To be recognized by the International Critical Incident Stress Foundation, a crisis intervention team must have properly trained peers and a properly trained clinician. Although intervention is peer driven, a clinician must be present at debriefings to guide peers if responders require a higher level of intervention. Having a clinician present also brings a further measure of validation to the process.

The Critical Incident Stress Debriefing (or CISD) process consists of seven phases:

1. *Introduction*: The introduction phase is when the team leader introduces the CISD process, encourages participation by the group, and sets the ground rules by which the debriefing will operate. Ground rules include confidentiality, attendance for the full session, non-forced participation in discus-

sions, and the establishment of a noncritical atmosphere. Emphasis is placed on the fact that this is not an operational critique.

2. *Fact Phase*: During this phase, the group members are asked to briefly describe their roles during the incident and, from their own perspective, what happened. The basic question is, "What did you do?"

3. *Thought Phase*: The CISD leader asks the group to discuss their first and subsequent thoughts about the critical incident. The question then is, "What went through your mind?"

4. *Reaction Phase*: This phase is designed to move the group participants from a predominately cognitive and intellectual level of processing to a more cathartic, emotional level of processing. The question here is, "What was the worst part of the incident for you?" It's at this point that members begin to vent their distress.

5. *Symptom Phase*: This stage begins the process of moving participants back from the emotional level toward the cognitive level. Participants are asked to describe cognitive, physical, emotional, and behavioral signs and symptoms of distress with the following question: "What have you been experiencing since the incident?"

6. *Education Phase*: This phase continues the move back toward intellectual processing. Information is given about the nature of the stress response and expected physiological and psychological reactions the participant may experience due to the critical incident. This helps normalize the stress and gives participants coping mechanisms. Here we reinforce the lesson: "You are having a normal reaction to a critical incident."

7. *Reentry Phase*: This is a time for answering questions and referral, if necessary, with follow-up questions such as "What have you learned?" or "Is there anything positive that can come out of this experience that can help you personally or professionally?"[2]

It has been my experience that debriefings rarely follow the script. They usually become a free-flowing discussion that the leader gently guides back to midstream. Eventually, the seven steps are touched on, and the end result is usually very positive. Debriefings can be as emotionally draining for peers as they are for participants.

I became involved with the CISD team in the mid–1990s. There had been a change in leadership, and Laurence Miller, PhD, was the team's new clinician. We were becoming better known in the emergency response community and, as a result, busier. It was apparent that we needed to recruit members other than firefighters, so we actively recruited and trained police officers, dispatchers, and nurses.

It's important to pair the right peers with emergency personnel. Sending a nurse as a peer to debrief a police officer doesn't work. The concept hinges on the peer's ability to intimately understand the job of the person in crisis. Occasionally, nurse, police officer, dispatcher, and firefighter peers will participate together in a debriefing. This makes sense when a call comes in where a dispatcher may be involved in providing medical information, such as explaining to a mother whose child may have drowned the steps of CPR. Other responders would include police, fire, and nursing staff at the hospital. If the child dies, and it's obvious that people are having a hard time coping, a debriefing involving all emergency response participants might be held. I have attended many successful interdisciplinary debriefings, and one of the benefits is a better working relationship between different agencies.

The call for CISD services is usually initiated by the responders. Once initiated, an assessment is made by the on-call CISD team member to determine whether a defusing or a debriefing is required. A defusing is a response by one or more peers to speak with responders as soon after the event as possible. It is much less structured and serves as a means to assess the responders' need for a follow-up debriefing. Debriefings are typically held 24 to 72 hours after the event. This delay gives people time to begin processing the traumatic event. Attending a debriefing or defusing is never required.

Prior to CISD, gallows humor was the accepted way of dealing with bad calls. That still occurs, but follow-up discussion is a better long-term fix and something that is now becoming routine, at least in our department. I remember one firefighter telling me if it were not for a debriefing that he attended after a horrific car accident, he would have resigned.

In the late 1990s Doctor Miller resigned as our clinical director and Stephanie Dill, MSW, from Horizons Bereavement Center in West Palm Beach, Florida, became our new lead clinical director. Stephanie and her staff are superbly trained grief counselors, and with the additional training in the Mitchell Model, they have brought a wonderful new dimension to our ability to deliver crisis intervention. We now have three highly trained clinicians available to the team, bringing a level of empathy from their grief counseling training that adds a new and very positive dynamic to debriefings.

Everyone on the team volunteers their time. When I retired, Captain Chuck Salustri, a long-time member of the team, became the team administrator. He is continuing the work that rarely receives recognition but is a vital component for the emergency service community. Serving with the Palm Beach County Critical Incident Stress Management Team was one of the most satisfying aspects of my career. Perhaps Carl Jung said it best when he talked about privileged conversations: "The finest and most significant conversations of my life were anonymous."[3]

14 — Special Operations

In the spring of 1996, Ed Hines called to ask me if I wanted to transfer into Special Operations, an assignment that would involve hazardous materials response, high-angle rescue, dive rescue, heavy rescue, and trench rescue. I was happy working as the captain at Station 55 but knew this was an opportunity for specialized training.

The Special Operations Team worked out of Station 31, located at the midpoint of the county with quick access to I-95 for a north or south response or east and west via Lake Worth Road. In the 1990s we were the only hazardous materials team in the county, so the location was ideal for a quick response in any direction. The team on each shift consisted of a district chief, a captain and a driver on the special operations truck; a lieutenant, driver and firefighter on the engine; and two firefighter paramedics on the rescue truck. Although Engine and Rescue 31 stayed busy running fire and medical calls, we all responded as a team whenever there was a need for our specialized training.

We fondly referred to the station as a "shit hole." It was built on an old landfill and had all the attendant problems that come with building on that type of site. The quality of the drinking water was suspect, rats and other vermin staked out their own territories, and an eight-foot chain-link fence with razor wire at the top helped keep out two-legged vermin, though not always successfully. It wasn't unusual for a crew to come back from a call and find a bum sleeping in a bunk.

Johnny Wright was our district chief, extraordinarily competent in a number of disciplines with the gift of being able to teach technically demanding subjects with infinite patience. I can still hear his voice coaching us through the complicated ritual of rope rescue. Our training cycles were varied and always interesting. One day we might be rappelling off the 50-foot tower at the 4th Anglico (Air Naval Gunfire Liaison Company) Marine Corps Reserve Base off Belvedere Road. The next shift we might be practicing heavy vehicle extrication at the local junkyard or else practicing dive rescue techniques in a lake or municipal swimming pool. Every day during vehicle checks we were hands on with the monitoring equipment used for hazardous materials mitigation.

Rope rescue is technically demanding and requires ongoing, focused training. This photograph shows Special Operations personnel practicing what we call a pick-off. This technique would be used to rescue a window washer on the outside of a building or anyone trapped in an inaccessible area. The equipment we use now is state of the art, a far cry from hemp rope and ladder belts (courtesy Arthur Werkle).

For a short while there was talk of deploying divers from our helicopter, a Bell 412. We went through a number of training cycles at the pool, practicing insertions into the water off a 10-meter diving board to mimic the height of jumping off the skid of the helicopter. Practicing the protocol for water insertion from a helicopter required us to stand at the end of the board, hold our mask in place with the right hand, hold our PFD in place with our left hand, step off the board and make a quarter turn to the right, and remember to keep our fin tips up.[1] I'm the guy who rides the Ferris wheel at the fair, so jumping 30 feet into the water with a mask, snorkel and fins scared me even more than the church raise back in fire school. They gave up on the idea after a while, to my immense relief.

When Battalion Chief Hines asked me to come to Special Operations, I told him I didn't have a lot of the necessary training, including dive certification. He said that wouldn't be a problem; the department would train me. I went to school for a number of weeks, taking classes in hazardous materials, gasoline-tank truck fires and liquid propane fires, and dive rescue. The first class I took to qualify for dive rescue training was a PADI (Professional Association of Diving Instructors) class in basic open-water diving. I had always enjoyed snorkeling and was looking forward to becoming a certified diver. I will always remember the sight and sound of a cargo vessel rumbling over my head during one practice dive. We were practicing ascents in 30 feet of water on the edge of the main channel for the Port of Palm Beach when that ship went over. The water was clear enough for me to see the barnacles on the underside of the hull and watch the slow turn of screw.

The next step in my dive training after PADI basic open water was advanced open water, which meant more classroom instruction and more time in the water getting qualifying dives under my belt. These were the basic classes needed to take Dive Rescue I, entry-level training for rescue and recovery, during which we learned how to use specialized equipment including full-face masks with built-in two-way communication capability.[2] We learned various search techniques for open bodies of water like lakes and ponds, as well as more confined bodies of water such as canals. This training enabled us to put highly trained divers in the water; however, it was usually a recovery operation, rarely a save.

During my tenure as a Special Ops captain, we never had a successful rescue — only body recovery. That's not to say we weren't good at our job; it was simply a function of time and distance. A person isn't going to survive a drowning event longer than five or six minutes, especially in the warm waters of South Florida. And even though a closer engine company would be on scene with Level I divers deployed in the water with masks and snorkels, it was never a good outcome.

One call in particular stands out in my mind. We were paged late in the afternoon on a beautiful fall day for a child who had fallen into the Palm Beach Canal. The father was intoxicated and had allowed his child to ride on the bow of the boat without a life jacket. It was just a matter of time before the four-year-old boy fell out of the boat. The most important information a dive team needs is a last-seen location; without knowing where someone went into the water, it is almost impossible to mount a successful rescue. The father narrowed it down to about a quarter of a mile — too broad an area to be useful.

There is a misconception among the lay public that a body floats after drowning. Bodies do not float upon initial immersion, but over time decomposition forms gas in the chest and abdomen, causing the body to rise to the surface.[3] Tom and I were the first divers into the water, and we conducted a basic sweep pattern, following a rope tended by other Special Ops personnel. The Palm Beach Canal runs parallel to Southern Boulevard, and the area we were searching was to the west of Military Trail. The canal in this area is approximately 70 feet wide and at least 30 feet deep, still well within our depth limits.

Tom and I would grasp the rope, one on either side, and slowly sink below the surface, rhythmically kicking our fins as we swept the bottom contour of the canal with our hands. We would do this repetitively, gliding back and forth while guided by the rope held by the line handlers as they moved over four feet on each pass. Visibility was nil; the only way we could stay on course and swim a straight pattern was to rely on the rope tenders to keep our line taut and for us not to pull from side to side. It was very disconcerting to swim a pattern and bump into the opposite bank, which was the only way to know that it was time to start swimming up. It was even more disconcerting to swim up and encounter a shelf, forcing you to swim underneath an overhang until you could once again begin a vertical ascent. I didn't know if I was in a gator hole or if it was just natural erosion, but it was a very uncomfortable feeling.

Controlling fear is a balancing act between executing a mission properly and understanding at all times whether you are still working within your training parameters, something that should be uppermost in every rescue diver's mind. When a diver is consumed by fear because of the circumstances, then he or she can't be effective. I was never comfortable as a rescue diver, but the training allowed me to do the work. Earlier training in smoke diver school also helped me overcome the feeling of claustrophobia that comes with being underwater in a zero-visibility environment.

On each sweep Tom and I would encounter debris: shopping carts, tires, unidentifiable rubbish, and monofilament fishing line. Diving is always a risk-versus-benefit decision, and I was beginning to question the benefit. We knew the likelihood of finding this child was slim, and Chief Wright was moving toward handing the search off to the Palm Beach County Sheriff's Office dive team. They were in the business of recovery, and after a half-hour on scene we were well into the recovery phase. When I swam into a ball of monofilament that threatened to entangle me, it was an easy decision for Johnny to turn the scene over to the PBSO.

I'll always remember my friend, Ted Randall, helping me out of the water. He happened to be driving by and stopped to watch the operation. Ted was a staff sergeant in the United States Marine Corps on recruiting duty in the West Palm Beach area, and we had become friends while attending the same class at Palm Beach Atlantic University. He hated recruiting duty. He was in Recon and wanted to be back in the fleet, but his superiors assured him it was great for his professional development. He was standing on the bank in his dress blues when I surfaced and extended his hand to me as I struggled out of the water. Ted had been riding with us whenever he had the chance, trying to make up his mind whether he wanted to get out of the Corps and join the fire department. He told me later that what we did in Special Ops reminded him of some of the training he did as a Recon Marine. Kind words from someone who served in such an elite unit.

The sheriff's divers recovered the boy the following day. He had been in the water long enough that body gases floated him to the surface. Doing this kind of work takes a toll; I was glad that dive rescue response wasn't something we did every day.

Our response zone for hazardous materials mitigation was county wide, an area bounded on the east by the ocean and on the west by the Everglades, and from the Broward County line north to Indian River County. The funding in the 1990s came out of Battalion 1 and 3's budgets, a measure of how expensive hazardous materials mitigation can be. The cost in salary and benefits for an eight-person team during my tenure was over $900,000 a year. Now, hazardous materials response is divided between Palm Beach County Fire-Rescue, Delray Beach Fire Department, and Boca Raton Fire Department, with much of the funding coming from the Palm Beach County Solid Waste Authority. Salary, benefits, and the cost of equipment for Palm Beach County Fire-Rescue's portion of hazardous materials mitigation now runs into millions of dollars each year.

Although we didn't run a lot of calls involving hazardous materials, we spent hours each month training. You get one chance to do it right in this business; it wasn't an option to think you knew the right procedure to mitigate a chlorine leak — you had to be certain of the procedure or someone was going to have a very bad day.

Chlorine is ubiquitous in every community. It can be found in small quantities at pool-supply companies and in much larger quantities at water treatment plants. We also had transportation corridors— I-95 and rail — that routinely carried bulk containers of chlorine as well as many other types of hazardous materials cargo. We trained for every eventuality, including railcar incidents.

A lot of the equipment we use requires a high degree of technical competence and physical conditioning, especially when working in entry suits. Working in a Level A entry suit is a debilitating experience in the heat and humidity of a South Florida summer afternoon. The suits are designed to keep the bad stuff out, and even before you are fully encapsulated and on air, you begin to sweat. Whenever a haz-mat technician is placed in a suit, hydration and physical fitness are key concerns. I always encouraged my guys to stay hydrated throughout the day so we would have one less thing to worry about if we were called to an event where crews were required to work in entry suits. Medics would take vitals prior to a technician suiting up, using pulse rate, blood pressure and temperature as a baseline measurement. Vitals would be taken again when the technician was done with the assignment and recuperating in a rehab area.

Working a hazardous materials incident is a choreographed event from start to finish.[4] Cold, warm, and hot zones are identified, usually with some form of visual marking such as traffic cones or tape. The incident commander establishes a command post in the cold zone, where a strategy for mitigation is developed and research is conducted. Our haz-mat truck has an onboard computer workstation with various software programs that enabled our team to identify hazardous materials and access industry information on the best way to deal with an unintended release. The warm zone is used as a staging area for crews prior to entering the hot zone, the area requiring our attention. A supervisor would also stage in the warm zone — sometimes with line-of-sight supervision, always with radio monitoring — and a lead technician would supervise all aspects of the mitigation within the hot zone.

Working on a haz-mat unit meant enhanced medical surveillance during

Special Operations personnel in Level A entry suits investigating a spill of unknown origin (courtesy Palm Beach County Fire-Rescue photo archive).

our annual fire department physical. Instead of one or two tubes of blood, the protocol called for eight tubes of blood. Instead of peeing in a cup, we had the honor of peeing in a gallon jug over a 24-hour period. I had a window-washing business that my wife and I worked at on my days off. She was always embarrassed when I had to pee in the jug while standing in the bushes of some lady's backyard. I told her it was a guy thing.

One of the defining moments of my physical was the dreaded prostate exam. One year the clinic we used had hired a young, very pretty female physician's assistant. When she told me she had to check my prostate, I tried to put a brave face on it and glibly said, "If you give me an erection, we'll have to talk."

She didn't miss a beat and remarked, "If I give you an erection, can I call you by your first name?"

Steve Hobbs was the engine company officer, and he and I shared a small bunkroom. Steve suffered from sleep apnea and snored like a rhinoceros. I would try and get to bed, and get some sleep, before he started in. Once he started snoring, it didn't matter how soundly I was sleeping, I would eventually wake up. In self-defense I would keep a broom handle under my bunk and whack it on the wall about a foot above Steve's head when he began to snore. That would wake him for a few moments but then he would go back to sawing logs. One night I awoke, not because of his snoring, but because I smelled smoke. I turned on the light to find the window air conditioner on fire. Being trained firemen, Steve and I leaped into action, unplugging the unit and dowsing the fire with a glass of water before going back to sleep. The thin layer of smoke just above our heads didn't bother Steve in the least; he was snoring as loudly as ever three minutes after I turned off the light.

It wasn't unusual for Chief Wright, my driver, and me to be the only ones at the station in the middle of the night; Engine and Rescue 31 were constantly running calls, and we were very good at listening to a page for a medical call or a car fire and then drifting back to our dreams. Johnny was something of an insomniac and was in the habit of wandering into the kitchen in the middle of the night to get a sandwich and glass of milk. One night in early December, when the engine and rescue were out, he was busy making a peanut butter and jelly sandwich at two in the morning. The kitchen has two entrances: one a framed opening that leads to an office area, the other a restaurant-style kitchen door that swings both ways and opens into the truck bay. While he was standing in his underwear enjoying his sandwich, he noticed the door to the truck bay gently swinging in and out a few inches each way. He looked through the tiny window set into the door and couldn't see anything, so he went back to eating his sandwich. Again, he noticed the door moving, looked out, didn't see anything and resumed eating. The next time the door started to move inward he caught a glimpse of a shiny black nose poking its way into the kitchen. A large boar raccoon wanted a bite of Johnny's sandwich.

Johnny put his foot against the base of the door to keep the raccoon out, but it didn't take long for the animal to slip its paw under the door, trying to pull it open. Johnny abandoned his sandwich and put all his energy into gripping the ledge of the window, trying to keep the raccoon out, not an easy task when his only purchase was the small lip around the edge of the window. This tug of war went on for an hour until the engine returned from its call. The raccoon then turned its attention to the guys on the engine, trying to climb aboard. Fearing that the raccoon might have rabies, one of the firefighters killed it with a halligan. Some bright soul couldn't leave it at that and drew a chalk outline around the animal before disposing of it in the dumpster.

I slept through this drama and was regaled with the story over morning coffee before going off duty. The next shift we didn't think it was all that funny when we learned a little boy who lived behind the station had come by looking for his pet raccoon. We didn't have the heart to tell him what had happened. We all knew a raccoon doesn't make a good pet, but that was little consolation after looking at that boy's face. All three crews kicked in to help make that child's Christmas merrier than he, or his single mom, ever expected.

I had spent two years in Special Operations and decided that my opportunity for advancement would come sooner if I transferred back to Battalion Five. I was promoted to district chief shortly after returning to my old assignment at Station 55 and was transferred to Battalion Two. My transfer came through two years before the country, and South Florida in particular, was rocked by domestic terrorism involving anthrax. In October 2001, U.S. Senator Tom Daschell, the Senate majority leader, and U.S. Senator Patrick Leahy of Vermont received letters postmarked from Trenton, New Jersey, that contained traces of anthrax. This was part of a series of escalating events involving anthrax, and Palm Beach County was ground zero for this war.

Emergency workers in South Florida had been dealing with white powder calls since September 2001, when the American Media newspaper company based in Boca Raton, Florida, experienced the first casualty in this new war. Bob Stevens, a photo editor for American Media, was admitted to JFK Medical Center on October 2 and died October 5, 2001, from exposure to anthrax.[5] This was a sobering reality check for all emergency service workers in Palm Beach County.

Although I was no longer in Special Operations, my training served me well. I responded to numerous calls involving white powder during that time period and felt comfortable supervising crews because of the extensive training I had received during my tenure in Special Operations. Our training had prepared us for every eventuality, including the terrorism that, unfortunately, would now be part of our lexicon.

Several years before planes were used as instruments of terror, I had a conversation with a woman who was attending a fire department open house with her two young children. Part of the static display was our equipment from the trucks laid out on two huge salvage covers. I was telling her about our capabilities and the types of calls we responded to, and she asked me about terrorism. I looked directly at her and said, "Ma'am, it's not a matter of if but when."

15—Women in the Fire Service

"Come on, Madigan, you can do better than that!" We were doing basic hose evolutions, and I was getting tired of telling M.C. to stretch the hose until all the kinks were out of it before calling for water. She had been on the job for only a few weeks, hadn't been through fire school, and didn't have a clue. She had been hired as a paramedic, and I prayed she would never be assigned to an engine. Del-Trail, along with most of the other departments in the county, was now providing paramedic service. Madigan was the first woman hired by the department, and no one was happy about admitting her into our ranks, including me.

According to Palm Beach County Fire-Rescue's payroll department, in 2010 there were 93 women in operations working as firefighters, paramedics, driver engineers, lieutenants, and captains, to say nothing of Mary Catherine Madigan as a district chief. When we first consolidated in 1984, there were 10 women on the job, approximately 2 percent of the workforce. Now, women comprise a little over 6 percent of the workforce, and we are a better department because of this diversity.

Over the years attitudes have changed. I'm sure there are a few who would like to see an all-male workforce, but the majority of male firefighters accept women as equals. That's not to say it is easy for a woman to enter this profession. During recruit training, and after, there are the same expectations, the same physical requirements, and the same training requirements for women as for men. This includes a grueling 12 weeks of recruit training and then a probationary period of a year, during which firefighters have to meet a number of demanding benchmarks. Not meeting those benchmarks means termination.

I knew that writing about women in the fire service from my own perspective would be a disservice to women firefighters and biased because of my gender, so I distributed a questionnaire to women of all ranks and tenures, asking them to tell me their stories. In that questionnaire I asked them to describe their thoughts on why they decided on a fire service career, their dates of hire, their first assignments, and how they felt that first day reporting for duty. I wanted to know how they were treated by their peers and their supervisors, what their assignments were, then versus now, and how they adapted to daily station life. I inquired as to whether they were accepted in the same manner as male recruits and whether the training and educational opportunities met their expectations. I also wanted to know how they balanced their personal and professional lives.

The response I received was better than I ever imagined, both straightforward and heartfelt, and gave me an intimate glimpse into the process a woman goes through to become a professional firefighter and what it is like for them to go to work every third day with their male colleagues. I have chosen the stories of seven women and will present them as they were presented to me, with editing only when necessary to clarify a point. I wish to thank Fire Inspector Carey Tiersch (retired), District Chief M.C. Madigan, Division Chief Vicki Sheppard (retired), Lieutenant Jody Black Meidama, Driver Engineer Cecilia Yolanda Perales Eaton, Firefighter Paramedic Vanessa Ramos, and Captain Karen Walshe for their insightful and thorough responses to my questions and for giving me permission to reprint their stories.

Fire Inspector Carey Tiersch (Retired)

I applied for a job as a dispatcher with Del-Trail Fire Control in the winter of 1983. I had worked as a dispatcher for the City of Boca Raton Fire Department and was currently working for a local ambulance company as an EMT. I felt good about my chances of being hired.

My hiring interview was at the Central Station on Military Trail, and I was not at all prepared for the process. I was placed in a very uncomfortable chair in the middle of the room and was surrounded by men who never bothered to introduce themselves— they simply started asking questions. There was no rhyme or reason to the questioning, and the questions came from all sides of the room. I was asked if I planned to marry and did I plan to have children. The only thing missing was the swinging light bulb! When I thought that there couldn't be any more personal questions, Chief Frye asked, "Carey, you're a cute little girl, what are you going to do when these boys make a pass at you?" I was floored. This was 1983, not 1950. I answered, "Don't worry about me, Chief. I grew up with a house full of brothers and can take care of myself."

Two days after that interview I was notified that I had the job. Three hours after that call I was called again by Larry Manley, the training chief. He told me they had decided to give the job to someone else, a bank teller with no experience. I informed him that he would hear from a lawyer. After a little more negotiating with the lawyer card still in my pocket, I was told they would definitely hire me but not right away. I told them I wasn't going through any more of their so-called interviews and was hired as a dispatcher on June 16, 1984.

My first day on the job I was issued uniforms, all men's clothing, and wore a pair of men's dress shoes that I think they found at K-Mart. None of the stuff fit, but I had a job! I thought I was done with the questions, but as I was walking through the bay to go into the dispatch office, a guy started asking me more questions. Did I know the ten codes? Had I ever dispatched? That was the last straw for me, so I answered him in my best stutter, "T-they said t-they were going to t-teach me!" and turned around and walked into the building. It was worth a million bucks to see the look on the guy's face when he learned they had just hired a stuttering dispatcher! Lieutenant Boike was in charge of the dispatchers, and when he found out what I had done he cracked up. He put the word out that I was like Mel Tillis, I did not stutter when I was on the radio.

After two weeks of training I was assigned to A shift, and that was the beginning of a 25-year career in the fire service. The firefighters were very supportive of the dispatchers. They knew if I didn't show up for work, they would have to dispatch. I quickly learned how much power a dispatcher had. One night a medic from one of the out stations was very rude to me over the radio. I waited until after midnight and paged that station, waited a minute or two until they were all out of bed, then canceled them. Of course the proper station was already on the road answering the call. After the fourth canceled call after midnight, the officer called me to ask what was up. I said, "Here's the deal: if I'm up, you're up."

He said, "What do you want?"

I told him about the medic being so rude to me and said, "I want an apology."

They dragged him out of bed and I got an apology. It was only then that I stopped paging out that station, "by accident." From then on I didn't have any problems with the guys. In fact, I have fond memories of hanging out late at night with the guys at Central Station, eating cookies, chatting, and waiting for the next call.

I had more problems from the firefighters' wives and girlfriends than I did from the firemen. Back then, dispatch handed out paychecks, and a lot of the wives would come in to pick up the checks. Some of them were very unpleasant towards me and M.C. Madigan, the only female firefighter. Captain DeVries was the shift officer, and I give him credit for putting a stop to the abuse we were receiving. In 1983 most station officers would not have stood up for us.

In October of 1984 Del-Trail and the other fire control departments consolidated to become Palm Beach County Fire-Rescue. I was elected union representative for the dispatchers and my first job, when they moved us into our new facility, was complaining to the Health Department about the working conditions. Everyone working in the building we referred to as The Hole was sick. The Health Department discovered that the AC filters were full of mold. They had been bypassed to help keep the computer equipment cold.

I spent three years as a dispatcher and then trained as a fire inspector. Working for Palm Beach County Fire-Rescue opened up doors that I thought would always be closed to a woman. I found that women were treated with respect and had the same opportunities for advancement as men. Starting out as a dispatcher in 1983, I could never imagine spending 25 years in the fire service, 22 of those years as a fire inspector.

I was one of those guys who used to hang out with Carey late at night eating cookies and chatting. She was a wonderful coworker, and I count her and her husband John among my closest friends.

District Chief M.C. (Mary Catherine) Madigan

After I graduated high school a good friend of mine, Holly, got a job at Boca Raton Community Hospital in the emergency room. Through that job, she met some of the ambulance company folks and decided to become an EMT. She convinced me to go to EMT school, and I got hired part time at Quality Ambulance Company in Boca Raton in 1976.

After working part time for a couple of years, I decided to work full time in the ambulance service and was hired by JFK Hospital Ambulance Company. They sent me to paramedic school in 1980, where I worked a 24-hour-on, 48-hour-off schedule, serving as a primary ALS provider in the Lake Worth and Lantana area.

It was clear that most of the fire departments in the county were going ALS and there was a big push to hire paramedics. The fire department had never been my goal for a career, but it was clear that if I wanted to stay a paramedic I would need to get hired at a fire department or find another hospital-based job. I was married to a firefighter, and I understood what the job would be like. I also knew there were very few women in the profession.

When I went for my interview with Del-Trail Fire Control District I drove my husband's truck, thinking it would help me get hired. I felt like I had a good reputation as a paramedic, but I also knew that if I wanted to get hired, I would need to appear as if I would fit in.

I was offered a job along with another woman that had interviewed. However, part of the stipulation of being hired was cutting my hair to conform to the hair policy. I agreed, and was hired in February 1984; the other applicant did not agree to cut her hair and wasn't hired. When I first looked in the mirror with my hair cut short — off the collar and not past the middle of my earlobe — it was quite a shock. This was my first realization that this job was going to be a challenge.

As I was preparing for my first day, some firefighters I knew from the ambulance company told me to "watch out." They had heard from Del-Trail people that the only reason they hired me was to show they had hired a woman and that Del-Trail had no intention of letting me get off probation. I knew Del-Trail was all men and I would be the first woman, but the realization that there were firemen out there that were intensely opposed to women in the fire service became crystal clear. It did not appear that I would just be able to "fit in" like I naively thought.

On my first day I was very nervous, excited, and scared. I had not been to fire school yet, so I did not think I would have to do any firefighting, but I had to learn everything, from how the alarms were sounded to where the bathroom was. My first task was to clean and mop the floors. Since I was going to be on the rescue truck, I thought I would be learning about the equipment and protocols, but not a chance. My first year was all chores and cleaning.

Within a couple of shifts of starting, the paramedic I worked with said he wanted to talk with me. He said the out stations were calling and had questions about working with me. I thought they were asking about my skills or if I could lift patients, but no, they wanted to know what I slept in! The bunkroom was very dark, and I never walked around in what I slept in, so he didn't know the answer. I didn't tell him either!

One morning after I had been working a couple of weeks I was doing my morning chores mopping the bunkroom. The next thing I saw was one of the paramedics walking around naked after taking a shower. I knew he did not like me and did not want women on the job. Apparently, this was an attempt to see what I would do. Well, I finished mopping and left. In my mind there was no option about making a complaint; I would have been labeled for the rest of my career. I would have also proven the naysayers right.

There was a lot going on in my mind. Was this just the beginning? How much worse would the harassment be? What was my limit? Was this going to be worth it? Was I going to be fired anyway? I finally decided to just take it one shift at a time. Each morning I would think, just 24 hours. The bathroom was a good hiding place, and I would go in there for some privacy and to think. This turned out to be a good strategy for years to come.

When I started fire school, I worked my regular shift and went to school off duty if it was a weekday. When I came back to duty after school I ran calls and covered dispatch during the night. If an EMS call came in, I would run the call, and then go back to the dispatch desk, sleep if I could, and then off to school the next day.

There was a tremendous amount of pressure on me to pass school because, in addition to being embarrassed, I would be out of a job. During these first few months I did not think about being a pioneer or paving the way for other women. I just wanted to be a good paramedic, learn to be a firefighter, and keep my job.

One morning during this time my partner told me his wife was coming by the station and would I mind hiding while she was here. Needless to say, I was *very surprised. I had begun to learn that not only did some of my coworkers not like me, their wives did not like me either. He had never told his wife that the department had hired a woman and that I was his partner. Apparently she was a very jealous woman. I got a call and was not at the station when she came by, but I had no intention of hiding.*

It was a huge relief when fire school was over. But then it was on to recruit school, better known as Camp Gribble. At that time it was a two-week orientation run through the training division to teach us how the fire department wanted things done. The union and the department were at odds over a lot of issues and the recruit class was one of them. Every time we had a training burn or exercise, a union member would attend to ensure we were not being abused. Not a good feeling and it certainly didn't give me a sense of belonging.

Have you ever known firefighters to play pranks on each other? It is common knowledge that firefighters like to have fun and during downtime horseplay does occur. For six months no one played any practical jokes on me. I assumed that it was because I was an outsider, not part of the group, a girl. I think that was true to a degree but apparently my coworkers had been ordered not to haze me whatsoever or there would be severe repercussions. Then that night, with six months on the job, my bed was short-sheeted and the mattress fell through the frame when I tried to get into bed. It was the best practical joke ever. I was IN!

It is hard to explain how I was being treated differently because everyone was trying not to treat me differently. I was learning about my coworkers and put them into three categories. There were those who didn't like me and thought women should not be firefighters. This group was generally vocal and sometimes outwardly hostile. There were those who did not think I personally was too bad, but they didn't approve of women in the fire service. As long as I was on the rescue truck it might be OK, but they didn't want to see me riding an engine as a firefighter. The last, and smallest group of people, thought I was a good employee and were accepting of women in the fire service. However, they would only express this opinion when no one else was around.

I made it through the first year with a sense of relief; I passed fire school and made it through Camp Gribble. The wives still did not like me, and I was not invited to shift parties or any outside activities. I had made some inroads with my crew and felt more a part of the group. By far, my biggest achievement was not being fired. Writing these reflections is the first time I have allowed myself to think about the changing role of women in the fire service and my part in that process.

M.C. went on to excel as a firefighter and chief officer. She is still on the job, though close to retirement. She is one of the pioneers and should be recognized as such. Working with colleagues like M.C. is what I miss most about the job.

Division Chief Vicki Sheppard (Retired)

In 1980 I was working full time in the ER of a local hospital and part time as a paramedic for a local ambulance company. Most of my friends were men, working as firefighter paramedics, and I was envious of their schedule. It was natural for me to want to go to work for a fire department.

I applied at several fire departments that I thought were good. Unfortunately, there were no female firefighters in any departments in Palm Beach County, and no one wanted to take a chance on hiring me. It was frustrating looking for a department to hire me, but I understood their apprehension. I admit I looked like an unlikely candidate at 5'3" and 103 pounds. Word got around that I was looking for a job, and a friend recommended a department that I didn't think highly of, but beggars can't be choosers. I applied, and on December 1, 1980, I was hired as a paramedic by Old Dixie Fire Control with the stipulation that I had to successfully complete fire school.

I started fire school in January, 1981, going to school by day and coming back to finish my shift after school. There was one other female in my class, so I did not feel alone, but she dropped out halfway through the class. I am the first to admit I had difficulties along the way. I didn't have a lot of upper body strength, and survived on anti-inflammatory medicine and hot baths. Fire school was difficult, but the instructors and my classmates were fair. I had a lot of male friends that were firefighters who gave me helpful tips and helped me train. I passed fire school in April 1981.

Early in my career I read about other female firefighters who were having problems working in an all-male environment. I felt so fortunate to not experience the harassment experienced by other female firefighters across the country. Many of the firefighters, and their wives, did not want me to sleep in the same bunkroom. I worked at the central station, but had to sleep upstairs with the female dispatchers. I didn't like being separated from my coworkers, but I understood the concerns, even though they were unfounded. After a while they scheduled me to work in other fire stations and decided I could sleep in the same bunkroom as the men, provided I wore a shirt and shorts to bed. The guys just wore underwear.

The crew I worked with said there were no females in the fire service and no firefighters named Vicki. Therefore, I needed a new name. They came up with Max as my new name. To be honest, I liked the name and felt accepted because they all had nicknames too. To this day when I see any of the old gang they still call me Max.

The trend back then was to wear the gear from someone who had either been fired or was on another shift. The gear that was issued to me did not fit at all — it was way too big. I stuffed socks into my boots and rolled up the sleeves of my bunker coat. They sent me to the local hardware store to find a pair of gloves. I looked like a mismatched kid in that gear. The department wasn't known for having the best, including gear, equipment, and stations.

The Women's Auxiliary had a lot of power with the Board of Fire Commissioners. I was advised to get on their good side, so I joined the Auxiliary. We held Wednesday night spaghetti dinners to raise money and sold sandwiches on Saturdays. The Auxiliary also responded to large fires and provided the firefighters with food and beverages.

I made it through my one-year probationary period and became involved in the firefighters' union. They were in debt, and I had a background in fundraising. Soon I became union president and truly felt like I was part of a team. I never felt that my gender was a consideration. I helped organize summer barbecues and concerts to raise money, and we were soon out of debt.

In 1983 I was promoted to lieutenant and then in October of 1984 all the county fire control districts merged to become Palm Beach County Fire-Rescue. As a union president, I was asked to help merge the 10 individual fire control contracts into one cohesive contract. This was the single greatest piece of luck in my career, as it put me in an early leadership position within the new fire department. I felt as though I had hit the career lottery. Our benefits, salaries, and chances for promotion increased overnight. While I loved my small department, I was now part of a large metropolitan fire department. I was in the big time now!

In 1986 Palm Beach County Fire-Rescue offered a district chief promotional exam. I felt this department had the potential for a lot of growth, and I wanted to grow with it. Bruce Hill, from the Old Dixie Fire Control, and I studied together. The promotional process was unbiased in regard to race or gender; personnel were ranked according to score. Both of us passed and we were promoted to district chief in mid–1986. I was assigned to the Training and Safety Division, and to this day I believe this assignment provided me with critical career development opportunities.

First, I greatly improved my technical skills, since I was part of the teaching team for the recruit academy. By then the academy was 18 weeks long, and we taught both the firefighter and the EMT curriculum. Teaching helped me perfect my skills and placed me in a position to serve as a role model for new recruits. This was especially important for women recruits. To see a woman instructor in a position of authority gave them hope that they too could succeed. For the men joining the department, they saw a female as a normal part of the teaching cadre and learned to accept and respect women. Second, I became viewed by the administration as a knowledgeable and respected officer. I was invited to join the department's Policy Committee, where I learned more about the department and greatly improved my written communication skills.

I carefully selected mentors based on traits I admired: integrity, knowledge, and loyalty. I learned there is a way to respectfully disagree with others, to follow your heart and not the crowd, and to fight for what is right and not what is popular. I was fortunate to rise through management to the final position of division chief in the Training and Safety Division. I loved the opportunity to shape the minds of new, and not so new, employees, and the opportunity to show people that an organization can only succeed if every member is involved and pulling in the same direction. I was blessed to work with great instructors, and I strived to support their professional development so they could in turn help others.

Finally, here are my observations over the last 30 years:

The fire service is now a diverse organization and represents the community we serve. While other departments continue to struggle with accepting diversity, it has provided us with many advantages, including the ability to respect the differences in others and the willingness to embrace change. Diversity has also had a positive impact on fire service manufactures. Personal protective equipment is now available in sizes that fit everyone, and apparatus design and equipment placement is safer to accommodate the diverse size of today's firefighters.

Most new people entering the fire service view it as a job, not a career. They enjoy the pay and benefits, but they don't get involved in the fire service. I encourage all new people entering the service to read and learn about the history of the fire service: we have a great tradition — embrace it; we have the trust of the public — earn it; and we have firefighters who lost their lives to save a stranger — honor them.

Chief Sheppard is one of the smartest people I ever worked with. If she didn't know the answer, she would have it by the end of the day. I loved walking into the training office and feeling the energy and excitement, a direct result of her leadership and the dedicated and talented instructors who worked in that shop. She had a clear understanding of what makes an organization successful.

Lieutenant Jody Black Meidama

I grew up as a tomboy and loved to ride dirt bikes. I was never bothered by the sight of blood, mine or someone else's. After college I returned to Miami and worked in restaurants and bars, living a pretty carefree life. A lot of my friends were firefighters, and when one of them told me they had just hired a girl, it got me thinking about a career as a firefighter.

I went up to Ocala and enrolled in the State Fire Academy. There were 100 recruits and only six were girls. The six of us roomed in the same dorm room on campus. Throughout the training a lot of people quit or washed out of the program, boys and girls. I knew I would never quit. I loved heights, confined space, fire, sweat, and busting my butt. They would have to drag my dead body out of the burn building before I would ever quit!

The first day of class one of the instructors walked down the aisle of the classroom and grabbed my blond ponytail in his hand. In a thick southern drawl, he said, "This ponytail will look mighty pretty on fire." I just looked up and smiled and thought to myself, "Yup, it would!" Some girls might have been offended or scared by that. Not me. I had a lot of love in my heart for the good old boys and didn't want them to think their club was being infiltrated by girls. I just wanted to be a girl in their world, but one who could pull her own weight. I wasn't a woman's libber and most of the girls I know feel the same way. We all strive to pull our own weight and perform at a very high level. We feel like one incompetent woman will make us all look bad. It's embarrassing to see a girl who can't do the job; it belittles all the hard work the girls who came before us did.

I completed fire school and started EMT school, finished that and started paramedic school. This was 1993 and jobs were scarce, but I got to see the inside of a lot of fire stations because of the ride time that was part of my medic training. I loved the ride time in all the different fire stations, and I loved the guys. They all treated me great, and I think it's because I pitched in. I would do dishes, mop floors, and bring in ice cream. That was part of the tradition, and I wanted to be treated as one of the guys.

I had been applying to all the departments in the area and one day I got a call from Palm Beach County Fire-Rescue to come in for a drug test. I was stoked. I knew they weren't going to spend money on me unless they were hiring. There were 22 people in that hire, 18 guys and four girls. Training went well for me. I loved it and threw myself into it, staying late to practice knots and other things.

I made it through recruit training and started on shift in May of 1993. I was a coffee-making, phone-answering, cleaning machine. I didn't want anyone to look at me as just a girl. I wanted to be like every other rookie, do my part, and learn the business.

Even though I was the first one to jump in when something needed to be done, I still felt as though the guys were walking on eggshells around me. It was almost like they were testing out what could and couldn't be said around me. I let them know that I didn't curse or tell dirty jokes, but I didn't care if they did. If I was offended by a conversation, I would leave the room. I didn't want the guys to feel they had to change because I was part of their crew. I know there are some women's rights people out there who would not approve of my approach, but getting in someone's face just isn't my style.

I was assigned to an engine during my first year and learned so much from my captain and the guys on the engine. I was even hazed a little bit, but I knew that meant I was fitting in. It was like being part of a family but with a handful of dads, lots of brothers and me as the little sister. Even though on the first shift every wife and girlfriend just happened to drop by, I was treated with respect. There was never any thought of romance in the station. I never dated guys I worked with. It would be weird to even think about dating someone who I looked at as a brother!

I've been on the job for 16 years and hold the rank of lieutenant. I always tell people that I'm not one of the guys, and I don't want to be. I am a woman in the fire service doing the same job and loving it just like the guys. I have certain things that I excel at, such as fitting into small spaces like an attic that needs to be checked for fire or humping a high-rise pack up as many floors as necessary. We all have unique qualities and are part of a team.

I am married, not to a fireman, and have two daughters. My husband and mother help out when I'm on duty and I give my girls 100 percent of my time when I'm off duty. I get to spend quality time with them, volunteer at their school, and I'm not being pulled in a lot of different directions like a lot of other working moms.

I supervised Jody after she had been on the job for about a year, and she was a joy to work with. At one point I had three women working for me, including Jody, and never thought about treating them differently than the men. They were expected to do their job and pull their own weight, and they did just that. My tenure as captain at Station 55 working with that crew were among the best years I spent as a fire officer.

Driver Engineer
Cecilia Yolanda Perales Eaton

I was hired by Palm Beach County Fire-Rescue on March 27, 2000. I went through Recruit Class 30 and there were 28 men and two women. It never crossed my mind that I could fail; I thought I knew it all because I had been a volunteer firefighter in my native country of Peru in the city of Lima.

After recruit training and two weeks of ride time in different battalions, I was assigned to Battalion Three at Station 34. The guys there were older and although I didn't feel uncomfortable, I didn't feel great. I have a vague memory of talking to the chief and I remember that the station officer was an odd man.

My first shift I was told to drive the brush truck if a brush fire call came in. I was intimidated by the size of the truck but knew I could do it. We caught an apartment fire that shift, and I rode on the engine. There were six apartments on fire and I was ready to fight fire, but the captain told me to take off my mask and air-pack, that we were assigned water supply. I pulled a lot of hose that day.

After several shifts I was assigned to Station 33. We had a lot more calls at this station. The guys were a lot younger, and I was assigned to ride on the rescue. This was a problem for a while until I learned the area. I was supposed to drive the truck to the hospital, but made more than a few wrong turns.

As a rookie, I was expected to answer the phone. I was scared because English is not my first language. I couldn't ever tell what they were saying and they would have to call back. It was embarrassing for me, and sometimes I would try and hide in the bunkroom and hope that someone else would answer the phone.

I was once again transferred, this time to Battalion Nine, the Special Operations Battalion. I learned the reason for the transfer was because people were complaining about me, but I didn't know this at the time. No one ever said anything to me. It turned out to be the best transfer ever. The guys at Station 31 were an awesome crew. Captain Gardner was a kind and competent officer and Chief Newport was the best chief ever. I had to do all my performance objectives all over for the captain, but I didn't care. I was finally at a station where I knew that I was accepted. I took all the required training for Special Operations, ran a lot of good fires and amazing trauma calls, and until this day treasure my life there.

The guys at 31 pushed me to go to paramedic school, and I did. I then decided to take the driver exam and was promoted to driver engineer in October 2004. Once promoted, I floated around the battalion as a driver. I was out of my comfort zone, but that was just what I needed. I did meet some guys that tried to belittle me, but every day I grew and learned.

I was married December 29, 2006, and my son Mateo was born November 30, 2007. I took three months of maternity leave and felt I was ready, mentally, to come back to work, but physically I was not ready. I did an extra month in light duty status before coming back to operations. I was able to manage being a mother and working, but when my daughter Lucia was born on July 7, 2009, my world collapsed. This was the first time in my life that I wanted to stay home with my children. It took me a couple of months, but I came back to work. My feeling for work has changed since my children were born. I am more empathetic. I know that men are stronger than women physically, but I think women are tougher emotionally.

During my tenure in Battalion Two, I crossed paths with Cecilia and was always impressed with how competent, thoughtful, and serious she was about her profession. I expected no less given the training she had received at Station 31 from Captain Gardner, Chief Newport, and the other crew members in Special Operations.

Firefighter Paramedic Vanessa Ramos

My name is Vanessa Ramos, and I felt it was important to involve myself by offering my perspective as a female in the fire service of today. I have been with Palm Beach County Fire-Rescue since October of 2006, so I am still the newbie despite being almost 35 years old. My journey to becoming a firefighter started in 2002 when I saw a woman in a fire truck as I was walking down a sidewalk in Miami.

It never occurred to me that I could do this job. I recall hearing my mother talk about Uncle Barry, a New York City firefighter, and what a noble job he performed and how exciting and dangerous those men were. I remember visiting Uncle Barry's station and going to parties held by his FDNY brethren. I can still hear the men reminiscing about abandoned building fires, griping about the new NFPA standards that required they actually wear their SCBAs, and [revealing] how they acquired their nicknames. Wives and girlfriends and mothers and daughters were always present, but never did I set eyes on a female firefighter. So I guess it never occurred to me that women could do the job. But I was drawn to it, sucked in by those stories to the point of hiding in trees in the backyard so that I could hear those grownups tell those very adult stories. I would try on my uncle's gear and play rescue games and fantasize about being the "hero" as a child.

So once I saw this woman in the fire engine years later while walking down that sidewalk, I went on a mission to find out how I could do this job. I went through fire school and got my EMT certification, submitted an application to Palm Beach County Fire-Rescue and before long I was sitting in a recruit class with 35 people, only three of us women.

Recruit class was not easy, and I do feel that if not for my gender it would have been a different experience. Not necessarily harder, but certainly there would have been more profanity. I felt as if people were careful about what and how they said things. However, I was treated with respect and dignity by my instructors and fellow recruits. I never felt like I was singled out or treated differently. I worked very hard and was chosen class leader. I think if I had shown anything less, I would have not been as respected by my classmates.

My first day on the job was extremely tense for me. I showed up at the station in my pressed uniform and spit-shined boots and was overwhelmed with information, rules, expectations, and station duties. It was like trying to stuff 10 pounds of crap in a five-pound bucket. This continued for the next eight months. I barely said a word. I barely slept. I barely sat down. I barely felt welcome and I did feel like that was gender related. I barely liked the job.

After surviving my first year, I started to come out of my shell and began to feel more welcomed by my shift mates. The guys saw that I could take a joke. Cursing didn't offend me, and I always pulled my own weight and sometimes the weight of others. Just as I was beginning to appreciate this amazing profession, I was deployed to Iraq with my United States Army Reserve unit as a combat medic.

I spent over a year away from my Palm Beach County Fire-Rescue family, and during that time I must have received over 30 care packages and tons of cards from the guys at the station. They went all out, sending me beluga caviar, canned octopus, and lots of other stuff that was considered contraband by the Army! Not to knock my real family, but I received far more from my fire rescue family than I did from my real family.

I would come back from a five-day mission, mentally, physically, and emotionally exhausted, and see a big box on my bunk and know it was from my fire rescue family. No matter what happened during the mission or how nasty and tired I was, I was so happy to sit down and tear into that box. It would cure whatever negativity was afflicting me. I'd walk to the showers with a lighter step with some newfangled candy in my mouth. Thinking about that now makes me misty-eyed. My sisters at the department were involved too, but the majority of my coworkers are men, so it's only logical that the majority of those care packages were packed by those callous, rugged, macho men. Their third grade handwriting on the notes, telling me to keep my chin up and my ass down, will never be forgotten.

Eight months into my deployment, I left Iraq on a medivac flight on life support and woke up weeks later in Germany. I eventually entered lower echelons of care as I got better and found myself in a Warrior Transition Unit in Fort Gordon, Georgia. As soon as I could, I made contact with the people from the department, and the first thing I heard from my chief was, "What can we do for you, Ramos?" I continued to hear that during my months-long recovery from everyone I came in contact with from fire rescue. They wanted to know my new mailing address, and the packages continued.

I'm not sure what the changing factor was, but I now feel comfortable wherever I work in the department. Even when I'm shipped out to a station where I don't know anyone, I never feel uncomfortable or ostracized. Maybe being a war vet has something to do with it, but I would rather think it is because of my never-stop, OCD work ethic. I fully love my job.

I never met Vanessa Ramos when I was on the job. I wish I had. She is the type of person who will uphold the traditions that are so important in the fire service profession, and she clearly makes the point about no longer feeling uncomfortable, regardless of where she works. This is the best indication that women are fully accepted within the department.

Captain Karen Walshe

My brother Brian talked me into volunteering at Plantation Fire Department, and I found that I loved it. There was a sense of family and camaraderie that I had never experienced before. I soon realized that this fun hobby could be a profession for me, so I attended the Broward Fire Academy and became a certified firefighter. Next were EMT school and then paramedic school.

I applied for a job at Palm Beach County Fire-Rescue and was hired on October 10, 2000. I was in Recruit Class 31, which I found to be mentally and physically challenging. I was always treated fairly by the instructors and my peers, which I found only reasonable. I expected no freebies and knew that I needed to earn trust and respect. I gave 110 percent effort and at the end of the training I was named Top Recruit, the first female to do so since the inception of the recruit academy.

I am in my tenth year and have climbed the career ladder to captain. I have no idea what else I would do if I couldn't be a firefighter; it's the best job in the world. Just ask a fireman! Yes, there are the bad calls we wish we hadn't seen and will never forget, but these are outweighed by the good calls where we were able to make a difference in someone's life. That's a great feeling.

I am part of a large family. If you have never done so, go to a firehouse and sit around the table with a bunch of firemen. You will cry with laughter at the stories and shake your head at the wisdom that is always a part of those stories. In my mind there is no gender issue; we are all just firefighters.

Thank you to the women who told their stories. From left to right: Carey Tiersch, Vanessa Ramos, Vicki Sheppard, Karen Walshe, Jody Black Meidema, Cecilia Perales Eaton, M.C. (Mary Catherine) Madigan (courtesy Douglas Watson).

I had the pleasure of working with Karen for a short time. Like all the other women who have told their stories, Karen is a competent, professional firefighter with a passion for the job.

I hope the reader has gained a clearer understanding of the progress women have made in this profession. It's certainly evident when you compare the experiences that M.C. Madigan and Carey Tiersch and Vicki Sheppard had with the experiences of the women who came into the business after consolidation. Becoming a part of this profession is not easy, regardless of gender, but at least the playing field is now level.

In a few years there won't be anyone left in the fire service who can remember working only with men. M.C. and Carey and Vicki didn't know about a glass ceiling; they did their jobs, pushed back when they had to, and made it possible for all the other women to enter this profession and excel. The fire service is now comprised of a diverse workforce that reflects the community it serves. As an organization, we are better for that, and so is the community.

16—Bill Rogers

Bill Rogers and I used to play "Palm Frond" at the beach in the early spring before the place was overrun with tourists. Throwing a Frisbee was no longer a challenge, so we borrowed a page from the jai alai games that are ubiquitous in South Florida. But instead of a cesta, we used a palm frond, and instead of a pelota, we used a tennis ball wrapped in yards of duct tape. We would stand 50 yards apart, throwing and catching for hours before jumping in the ocean to cool down. The few tourists who were on the beach were always amazed at the velocity of the ball and our ability to catch and throw it. Firemen are known for doing some crazy things, but we simply looked at it as another way to stay in shape. That's not to say that Bill and I didn't do some crazy things, such as going body surfing when the waves were 10 to 12 feet high. Getting out was easy—catching a wave in and surviving was not. We were both fortunate we didn't drown. If we weren't swimming, or body surfing, or snorkeling, we were running. Firefighting is a demanding occupation, and most of us lifted weights at the station and worked on our aerobic fitness off duty.

Bill grew up on German Town Road in Delray Beach, Florida, acting out childhood fantasies with Jimmy Weston, Larry Creasman, and Eddie Everette in the palmetto scrub and pine forests that have long since been paved over. Jimmy and Larry would spend more time at Bill's house than anywhere else, where Bill's mother, Juanita, would care for them as if they were her own sons. Bill was playing keyboard and strumming a guitar from about the age of 10, laying the foundation for a talent that would enthrall all who knew him. Later, he began writing songs, something he would continue to do for the remainder of his life. One particularly poignant song titled "Giants" is a tribute to his father, William Ernest Rogers, Sr. His father was a giant in the eyes of his son, and Bill's lyrics capture for all of us what we would like to say to our fathers but are never quite able to express. Another song Bill wrote about his childhood tells the story of Jimmy and Larry trying to hang him; thankfully, Bill's grandmother intervened just as they were getting ready to push him off a stack of books. Maybe those early years were good preparation for a life that sometimes places demands on a man that no one can adequately prepare for.

Bill played in various bands in high school, including Keith Austin's band, the Avengers. By then he was writing serious music. Two songs, "Sad Boy" and "Flake Off Baby," were made into a 45 record by Ducoff Recording Studio in Miami.[1] Bill entered the Navy as soon as he graduated from high school, and while stationed in Jacksonville at the Naval Air Station he played keyboard in a band with Ronnie Van Zant and Steve Brookins before they went on to fame with Lynyrd Skynyrd and 38 Special. Bill grew up during the beginning of the Southern rock genre, and soon after getting out of the Navy, he started a band called Thunder Blu that was based in Lake Worth, Florida. Brookins played in that band, standing in for Bill when he was too sick to play some of the gigs. According to Bill's mother, Bill roomed with Brookins during the early 1970s. Thunder Blu would go on to become Hot Lanta Band.[2]

Leading the life of a rock-and-roll musician in those early years was a wild time for Bill. He continued to hang out with his childhood friends, including Keith Austin, who also became a Del-Trail fireman. Keith once told me a story about a girl Bill was interested in. One evening Bill and Keith drove over to the girl's home, having been told her parents would not be home. They parked the car out of sight of the house on an old farm trail leading into a cow pasture, just in case their intelligence about the girl's parents was wrong. Shortly after they arrived, the girl's parents drove into the yard. Bill and Keith ran out the back door and crawled under a fence into the cow pasture, trying to make their way back to the car before being discovered. Keith said they were covered in cow manure by the time they reached the car and then ran out of gas a half mile down the road. They tried hitchhiking, but no one would pick up two boys smelling the way they did.[3]

I met Bill in 1977 when he joined Del-Trail, and we immediately became friends. Jimmy Weston and Keith Austin were already working for Del-Trail, and I had heard many stories about Billy before ever meeting him, including the time he thought Frankenstein and the Wolf Man were after him. Growing up in the late 1960s and early 1970s will do that to you. Keith told me that Billy was pounding on his door late one night, screaming, "Let me in. Let me in. Frankenstein and the Wolf Man are following me!" We were all pretty wild in those days, and Billy did love his Jack and Ginger.

We worked together in the same stations over many years. Bill was always one of the first to check his truck or clean the dishes, and he loved talking music trivia. We would name a song, and he would tell us who wrote it. Around Christmas one year I heard an advertisement for old records, including songs by Burl Ives. I thought I had him when I asked, "Who wrote 'A Little Bitty Tear'?"

Without hesitation he replied, "Burl Ives!"

This went on for years, and we never stumped him.

He told us a different joke every day and was equally quick to play a practical joke. Firemen are known for their practical jokes, and I will never forget the time he returned from a call with a live alligator in the back of the rescue truck. I was taking a nap on a Sunday afternoon when Billy shoved that thing under my nose. It was only three feet long, but frisky, and it certainly looked a lot bigger from six inches away.

Billy was a big-boned, lean man with a bushy mustache and eyebrows to match, plus a perpetual five o'clock shadow. His dark brown eyes were a mirror to his soul — twinkling or sad, it was easy to read his mood. At six three and 220 pounds, he was immensely strong, with huge hands that were made to play the keyboard. He had a wonderful baritone voice that I can hear even now. An extraordinarily gifted musician, he was as talented on the acoustic guitar as he was on the organ, and I have fond memories of listening to him play his songs of lost loves, new beginnings, and old Florida while we waited for the alarm to ring. Even those who didn't appreciate music sensed they were in the presence of something very special as Billy played his songs while sitting on the back step of an engine.

Bill was a great cook, especially at breakfast, and his specialty was something he called Huckle Buckle. He assured me it was an old Southern standby, but you could never be sure when Bill was pulling your leg. That aside, he would fry thinly sliced potatoes, onions, and peppers in a large cast-iron skillet and, once the potatoes were browned, crack eggs on top. It's a delicious dish, and one I continue to make on lazy weekend morn-

Bill Rogers playing the keyboard at Country Jam IV (courtesy Lee Tenney).

ings. He also taught me how to make biscuits and gravy, though he called them cat heads and gravy. I was making biscuits and gravy early one Sunday morning at Station 42 while Bill and the rest of the crew were cleaning the station and checking equipment. As I was adding flour to thicken the gravy, I noticed small black bugs scurrying around in the flour. The gravy was well under way, so I looked over my shoulder to make sure no one noticed, turned up the heat, and added a lot more pepper. When the eggs and bacon were ready, I called the boys for breakfast. I never said a word, until later, and I passed on the biscuits and gravy. That was one of the few times I ever put one over on Bill.

Billy agonized about going to paramedic school. Unlike now, the potential for career advancement wasn't good if you decided to become a paramedic. The traditional route to attaining rank was to become a driver engineer and then sit for the lieutenant's exam. But Bill had a love for medicine and wanted to pursue the training. He became a gifted paramedic, and I was fortunate to have him in my station when I became a station officer.

This photograph was taken at one of the many pig roasts held at the home of Bill and Roseanne Rogers. All of the people in the picture began their fire service career with Del-Trail Fire Department. Front row from left to right: Richard Cromwell, Henry Cusell, Kelly Browning, Eddie Schnabel, John Gloskowski. Back row from left to right: Tony Scott, Bill Rogers, Keith Austin, the author, Jay Little, Lee Tenney, Jim Weston, Fred Russell, Everett Frye, Larry Manley, Carey Tiersch, John Tiersch, Lenny Volpe (courtesy Lee Tenney).

I remember running a bad wreck, I think it was a head-on collision, where a woman was pinned in her vehicle. Bill was assessing her condition as we worked around him with extrication tools, trying to free her from the wreckage. There is a fine line between quickly removing someone for more definitive care and, at the same time, trying not to injure the patient even more through extrication efforts. Billy pulled me aside and told me if we didn't get her out immediately, she was going to die. He recognized the signs of cardiac tamponade — distended veins in her neck, weak pulse, cyanosis, and weak blood pressure — and knew she wasn't going to live long without immediate treatment. She was pinned between the steering column and the seat, and he had been evaluating her condition as the rest of the crew used rams to roll the dash.

Cardiac tamponade is a life-threatening condition of fluid buildup in the pericardium, caused in this case by blunt-force trauma from her chest striking the steering wheel.[4] She had a massive amount of blood in her pericardial sack, as well as a flail chest, which is life threatening in itself. I told my guys to get her out, now, and not worry about aggravating her other injuries. Once she was extricated and in the back of the rescue truck, Billy shoved a needle through her left costal arch into the pericardium and aspirated a large amount of blood from her pericardial sack. She didn't like that one bit, but she survived the accident. There are many calls where the outcome is never certain; however, it is certain that a number of people owe their lives to Bill Rogers' skill as a medic.

Bill's career was cut short because of doing what he loved most. One of the hazards of working in the EMS field is back injuries caused by repeated lifting. Billy retired early because of his back and moved to Branford, Florida, with his wife, Roseanne. They lived on a beautiful piece of property on the bank of the Santa Fe River, and he named the property Rosie Oaks after his wife. Bill started an annual tradition the year he moved to Branford, holding a pig roast that became an informal reunion for Del-Trail firemen. The year Bill Clinton was having his proclivity problems, Bill made up a sign that he hung over the roasting pig, proclaiming, "Here Lies Linda Tripp!" (a not-so-subtle jab for her selling out Monica Lewinsky to independent counsel Kenneth Starr). The pig roasts brought chief officers and firemen together without the formality of rank. It was a time for reminiscing, renewing friendships, and even burying the hatchet with Chief Frye. In addition to roasted pig, Bill would fry whole turkeys and chickens, which would disappear off the cutting board as fast as Roger Hackle or Lenny Volpe could cut them up. Wonderful food and lots of beer, horseshoe matches, swimming in the Santa Fe River, and relaxing with good friends was something we all looked forward to each year. Bill's back eventually gave out completely, and it was no longer possible for him to host such a large event, so Lee and Eva Tenney kept the tradition alive with an annual chili cook-off. Lee, also one of the original Del-Trail firemen, and Eva bought property just down the road from Bill and Rose. My wife and I continue to reconnect with old friends at Lee and Eva's house every year in March at their chili cook-off.

Bill's health continued to decline; it was hard to see him slowing down, no longer the strong, robust man I had worked with for so many years. He contracted throat cancer in 2006 and called me when he received the diagnosis, saying he was going to beat it. I remember thinking what a cruel disease throat cancer was for someone who had such a fine voice. He fought a hard battle, but passed away on September 4, 2008. After the funeral service his son gave me three CDs of Billy's original songs, including many I had never heard. Bill had set up a small recording studio in his house, and when he realized that he wasn't going to recover, spent a year laying down tracks of all the music he ever wrote. He managed to finish this project before he became too sick to sing, and one of the last songs he wrote when he knew he wouldn't recover was "Captain of My Soul." I can't imagine a better legacy, and I play these songs whenever I want to hear his voice.

People in other professions have coworkers they call friends, but in most professions friendships are not forged in fire. When you work with guys who will put their lives on the line for you, friendship becomes a sacred trust. Bill Rogers was a true friend to me and all who knew him. Billy was one of the finest men I will ever know.

Captain of My Soul

There comes a time in all our lives
When we hear a distant thunder
And think — is this really all there is
To life's amazing wonder?

The answers have been there all along
All you have to do is ask
The good Lord will provide for you
No matter what the task

I'll sail my ship to heaven's door
Where Jesus has control
He's the master of my fate
And the captain of my soul

When you feel the love inside you
And hold it to you dear
The dreams that you imagined
Will suddenly be clear.[5]

On the Job: Near Miss

Fighting fires is a science, but with so many variables, it's never an exact science. Building construction, building content, area of fire origin, and how long the fire has been burning all play a part in what we, as firefighters, are presented with when we pull up to the front of a burning building. Although we don't have any control over those variables, we do have control over how much and what type of training we have had in all the various aspects of the firefighting profession. As an experienced fire officer with 30 years on the job, I relied on that training and on past experiences to make decisions about where to place lines; how, when, and where to ventilate; and the number and type of resources needed to safely extinguish a fire that almost killed some of my people.

We received a page for a house fire in a residential neighborhood of cookie-cutter homes in Royal Palm Beach. The single-story house was constructed of concrete blocks with a floor area of approximately 2,500 square feet. Children's toys were scattered around the yard, and a doghouse with a steel cable for a run was positioned between two trees in the backyard. It was late September 2006. The sun was low in the sky, and humid air forced acrid brown smoke curling from the eaves to drift down the side of the building. There was active fire at the back of the house in a kitchen area. As I walked around the house, my mind was sorting through all the kitchen fires I had seen in the past, helping me decide how this one should be attacked. The first alarm assignment included Engine and Rescue 28, Engine 21, Quint 29, EMS 2, and me as the district chief. I filled the alarm for another engine and rescue, knowing the 90-degree late afternoon heat would limit the time crews could work effectively.

I ordered a line to the front door and a crew to the back to vent on my orders. The ladder company forced the front door, clearly revealing an open floor plan leading to the back of the house. There was a well-established free-burning kitchen fire rolling across the ceiling into the living room area, pushing lazy smoke through the top of the front door opening. I ordered the vent team to take a window at the back of the house and told Lieutenant Earl Wooten to check the overhead before advancing a line through the front door.

Opening up a roof is a dangerous job made easier and safer when it can be done with the help of an elevated platform. This house was hit by lightning, and the crew from Platform 29 is cutting a hole in the roof to release fire and heated gas, allowing crews inside the building to reach the seat of the fire and extinguish it. This fire went to a third alarm (courtesy Arthur Werkle).

He used a pike pole to open the ceiling just inside the door and informed me that it was very hot but there was no fire. I remember thinking to myself that it should be hot; the damn house was on fire. The lazy smoke I observed coming from the eaves during my size-up told me there might be fire in the attic, but the conditions I observed with the front door open and fire blowing out the back told me that likelihood was remote. It didn't take long for me to reconsider that thinking.

I ordered Wooten and his crew to advance a one-and-three-quarter-inch line, ordered Lieutenant John Przybylek's crew to position a back-up line at the front door, and ordered the truck company to do a left-hand search for occupants. Conditions started to deteriorate almost immediately. The lazy brown smoke that had been coming from the top of the front door turned to angry black smoke, filling the whole door opening and lighting up at the top with fingers of red fire. For me, time slows down when I'm under pressure, seemingly giving me all the time I need to make the right decisions. When I saw conditions change from a relatively benign fire to a fire that was approaching flashover, I immediately ordered the crews to evacuate the building and told the crew on the back-up line to start penciling the ceiling to cool the overhead without disrupting the thermal balance. Within 20 seconds of issuing the order to evacuate, firefighters started stumbling out the front door. I knew I had six people inside, but only five had come out. Lieutenant Przybylek's crew was just inside the door, hitting the ceiling with short, hard blasts of water. I grabbed the lieutenant and told him we were missing one man. He didn't say a word; he and his crew turned and disappeared into that silent black hell.

They came out within seconds, dragging Steve Trimble by his air-pack straps. His gear was so hot they were burning their hands as they stripped it off. The rescue crew started evaluating Trimble, and I turned my attention back to a house that was still on fire and getting worse by the second. This fire had progressed from what appeared to be a small free-burning fire with a temperature of around 500 degrees to one at the point of flashover with a temperature of around 1200 degrees, all in under three minutes— an unbelievable display of raw energy, particularly when it's your responsibility to mitigate the problem.

The fire wasn't going to go out by wishing it out, or because I was all of

This picture shows fire venting from the roof only a minute after Platform 29's crew cut the hole. It's a balancing act to open a roof enough to allow a good vent but at the same time do so safely (courtesy Arthur Werkle).

a sudden having a very bad day. The fire didn't care that one of my men was injured, or that the strategy we had been using was no longer working. And the fire certainly didn't care that I was trying to get my act together after almost getting my people killed. As an incident commander, getting your own people hurt (or worse) is a nightmare none of us like to think about, but it is something that is always there, always a possibility; cold fear and loose bowels don't even begin to describe the feeling. Yet, as the officer in charge, I had to put that fear aside and continue to function effectively as a fire ground commander.

Fire officers receive training on command and control of major incidents at the National Fire Academy in Emmitsburg, Maryland. This training is high-tech and real world, utilizing video-based scenarios where trainees have to make decisions in real time. The videos present different scenarios where decision making has direct consequences. If a trainee makes good decisions, the fire goes out. Conversely, with poor decisions, the situation continues to deteriorate. The rationale is that if you have seen a similar problem during training and dealt with it in an appropriate manner, you are more apt to make good decisions on a real event.

Although it doesn't matter how many times you burn a building down in the classroom, that's not an option in the real world. My training kicked in, and I ordered the ceiling pulled and fire streams directed into the attic space. After several minutes of hitting the fire hard with straight streams in the overhead area, I could see we were making progress. Soon, dark brown smoke began to turn white, and I knew we were finally putting the fire out.

Most district chiefs monitor incidents in their own and neighboring battalions so they will be prepared if they have to come in on a second alarm. Kermit Russell was the district chief from the neighboring battalion, and he cruised by just about the time I thought I was getting people killed. He asked if I wanted help, but I declined. Incident commanders never want to admit that their strategy isn't working or they might need a few more people. As it turned out, we were able to put the fire out with the resources on scene. He came around again as we were overhauling and was amazed that the building was still standing. So was I.

There are distinct phases of fire suppression, from initial attack through salvage and overhaul and finally determining cause and origin. Every phase of firefighting is hot, heavy, dangerous work. Even during the overhaul and salvage stage of the fire, when the fire is out and crews are pulling ceilings and searching for hidden fire and possible victims, crews are still in full gear and on air. When I called re-hab for a fresh crew to continue with overhaul operations, I was amazed to see Trimble standing with his crew, awaiting another assignment. I thought he had been transported to the hospital, but he assured me he was all right. I assigned him and his crew to do a final sweep of the house to make sure we hadn't missed any victims. They came out a few minutes later to tell me there was a dead dog in a bathroom. By this time the family had arrived, and Steve didn't want to drag the dog out with the children watching. I told them to secure the dog in a salvage cover and leave it inside the front door. I then spoke with the father and told him about the dog and suggested that he talk with his children. I also told him we would help dig a grave for the dog in the backyard. The children learned a hard lesson about life and death, but we were able to soften that lesson through our empathy for their loss.

Several days later Steve told me what had happened, and his experience confirmed that training saves lives. He was on the first hose line, all the way at the back of the house adjacent to the kitchen area, when conditions started to deteriorate. When I gave the order to exit the building, he and the other two men on the line were already heading for the door. He told me it got so hot so quickly that they tried exiting through a sliding glass door adjacent to the kitchen, but it was locked and they weren't able to break the glass. Steve is six four, 240 pounds, and in superb condition — tall enough and strong enough that he was able to repeatedly punch the nozzle through the ceiling trying to cool the attic space. When it became too hot to stand, he started penciling the ceiling with quick, hard blasts of water with the nozzle set on straight stream, something that we teach in flashover training. He said they abandoned any attempt to cool the upper levels of the room and were following the line toward the door when he went down. Przybylek's crew found him on the line just steps from the front door.

I was one of a large cadre of instructors who helped teach flashover recognition, truly life-saving training. Our flashover prop was a 50-foot metal cargo container. The fire we ignited consisted of four 4 × 8 sheets of outside strand board plywood with hay and a stack of pallets to stoke the fire — the heat inside the container was absolutely debilitating. After 10 minutes working inside that metal box, the soles of my fire boots would be degraded to the point that I could actually skate on melting rubber. Supervision inside the prop was very tight, with five instructors for 10 students. We would seat the trainees on a bench along the side wall and ignite the fire. They would then observe the progression of the fire from its incipient stage to a free-burning stage and then to a point just before flashover. We controlled the fire using a vent in the ceiling of the cargo container. When the fire was approaching flashover, one student at a time would use a hose line to pencil the ceiling with short, hard blasts of water with the nozzle set on straight stream. The reaction of the fire to the water was immediate: it would flow back across the ceiling toward the point of origin and the thermal balance within the confines of the steel box would not be disrupted. To demonstrate what happens when a fog stream is used rather than a straight stream, the instructor at the hose line would give the ceiling a quick sweep with a fog stream. This immediately raised the temperature and reduced visibility to nil. We would then exit the box and continue the lecture portion of the training.

All of our crews receive training in how to recognize and deal with impending flashover conditions, and one of the prime considerations is to not disrupt the thermal balance. When my crews started penciling the ceiling, it cooled the overhead without moving a lot of air around, allowing everyone but Steve to safely exit. That's not to say it wasn't getting very, very hot at floor level. Steve's helmet was degraded from the heat and had to be replaced, his air-pack was taken out of service for repair, and all the metal parts of his turnout gear were hot enough to blister the hands of the guys who were helping him. Although he wasn't hurt physically from this experience, it shook his confidence as a firefighter for a time. I think all of us were shaken, but at the same time we all gained valuable knowledge. Becoming a competent firefighter requires ongoing training and the ability to apply lessons learned the next time the alarm sounds. Becoming a truly great firefighter means becoming a student of the profession. The guys I worked with were students of the profession.

We learned several lessons on this fire: pay more attention to smoke patterns; look more closely at the roof; consider ventilation consequences; and think about people's storage habits. The light brown smoke coming from the soffits that I initially observed told me there might be a fire in the attic. The conditions I saw inside the house didn't support that observation, but we later found huge amounts of newspapers and magazines stored in the attic. Those amounts of class A combustibles aren't normally stored in attic areas, but you never know about the habits of people. The volume of newspapers and magazines in the attic contributed to heavy fire conditions that weren't immediately apparent and eventually contributed to flashover conditions. A closer look at the roof would have revealed sagging in the area of the attic fire, a sure sign that there was heavy fire involvement in the attic. I didn't see it because it was getting dark, and I didn't use a flashlight to get a better look at the roof. I could have used a thermal imaging camera, but I thought I knew what was happening in that house from the conditions that were immediately apparent in the kitchen. The biggest contributing factor to flashover was leaving the front door open as crews advanced a line into the house. This allowed a huge influx of fresh oxygen, which accelerated the progression of fire to the flashover stage. We always learn something new during firefighting operations, and I always preached to my guys that if you weren't continuing to learn, it was time to get out of the profession. That evening I was happy I only had another year in the business, because I wasn't ready for any more lessons of this nature.

17—Transition Process

Line officers are expected to think tactically; chief officers are expected to think strategically. That was a paradigm shift I struggled with for a long time. Even when I was comfortable standing on the street at a command post while making strategic decisions and managing resources, I still wanted to peek over the shoulders of the lieutenants and captains who were implementing those strategic decisions at the tactical level. I knew they didn't need my help advancing a hose line into a building that was on fire, but it was all I could do to let them manage their crews without input from me. It didn't take long to figure out that letting go of tactical thinking would be a very small part of moving from line officer to chief officer.

I got some experience in working as a district chief when I was given the opportunity to work in an acting capacity in Battalion Five for close to a year. That was invaluable experience in many different ways, especially with incident management. But earning the badge of district chief through competitive testing brought a level of responsibility that I never felt when I was working in an acting capacity.

I was promoted to district chief in December 1999, along with my good friend Daryl Newport. Daryl and I had come into the service at the same time and had come up through the ranks together. It was only fitting that we should be promoted to chief at the same time.

I was assigned to Battalion Two, a western battalion that straddles Southern Boulevard, a major roadway leading west to Belle Glade. The battalion encompassed the communities of the Village of Royal Palm Beach, the Village of Wellington, and the unincorporated areas of the Acreage and Loxahatchee. It was a very large battalion with a good mix of residential, commercial, and rural areas. I had nine stations under my command and Battalion Chief Al Sierra was my boss. Al and I went way back to the pre-consolidation days, when he was a lieutenant and I was a captain. He was the one who gave me the nickname Captain Happy, and after my promotion he changed it to Chief Cheerful.

Al was fun to work for, but he was a demanding boss. He loved to delegate work and used to delight in saying that if a project didn't require his signature, it should be delegated. He explained to me in his quiet way that it was all about time management. I would point out to him that he was managing *my* time, and he would reply that it was good for my professional development. Although I didn't appreciate the sentiment at the time, he was stretching my time-management abilities and, more importantly, developing my executive leadership abilities.

A battalion chief is involved in local politics as a necessary part of the position. Al attended council meetings and sat on various committees, including the safety committee for the Village of Wellington. Al hated going to those meetings, so he delegated. As a result, I would wind up sitting in on the best example of a waste of time that a municipality could ever dream up. I eventually came to hate those safety meetings even more than he did.

Another example of his delegation habits was assigning me to write the annual report of Fire-Rescue's involvement with the Village of Wellington. Wellington paid Fire-Rescue a lot of money each year for fire and rescue service, and the people wanted to know, in detail, how their money was being spent. This wasn't all that difficult, but it was time consuming. My day started at 7 in the morning and didn't end until 10 in the evening, and that was just the administrative part of the job; I still ran calls throughout the day and sometimes all night long. It didn't take me long to figure out there weren't enough hours in the day to get the annual report in on time, so I delegated a lot of the work to the three station officers assigned to the three Wellington stations. They complained bitterly that it wasn't part of their job description, but I pointed out that it was all about time management and would do wonders for their professional development. Al just smiled when he learned how I was managing that project.

Formal photograph taken after I was promoted to district chief (courtesy Palm Beach County Fire-Rescue photo archive).

There was a quid pro quo for this additional work. Because Palm Beach County Fire-Rescue is a large department, and well respected nationally, we would be asked to send fire officers to other fire departments to assist with their promotional processes. Most fire departments rely on outside subject-matter experts to oversee portions of a promotional examination. When the District of Columbia Fire Department asked for help in testing 500 candidates for promotion, Al gave me the nod. I spent two weeks working with 34 fire officers from the United States and Canada, helping the DCFD select candidates for promotion. It was a professional development opportunity that few people ever receive and a wonderful chance to network with other fire officers.

A necessary and sometimes unpleasant part of my job as a district chief was administering discipline to firefighters who had stepped over the line. Firemen are their own worst enemies, and I never had a problem correcting someone's behavior. But as a member of Local 2928, and before that a charter member of Local 2624 with Del-Trail Fire Department, it was difficult to punish a fellow union member, especially if it resulted in loss of pay or a demotion. As a district chief, I was still a member of the union, even though I was now considered part of management.

Joel Brier was the representative for union members facing a disciplinary procedure, and if you looked up "acerbic" in the dictionary, you would see his picture. He was the best advocate a firefighter in trouble could have, knew the contract and the Firefighter Bill of Rights (see Appendix G) by heart, and never gave ground. He's a big, hulking guy with fierce blue eyes who wasn't afraid to get in your face, regardless of rank. On several occasions I found myself seated across the table from Joel and a wayward fireman, and I always felt inadequate. I missed the days as a line officer when I could pull a firefighter outside and have a friendly chat, just the two of us, where I talked and the firefighter listened. A station officer has a lot of authority over a crew, and as a captain I used that authority judiciously and without any thought that someone would be looking over my shoulder. Certainly, no one questioned my authority. It was a strange transition to move to being chief officer, where you had even more authority, yet you knew it could be called into question at any time. With the checks and balances that came with a union rep like Joel, a lot of the joy was gone.[1]

When I came into the battalion the other two district chiefs went out of their way to help me become comfortable in my new position. The administrative work was overwhelming at first, and I learned a great deal from Chief Kimberly and Chief Neil Enos about how to manage that aspect of the job. They were also good at knowing when to step back and let me, as a new chief, find my own way. I was made to feel welcome and realized I had entered a new and exciting fraternity.

Perhaps the most daunting part of my transition from captain to chief was the dynamics involved in supervising nine station officers rather than my own crew of firefighters. A station officer lives with his crew, resulting in a close relationship almost akin to a family structure. As a district chief, I no longer had that intimate relationship with crews; establishing a relationship with my officers would take time.

I inherited a cadre of senior and very junior officers. The senior officers were great on calls but hard to motivate. The junior officers were easy to motivate and sometimes a worry on calls. It was an interesting mix, with the senior officers challenging my authority at every turn and the junior officers toeing the line. I could empathize with the old guard; as a senior captain I would have felt the same way toward a new chief, though I hope I would have been a bit more diplomatic. Although it was more like a skirmish than a war, I still had to pick my battles. I was a little more lax than I wanted to be regarding certain regulations but did insist that one of my more recalcitrant lieutenants cut his ponytail.

Cadre of fire officers posing in front of a building that was used to train recruits. Each time a class of recruits goes through the training academy, it takes a large number of experienced trainers to safely supervise this physically demanding work. When they are not assisting with training, they are working as line or chief officers. Left to right: Bruce Clark, Bill Morris, Skip Moser, James Guyn, Mike Kemp, Jim Gribble, Bruce Young, James Schaffner, John Przybylek, Ron Beesley, Ron Lowe, Daryl Newport (courtesy Craig Whitney).

The first year I was in the battalion, we did a lot of training. It was important for me to understand the capabilities of my crews, even though there was a lot of bitching about the training from the senior officers. That fell on deaf ears; we conducted multi-company drills each week, which revealed weakness in many areas. When it became apparent, even to the senior officers, that their performance was not at a satisfactory level, the bitching stopped.

Chief Jim Gribble, my counterpart in Battalion Three, and I would hold larger drills at least once a month. This required coordinating through dispatch because of the number of units we would pull out of service. Sometimes my crews would go to Battalion Three and train on commercial occupancy strategies, and sometimes his crews would come to Battalion Two and train on rural firefighting strategies. This type of training encouraged competition between crews, and everyone agreed it was relevant and well worth the time and effort it took to put the drills together. When I was satisfied with the performance levels of all my crews, we dropped back to a maintenance level of training, although still more than what they had been used to. Just to keep

Crews training with a deuce and a half are learning how to advance the line by rolling the hose in a circle. This two-and-a-half-inch nozzle has a solid tip that will flow between 200 to 300 gallons of water per minute, depending on the size of the tip. It requires skill and strength to operate, and is one of our best weapons against a large fire (courtesy Douglas Watson).

the crews on their toes, Gribble and I continued to conduct larger multi-company drills on a quarterly basis. And every once in a while, if a crew became too complacent, I would walk into a station at 10 o'clock in the evening and announce that we would be out of service for the next two hours so that we could train. That was a management tool that certainly didn't endear me to the troops, but it did remind them that the chief has the final word.

It seemed that I was always at the wrong end of the battalion whenever I was paged for a call. Battalion Two covers a huge geographical area, and it took me a long time to become familiar with the zone, especially the Acreage and Loxahatchee. Miles of dirt roads, missing street signs blown away from past hurricanes, and interlacing canals made for an interesting response, especially at night. It was hugely frustrating to see a house on fire and crews setting up, only to have to backtrack because the road I was on dead-ended at a canal. I would turn around until I found the right road, the one with a bridge over the canal, and finally make my way to the fire scene.

It took the better part of a year for me to become comfortable in my new assignment. Years ago, when I transitioned from driver to lieutenant, I could not have cared less if I never drove another fire engine. I had the same feeling moving from station officer to chief officer. I knew I wouldn't miss riding the right seat of an engine, especially at Station 55, where the engine was apt to run five or six calls after midnight. Although I missed the camaraderie of working with a good crew, it was time to let go once again and move on to different responsibilities.

18 — Incident Management

The page woke me from a restless sleep around 1 A.M., the synthesized voice we called Lulu dispatching us to a residential structure fire. I knew from the address that it was a house in Palm Beach Estates, a development in Station 27's zone with huge estate homes. I stepped into my boots and pulled up my bunker pants, shrugging into suspenders as I walked out to the apparatus bay. My bunker coat was hanging on the outside mirror of my command vehicle; it felt good to pull on that warm coat against the cold air of that February morning. Captain John Vanek was right behind me, donning his gear as well before getting into his vehicle. As I was rolling south, I heard the rest of the assignment checking in with dispatch on the radio.

Engine and Rescue 27 were first due, only minutes from the address, and I was pleased to hear Brush 27 responding. Even though the brush truck was not officially part of the assignment, we always took one for extra water in areas where there were no hydrants. Engine 20 and Tender 21 rounded out the assignment.

Engine 27 had been on the road about two minutes when I heard them advising dispatch of a large glow in the sky with a heavy column of smoke. That sort of information always gets your attention, so I wasn't surprised to hear Captain Dave Blount's arrival report: "Dispatch, Engine 27 arrival. Very large two-story residence, 20 percent involved. We'll be establishing a water supply. Fill the alarm."

Winning the fight against fire is all about getting ahead of the curve. I arrived just as Dave's crew had finished cutting a hole through a wood fence with a chainsaw in order to gain access to a pond adjacent to the driveway leading to the house. Many developments in the western area of the county do not have hydrants, Palm Beach Estates among them, and many home owners put in ponds to assist with fire protection. Captain Blount ordered Engine 27 to establish a draft from the pond, knowing we would need a lot of water to extinguish this fire. I looked at the amount of fire, and where it was headed, and knew it was going to take every bit of Engine 27's 1250-GPM pump capacity to slow this fire down. I also knew we were going to need a lot more help and requested a second alarm.

137

When I first started in this business, command and control was sketchy at best; freelancing on fire scenes was the norm. All fires go out eventually, even without a coordinated effort, but on those early fire scenes it seemed that people were responding to orders through some weird osmosis process rather than verbal communication. I'm still amazed that we didn't kill or hurt anyone in those early years. Radio communication was in 10 codes, something that always caused problems if other jurisdictions were working the same incident. We all used 10 codes back then, but they would differ from department to department. Since consolidation and the implementation of the National Incident Management System (NIMS), we communicate on the radio almost exclusively in plain language, which eliminates any confusion. But old habits die hard. We continue to use 10–24 to call for help in violent situations, Signal 7 for a dead person, Signal 20 for an emotionally disturbed person, and Signal 2 for someone who is intoxicated. Interestingly, many volunteer departments continue to use 10 codes, even though NIMS is a federal mandate and requires the use of plain language.[1]

The California Division of Forestry was the first agency to implement an incident management system after the state experienced devastating wild-land fires in the early 1970s.[2] Massive fires chewed through thousands of acres of brush fanned by Santa Anna winds, destroying houses and lives. Controlling those fires required thousands of firefighters from many different agencies, and coordinating so many people and resources required a new way of doing business. From that infancy, incident management changed many times, culminating in the form that all emergency responders now recognize as the National Incident Management System, an all-risk management tool that is used to manage diverse resources to mitigate natural and manmade disasters, regardless of size or complexity.[3]

The job of incident commander (IC) is to establish a strategy to mitigate the emergency with available resources. Working for Palm Beach County Fire-Rescue was a pleasure — we are blessed with almost unlimited resources and highly trained personnel. Before this fire was extinguished, I would call upon many of those resources, including command and support staff.

Arriving at a house fire in the middle of the night never gets old, even after three decades in the business. Pulling up to a mansion with one whole wing on fire is an adrenaline rush like no other, especially when it's your responsibility to put the fire out. I took the first step in that process by walking around the structure, assessing the extent of the fire, where it was going, and the number and type of resources we would need to extinguish it. This walk-around, what we call a 360, gave me a chance to look at the problem as a whole, slow down my thinking, rein in the adrenaline that is a natural part of the business, and begin the process of formulating a strategy that would cut off and ultimately extinguish the fire.

Fire officers are presented with the same set of problems on every fire. Assessing what has to be addressed immediately is the tricky part of getting things headed in the right direction, and we do this by prioritizing life safety concerns, incident stabilization, and property conservation, in that order. I knew from speaking to a caretaker when we first arrived that no one was in the house, information that alleviated the need for search and rescue. With life safety no longer an issue, fire suppression, safety, ventilation, a Rapid Intervention Team (RIT), medical, salvage, and necessary command staff were the remaining positions that needed to be filled on this fire.

Firefighting requires teamwork to accomplish most tasks, so we assign engine, rescue, or truck companies, each staffed with a minimum of three people, to get the work done. I knew that on a fire of this size we would have to deploy at least two large-diameter handlines to cut the fire off from the rest of the structure. We would also need several pre-connects inside to extinguish fire that would be found in void spaces in the walls and ceiling. Large-diameter lines are typically two-and-a-half inches in size and it takes, at minimum, one beefy engine company or two normal engine companies to operate. Pre-connects are one-and-three-quarter-inch lines, and one company of three people can deploy and operate that size line. Simple math told me I would need four engine companies just for fire suppression. Safety would require one, maybe two chief officers, due to the size of the building. I would also need one crew dedicated as a Rapid Intervention Team, one crew for ventilation and one, maybe two, for salvage. There was a lot of original artwork in the house, along with a Jesse James V-Rod motorcycle parked in the living room. If we weren't able to stop the fire, I wanted as many of the owner's possessions removed from the house as possible. I would also need at least two companies in reserve for crew rotation and another for medical support. Now we were up to 10 companies. The initial assignment was two engines, a rescue, a tender, an EMS supervisor and a chief. Blount had filled the alarm which gave us another engine and another rescue. I called for a second when I arrived, which doubled those resources, but was still not enough. As I completed my walk around the structure, I was on my portable radio, calling for a third alarm with a special call for a truck company. Now, the first alarm and all subsequent alarms receive three engines, a quint, a rescue, an EMS supervisor, and a district chief, something we were fighting for in 2004.[4]

I estimated the area of the structure to be 12,000 square feet. It was a U-shaped building with a central courtyard containing a swimming pool bigger than most average-size family homes. The top of the U on the bravo side, or the left side of the house, was completely involved in fire and it was rapidly moving toward the bottom of the U, or the front of the house. I could still see the outline of four garage doors on the bravo side. (We would learn later from fire investigators that the fire started in the garage area from improperly discarded rags soaked in teak oil.) I knew if we didn't work quickly, the fire would soon claim the middle living area of the house.

I grabbed Captain Vanek and assigned him personnel accountability: the job of keeping track of everyone's whereabouts on the incident at all times. On large incidents especially, it's critical that the incident commander be free to think at a strategic level. Being free of the minutiae involved in personnel accountability shifts a large amount of responsibility, and a constant time commitment, from the IC to a command aide.

Calling a third alarm early in an incident can be a double-edged sword. It's great to have the resources you need, but it doesn't give the incident commander a lot of time to think about how to manage resources before they are lined up with officers jamming the radio frequency while requesting orders. I made it very clear to dispatch that units coming in were to stage a minute out from the scene and wait for orders from me before they came all the way in. I wanted an orderly progression of assignments to give Captain Vanek the ability to integrate crews into the command structure. Tracking personnel and their assignments is a critical function, especially from a safety standpoint. John is very detail oriented, and when you have close to 40 people on scene, that's what it takes to run an accountability board. He would be my command aide throughout the incident.

The biggest mistake that incident commanders make is not decentralizing command as the incident grows. As more companies arrived, I started dividing the incident into divisions and group assignments, delegating responsibility and ensuring that the span of control (the concept of three to seven people answering to one individual, with five being the optimum number) was manageable. Having a clearly defined chain of command and manageable span of control is essential to effective command. Dividing the scene into geographical areas called divisions, and assigning a supervisor to oversee each area of operation, keeps span of control at an acceptable level (see Appendix H).

Every firefighter carries three small plastic tags on the underside of their helmet with their name stenciled on it, which we refer to as personnel accountability tags, or PATs. This is a passport system that most fire departments now use to track personnel; some are more high-tech than others, but all serve the same purpose. Implementing a personnel accountability system can be expensive, especially if a department uses barcode technology. Handing out plastic tags costs very little and they aren't subject to technical glitches. That's not to say they are fireman-proof; guys would lose them, but they were easily replaced.

As crews arrived at the incident, they checked in through command for an assignment, handing a PAT to whomever they were working for, a concept called unity of command. I assigned Chief Ron Beesley to Division Bravo, the left side of the U where the fire was most active. That area of the fire was now his responsibility. Engine 20 was already operating a deuce and a half on the left side, but I knew it would take two large-diameter lines to hold the fire in check and told Beesley that as soon as Engine 25's crew arrived, they were his for the second line.

All officers carry command boards, and Chief Beesley took Engine 20's PATs off Vanek's board and placed them on his board. Captain Vanek then placed Chief Beesley's PAT on his board with a notation that he was responsible for Division Bravo, along with a further notation of which engine companies were working for Chief Beesley. If Beesley needed more help managing his area of the fire, all he had to do was call me on the radio and request additional resources.

Communication on the fire ground would be chaotic if there weren't a protocol. The best form of communication is face to face because there is little chance that an order will be misunderstood, and I always tried to do that with officers prior to assigning them a task. Effective radio communication requires the receiver to repeat, or echo back, the order, alleviating any misunderstanding. Even though Engine 25 had been given an order over the radio, and I was sure they understood the order, I still had them report to the command post. I always found it useful to look crew members in the eye to make sure they were ready to go into the game and to take just a moment to do a visual safety inspection before sending them to an assignment. A minute or so later, Engine 25's crew was standing in front of me, fully geared with tools in their hands. I advised Lieutenant John Lobsinger that he would be working for Beesley on the bravo side of the structure and they would have to deploy a two-and-a-half from Engine 27. I also notified Beesley that Engine 25's crew would be joining him as soon as they could stretch a line.

Establishing clear lines of communication is critical for a smooth flow of information. I was in direct radio communication with the division supervisors, safety officers, rehab, ventilation group, salvage groups and dispatch. Any other communication would be face to face between crews and division supervisors. The only exception to this would be a crew member calling a Mayday if a person was lost or trapped, a radio message that none of us ever wants to hear.

It was 30 minutes into this incident and my strategy of cutting off the fire before it could reach the bottom of the U was beginning to come together. I had an engine at draft supplying two large-diameter lines operating in Division Bravo, each flowing 200 gallons a minute from a one-inch tip. I was getting ready to establish Division Alpha and place crews inside the house at the bottom of the U to open up walls and ceilings to stop fire from penetrating into that space. I assigned Chief Nigel Baker to Division Alpha and gave him a truck company to start opening up and two engine companies manning pre-connects to suppress fire as it was exposed. The interior of the great room on the alpha, or front side of the house, was 30 feet to the ceiling, so we placed three 24-foot ground ladders inside the living room against the wall facing the bravo side. Now Vanek had two PATs on his board and four companies working. Chief Baker had the PATs of the crews working for him on his own command board.

The next company in was assigned RIT. A Rapid Intervention Team is responsible for rescuing firefighters in trouble. Prior to establishing RITs, the fire service was killing too many people, mostly from entrapment. Palm Beach County Fire-Rescue runs regular drills exercising the concept of rapid intervention, so I felt confident in the ability of my RIT to effect a rescue if needed. RIT is typically assigned to the incident commander. Now Vanek had three PATs on his board.

Station 33's crew taking a well-deserved break from Rapid Intervention Training. These are the guys you want as RIT on a fire. Station 33 is the tenth busiest engine company in the country, and they train every day. They have a number of gangs in their response zone, so they always flash their sign—33—to gang members. Shown left to right: Joe Casella, Ric Jorge, Captain Sean Pamplona (courtesy Douglas Watson).

We also assign people to groups to accomplish certain tasks on emergency scenes. The most common group assignments are search and rescue, ventilation, and salvage, and they usually report to the IC unless the scene is big enough to warrant an operations chief. A group is a company that may have to operate anywhere on the fire ground to accomplish their task, which means working in or passing through areas that already have supervisors, such as Divisions Alpha and Bravo. It's the responsibility of the IC to let other supervisors know that a group has been assigned to accomplish a specific function and who they are working for, so there is no confusion about chain of command. There are three positions that report directly to the incident commander: safety, liaison, and public information. I had no need to fill the liaison or the PIO position, but safety is always staffed. I tapped Chief James Schaffner for that position. Now Vanek had four PATs on his board.

An hour into the incident everything was going smoothly, meaning we were holding the fire in check, but it was reluctant to go out. A rehabilitation area was now up, managed by an EMS supervisor and staffed with a rescue crew. I was requesting updates from my division officers, asking if they were making headway and reminding them there were fresh crews available if their people needed rehab. Firefighting is physically demanding work, and rehab is a critical component in keeping crews hydrated and healthy enough to continue working for extended periods of time. With rehab established, Vanek now had five PATs on his board.

Soon, division supervisors were sending exhausted crews to rehab, and I began sending them fresh firefighters. As a crew left the hot zone for rehab, they were given their PATs, as their passports as they walked to the rehab area. When they arrived at rehab, the PATs were handed off to the officer running the rehab. Rehab gives crews a chance to gear down, rehydrate, and have a medic take basic vitals. Most firefighters are ready for a break after being on air for 30 to 40 minutes, the length of time it takes to burn through one bottle.[5] When a person's vital signs are back within normal limits, they are released from rehab and command is notified that a crew is once again available for an assignment.

After an hour and a half of aggressive firefighting, we were finally starting to make headway. I now had six engine companies, three rescue companies, one truck company, one tender, two EMS supervisors, four chief officers (including myself), and a mechanic from the shop on hand, a total of 38 people. Palm Beach County Fire-Rescue spends long hours training crews in incident command. It's a testament to that training there was no confusion about assignment among those 38 people operating on a fire scene at 2:30 in the morning.

There are always teaching opportunities, so when a firefighter who was studying for an upcoming lieutenant's exam handed me a bottle of water, I asked her what we could have done differently. I knew this was her first major fire and wanted to take the time to assess her level of understanding about incident management and answer any questions she might have. She had a good understanding of incident management, but she told me she would have been overwhelmed if she were the incident commander. I assured her that her ability to manage complex incidents would come with time and reminded her that resource management is a function of prioritizing problems and then plugging in appropriate resources.

Releasing crews from a fire is a delicate balancing act. When so many resources are committed to one incident, there is always pressure to release units as soon as possible. There is an unwritten rule that first-in units are the first to be released, but many times that is difficult, especially when the first engine on scene is still at draft supplying water. On this occasion crews assigned to salvage and ventilation were the first to be released, and as we shifted into the overhaul stage and handed responsibility off to the fire investigators, more crews were released.

With the last section of hose packed, ladders placed back on engines, and hand tools and portable lighting secured, I was ready for coffee and a shower. The sun was starting to light the eastern sky as I did one more walk through the structure, satisfying myself that we had made a good stop and the scene was safe enough to leave to the investigators. My last responsibility would be writing a fire report, a dry, anticlimactic process after managing a fire scene for the last four hours.

19—Continuing Education

Training of every sort is a given in this profession, and due to the constantly evolving technical training, the demand to keep pace is relentless. Now that most firefighters are cross-trained as medics, and almost everyone at Palm Beach County Fire-Rescue is a firefighter paramedic, it is a constant time-management issue to ensure enough continuing education credits each year in the many disciplines that are required for those in the fire rescue profession.

I always enjoyed the technical aspects of the job and took advantage of any training that was available. This included vehicle extrication training; LP gas fire training; hazardous materials training; high-angle rope rescue training; Firefighter I, II, and III; Company Officer I, II, and III; water rescue training; and gasoline tank-truck fire training, to name but a few classes of a technical nature. I also became a State of Florida Municipal Fire Inspector and a State of Florida Fire Instructor. Inspector and instructor were mandatory for promotional examinations. Many of the classes I attended on my own time, while others were part of the normal training cycle that was part of the workday. Technical training was ongoing throughout my career.

The most difficult technical class I took, both physically and mentally, was Smoke Diver. The Florida Smoke Diver School, though closed now due to changes in training standards, was one of several in the country and considered the toughest in regard to the selection process and the training. There was an attrition rate of 70 percent.[1] This one-week class offered at the State Fire College in Ocala trained us in the use of self-contained breathing apparatus and quickly defined each person's physical and psychological limits. I still remember the lead instructor, Dick Kobe, who proudly wore a chrome helmet with the perfectly appropriate emblem of the devil on the front piece. We had a visceral hate for that man by week's end.

Ray Abel and I were selected to attend smoke diver training in the spring of 1980. I learned years later, after examining documents that were released from fire department archives, that the fire department allowed me to attend this training as an incentive for reinforcing positive behavior. Larry Manley was the training officer, and he wrote on the request I submitted, "Kit has shown a phenomenal improvement in his attitude over the past two months; I sincerely hope this indicates a turnaround in his attitude and not just a temporary change."[2] I'm sure this was in response to my days as union spokesman. Ray never gave the administration any trouble and his request was rubber-stamped. This management style was common during my early years as a firefighter and driver engineer. At that time, we had spent four bruising years in contract negotiations and there was still an "us against them" mentality.

Ray and I knew how physically demanding the class would be and had done a lot of weight training and running in preparation. We were both ready for the physical demands, but there was nothing we could have done to prepare ourselves for the mental demands of the class. There were 32 men who entered the training; only 13 finished. Each day, at some point, every man was crying, either from pain or exhaustion or fear.

The first challenge was a physical agility course that appeared deceptively simple but demanded absolute concentration. One of the exercises required us to carry an old brass two-and-a-half-inch nozzle. It probably weighed 30 pounds, which was not a big deal, but we had to carry it while walking across a 16-foot 4 × 4 timber. The 4 × 4 was lying on the ground and we were told, just before we stepped on to the timber, that if we stepped off for any reason we would be washed out of the class. Let the games begin!

Although most of the class involved hands-on activities, there was some classroom work. The morning of the second day, one of the instructors noticed a trainee exercising without gloves—we were required to work out in fire gear, including gloves. Everyone wore gloves from then on, even in the classroom. It didn't take us long to figure out they were going to screw with us every chance they had.

By Wednesday we had lost 11 men, most through a voluntary decision to quit. There were some evolutions that had to be completed properly the first time or you would be told to pack your bags, but on most of the evolutions the instructors would give us a second chance. Sometimes a particular evolution was too tough physically for a trainee to complete, but usually it involved psychological stamina.

Thursday we lost eight more men during an evolution that involved the burn building and the tower. We were told that one bottle of air would not be enough to complete both evolutions. We were also told that we would only get one bottle of air. I remember looking at the gauge on my bottle in disbelief—it showed only 1750 pounds per square inch. A full bottle should read 2250 PSI. My protests fell on deaf ears.

The maze in the tower was tough, but it was all mental. The instructors would change it each day, but there were only so many changes that could be made. I entered the maze and discovered that the smoke level wasn't that bad, especially in areas where there was water flowing. There was a stand-pipe system in the tower and at several points we had to crawl under an open two-and-a-half-inch port. The water would knock us flat on our bellies but it also helped displace a lot of smoke, so I turned off my regulator, disconnected my breathing hose, and shoved it inside my bunker coat. It was mighty stale air, but at least I wasn't breathing a lot of smoke.

Del-Trail Fire Department used Survive-Air breathing apparatus, state of the art in the late 1970s and early 1980s. Breathing apparatus during that era had a low-pressure hose from the regulator to the face mask, which allowed us to disconnect from the regulator and still keep our mask in place. Now all breathing apparatus have high-pressure hoses, and it's not possible to disconnect from the regulator. Smoke diver training changed as well. It wasn't uncommon for trainees to be injured, sometimes badly. There were even several deaths, which helped force changes in training procedures.

By the time of this exercise we had figured out that the point of smoke diver training was to force us to think calmly in a very high-stress environment, rely on our equipment, and improvise. Each of us learned, over and over again, what our physical and psychological limits were. I went through most of the maze without being on air, knowing that my bottle of air would have to carry me through the burn building evolution.

We weren't given a chance to gear down, take a break, or even drink water before going into the burn building. This was a two-story concrete structure with a burn room on the bottom floor. A typical fire in the burn room would involve class A combustible material in the form of pallets with a good measure of hay thrown in to increase the production of smoke inside the building. Heat and fire gases would then be funneled throughout the building by way of a chimney and an open stairwell. When I stepped off the ladder through a partially open window on the second floor, it was so hot that I could feel the heat beginning to burn my hands and knees as I crawled across the floor looking for the hose line.

This evolution required us to make five circuits through the building. We entered by climbing a ladder placed at a second-floor window. From there we had to find a two-and-a-half-inch charged hose line and follow that line as it snaked around the second floor, then to the stairs, and finally to the ground floor, where it led to an outside door. Fairly straightforward, except you also had to locate a brass ring each time and hand it to an instructor as you exited the building. The ring wasn't hard to find, since it was placed somewhere along the hose line, but that meant you couldn't take any short-cuts. I didn't want to take any shortcuts after finding out how hot the floor was. I tried to keep both hands and both knees on the hose to keep from being burned.

I knew that my air supply wouldn't last all five circuits through the building, so I did what I had been taught and improvised. There were scuppers along the walls on the second floor, so whenever the hose line was close to a scupper I would stop, disconnect my breathing hose from the regulator and stick it through the scupper, allowing me to breathe air from the outside and conserve what little air I had left in my bottle. The instructors would yell each time they observed someone breathing through a scupper, but smoke diver training was all about thinking on your feet; we would do anything to make it through the class. This only carried me so far, and I ran out of air on my fifth circuit. There was no way I was going to quit or be dragged out by an instructor, so I shoved my breathing hose inside my bunker coat and crawled out for the last time, hypoxic but triumphant.

Ray was among the eight men who washed out that day. With such a high attrition rate, it was sometimes a measure of luck as to whether a trainee made it through the class. I never thought any less of those who didn't make it through the course. Everyone learned something valuable about themselves and their abilities under extreme stress. In our business it's the little things that make the difference between success and failure, and sometimes between living and dying. What Ray and I learned gave us tremendous confidence whenever we were deep inside a smoke-filled building. Smoke diver training served us well throughout our careers.

Unfortunately, the smoke diver program was discontinued in 1996. There were new safety standards that prevented instructors from putting students through some of the more hazardous evolutions, and the smoke diver instructors were reluctant to reduce the difficulty of the training. Rather than compromise the difficult training standards that were a hallmark of the program, albeit a dangerous one, they decided to stop the program. I understand they had to comply with the new guidelines in regard to safety, but it's a shame such life-saving training can no longer be offered to today's firefighters. Cortez Lawrence went through the program in the mid–1970s and took the training concepts back to Georgia and started the Georgia Smoke Diver School. He is considered the godfather of that program and carries the designation of Smoke Diver #1, a very high honor indeed.

Another class that was difficult from a purely academic standpoint was Chemistry of Hazardous Materials. This was an off-campus National Fire Academy class that all of us assigned to Special Operations were required to take. It was a distillation of college-level organic chemistry, and I dreamed about carbon atoms for months after taking the class.

The two instructors for our class of 20 were exceptionally gifted and dedicated. This training lasted for two weeks, with class starting at eight in the morning and ending at six in the evening. At the end of each day they would announce, "Gentleman, class is over for the day. If anyone needs additional help, we'll stay as long as it takes." Even if only one person needed additional help, both instructors would stay. I would go home each evening and complete five hours of homework in preparation for the next day.

At the end of the course the instructors presented us with a one-hour video that highlighted the key points of the class. After studying our notes and watching the video, we all passed a very rigorous final examination. This was a testament to the skill of those two instructors, not at all unusual for National Fire Academy instructors. We showed our appreciation by taking them out for dinner, followed by a late-night round of gentlemen's establishments in Fort Lauderdale.

Formal education at different area community colleges was also available. I finally enrolled at Palm Beach Community College and earned an associate's degree in fire science in 1989, even though I had vowed after graduating from high school to never darken the doorway of another classroom. It took me six years to complete a two-year program, probably a holdover dislike of education from high school. Even though an associate's degree was not immediately required for promotion, I knew it would be in the future. Now chief officers must have an associate's degree, as well as many types of certification. I'm sure a bachelor's degree and Executive Fire Officer certification will be necessary in the near future.

In 1991 I enrolled in a human resource management program at Palm Beach Atlantic University. This was a wonderfully designed, extremely demanding program for working adults. I was able to use many of the general education credit hours earned in the fire science program, and graduated magna cum laude in December 1993 with a bachelor's of science degree.

We attended class on Monday evenings from five to nine and were expected to prepare at least 25 hours a week for those Monday evening classes. Palm Beach Atlantic University is a Christian-oriented school, so a class in religion was inevitable. I knew I was in trouble when the professor for Comparative Religion handed us a 20-page syllabus for a five-week class. It was a tough class, but it was also one of the best classes I attended.

The teaching format was similar in each class: animated class discussion of the reading, lecture from the professor, and a final at the end of the five-week class. The finals were also similarly structured. We were required to write a paper, typically 15–20 pages, and answer three questions: What did we learn from the reading and class discussion? How would we apply the learning in our professional lives? How would we apply the learning in our personal lives? I loved the introspective aspect the writing demanded and thought it a very good way to teach and learn.

Unusual for an undergraduate program, part of the graduation criteria was a thesis paper. I wrote my paper on the need to train future company officers in leadership and management skills prior to their promotion.[3] I gave a copy of the paper to the deputy chief of operations, Steve Jerauld, who is now chief of the department. I was hoping that it might spur some sort of training program for new lieutenants.

It took five years for the department to embrace the idea, but in 1998 Chief Jerauld called to gauge my interest in designing coursework for an Officer Candidate School. I jumped at the chance, even though I knew how much work would be involved. Transitioning from firefighter to company officer is daunting and can have a far-reaching effect on the department if the new officer doesn't get up to speed quickly. Too many times, I have seen new lieutenants floundering. This wouldn't be such a big deal in any other profession, but when we go to work, people's lives are at risk.

The first question I asked Steve concerned the budget and how much support and autonomy I could expect from the department. He told me to design a curriculum for a two-week class, and that I had carte blanche within reason. I started by sending out a questionnaire to all members of the department, polling them about training that would be beneficial for a new lieutenant. I had my own ideas, but knew this project would have to be inclusive if it was going to be successful. Chief officers have their own ideas about what makes a good company officer, just as experienced company officers have their own ideas. The same can also be said when polling driver engineers and firefighters.

While waiting on the poll results, I put together a team to help me, including firefighters, drivers, lieutenants, captains, and chief officers. When the results of the poll came back we locked ourselves in a classroom and wrote down every suggestion, categorizing them into broad topic areas. We also brainstormed our own ideas. From those topical areas, we began to narrow our focus until we had developed a curriculum that we thought was most beneficial and would take us through a two-week training cycle. It was a winnowing process that required a great deal of discussion and complete consensus before we discarded or adopted a topic. The final curriculum has changed over the years to keep pace with an ever-changing environment, but the original two-week class consisted of classes in ethics, leadership, station and personnel management, basic fire operations, professional development, labor relations, and understanding small group dynamics.

The first Officer Candidate School trained 24 prospective candidates for promotion to lieutenant. The first morning consisted of a parade of department heads, starting with the Fire-Rescue administrator, Chief Brice. Included among the department heads was the president of the union, sending a message that labor relations would always be an important aspect of being a lieutenant.

One of the unique ways that we coached each candidate was to give them a scenario at the end of the day. It might be a personnel issue or a fire scenario, but they were real-life problems we knew the candidates would eventually face. We gave them 10 minutes at the end of the day to write their answers. The next morning the instructors would discuss how we, as experienced fire officers, would handle the situation. Then we would hand the scenarios back to the students, along with written comments on what they submitted. We told the students there was no wrong answer, although some answers were intriguing. The class looked forward to this interplay because it was real world, yet allowed them to succeed or fail in a nonthreatening environment.

We established a tradition of awarding a plaque for Outstanding Officer Candidate. Billy Schmidt was the first recipient of this award, and he has measured up in every way. Billy will be teaching at the Fire Department Instructor's Conference in Indianapolis, Indiana, April 2012, the largest conference of its kind and an honor of the highest order. Only those at the top of their profession are invited to teach at this conference, and I am proud to say that two other members of Palm Beach County Fire-Rescue — Doug Watson and Ric Jorge — will also be teaching at the conference. Graduation of OCS Class 1 was a proud day for me, the other instructors, and the candidates who were about to receive their lieutenant's badges. Text of my closing remarks to the graduates of Officer Candidate School, Class 1, is available in Appendix I.

The department is to be commended for its commitment to this process. It's expensive to take people off shift, place them on days for two weeks with a 5 percent pay differential, and back-fill the shift positions with overtime personnel. However, the alternative was to continue promoting people without the necessary training to ensure their success. I am proud to say that the Officer Candidate School continues to be a part of the training new officers must undergo.

I knew we were doing something right when, several years later, I overheard a conversation in the Command Post, the on-campus pub at the National Fire Academy. A group of firefighters from different areas of the country were talking about Palm Beach County Fire-Rescue's Officer Candidate School training, praising how forward-thinking the department was, and lamenting the fact that they weren't doing it.

I was fortunate to have the opportunity to attend the National Fire Academy (NFA) in Emmitsburg, Maryland, for a number of technical classes, including Command and Control of Multi-Company Operations. One of the benefits of attending classes at the NFA is meeting people from all over the world. The knowledge that is passed on through conversations with other students and the attendant stories that come from two weeks on campus with

Aerial photograph showing the campus of the National Emergency Training Center, including the National Fire Academy and the Emergency Management Institute, located in Emmitsburg, Maryland (courtesy United States Fire Administration).

hundreds of firefighters was a learning opportunity in itself. There were some very impressive people in my Command and Control class, including the deputy director for the National Fire Service for Nigeria, John Obinyan. He spoke English with a British accent, as well as Swahili, Russian, and Japanese. He took a graduate degree in civil engineering in Russia and another in public administration in Japan. There is a story about him that is better left unsaid, except to say that he was "heavily pressed" during a tour of the Gettysburg battlefield. However, I can speak about buying a nun a drink.

I was relaxing in the Command Post Pub one Sunday afternoon, watching a football game on the big-screen TV, when two older women walked in and sat down at a table across from me. I was intrigued to see two women who obviously weren't students, so I went over to their table and introduced myself. It turned out they had gone to school on this campus when it was Saint Joseph College for Women, prior to the campus becoming the National Fire Academy. They were friends and had been classmates together at Saint Joseph and were now enjoying a quiet afternoon reminiscing about their college years.

We had a wonderful conversation about the history of the campus, and when I offered to show them around, the nun demurred and said she would rather drink a beer first. After I bought a round we took a walking tour, during which I learned more about the history of the campus than I had learned in all the years I had been attending classes at the NFA. Before the campus became Saint Joseph College for Women, it had been a convent, and during the Civil War the nuns hid Confederate soldiers in the catacombs that still exist under the campus grounds. The building that houses the classrooms for the Emergency Management Institute and the cafeteria was used as a surgical ward during the Battle of Gettysburg. Learning opportunities are everywhere; you simply have to look for them.

My next educational goal was to enroll in the Executive Fire Officer program at the National Fire Academy, but first I had to persuade the fire department to let me attend the program. It's a four-year commitment, though only one two-week class each year. Several chief officers had already been through EFO, and they and the administration felt the training was beneficial, so I was given permission to begin the application process.

A lengthy application soon arrived in the mail. I think there were 15 or 20 questions that needed answering, each requiring at least a page of writing. I was told that only one out of ten candidates would be accepted into the program, so I chose my answers carefully. Months later I received a letter of congratulations, informing me of my acceptance.

The next four years were the most demanding and rewarding educational opportunity I have ever experienced. Although there was only one class a year, it was an extremely time-consuming program. After each two-week class, students would use the information gained from the classroom learning to write a paper that addressed a particular problem in their own department. We were required to do original research in addition to a literature review and had six months to complete the paper, typically 50–60 pages in length. If the paper was accepted, you were invited back for the next year; there was no guarantee of completing the program. All my papers were accepted and are available at the National Fire Academy library for others to read. I was awarded the title of Executive Fire Officer in January 2001, by authority of the 93rd Congress of the United States.

The Executive Fire Officer curriculum is a master's-level program that prepares men and women to become leaders in the fire service. Each class had two instructors, both PhDs in their field. Our instructors for the first class, Executive Development, were Dan and Ann Fabyan, the same people who did early training in company officer development when Palm Beach County Fire-Rescue consolidated. They were very good then and even better the second time around.

The EFO program is a validation process for the fire service. Through this program, a body of knowledge about every aspect of the profession is being compiled, one that will continue to improve the way we do business. Executive Fire Officers are invited back to the National Fire Academy for an annual symposium. It's a time to renew friendships, gain additional knowledge in our ever-changing environment, and continue the networking process that is so important in any profession.

The last significant training I participated in was wildland firefighting. Throughout my career my work was predominately structural firefighting, but in Battalion Two, with its large areas of undeveloped land, brush fires were a constant threat. So it made sense for the fire department to spend the money and time to send me to advanced training in wildland firefighting. The fire school in Florida for wildland firefighters is located mid-state near the west coast in the small town of Brooksville. I was always reminded of summer camp whenever I attended — the décor and setting was fitting for such a rural area, right down to the campfire circle where we would sit around each evening socializing. I was fortunate to attend with Neil Enos and James Schaffner, both district chiefs and good friends. We slept in bunkhouses and ate breakfast and lunch in the cafeteria. We usually tried to find a local restaurant to eat supper; the food at the training camp was prepared and served by local prisoners— gourmet dining it was not.

I had taken the basic S130–190 class for wildland firefighting years earlier and received advanced training (S290–390) in Brooksville. I also attended and successfully passed Division Group Supervisor, an extremely demanding class that provided training at a strategic level. A division group supervisor manages multiple and diverse resources, up to 100 personnel.

Soon after completing this training, I enrolled in the State of Florida Burn Boss class.[4] This class was held at the 60,000-acre J.W. Corbett Wildlife Area, a beautiful wilderness area in the northwest corner of Battalion Two. It was a 40-hour class with 40–50 hours of independent study required before classroom and field work began. This training taught us the art and science of writing prescriptions for controlled burns. There are many reasons for controlled burning, ranging from habitat improvement for various species of animals to fuel reduction to prevent catastrophic wildland fires. One of the reasons fires were so destructive in Yellowstone National Park in the late 1980s was due to a policy of immediate fire suppression. Fire managers have since learned that it is better for the ecosystem to let periodic fires burn, thereby reducing the amount of fuel available. Fuel and catastrophic fires go hand in hand.[5] After the catastrophic fires in Florida in 1999, fire managers used prescribed fire as a tool for fuel reduction to prevent future fires of that magnitude. Now, Florida leads the nation in acres burned through the use of prescribed fire.[6]

A prescription is a detailed written report stating the reason for the burn and the parameters under which the burn can be conducted: relative humidity, temperature, wind speed and direction, dispersion index, smoke management, a safety plan, an incident command structure, and resource tasking to manage the burn, to name just a few of the criteria. This training, more than any other, gave me the confidence to make decisions on large, complex fires. After successful completion of the class, I was designated a Certified Burn Boss for the State of Florida.

In 1972 Richard Rothermal, an aeronautical engineer working for the United States Department of Agriculture Fire Sciences Lab in Missoula, Montana, developed a way for wildland firefighters to more accurately predict the movement of fire across the landscape. His model of calculating fire spread is the basis for the last training I received: Basic Fire Behavior Calculations (S-490). Rothermal developed a system of modeling that employs data about wind speed and direction, aspect and slope, relative humidity, fuel moisture, fuel type, and fuel loading to determine the rate of spread and flame length of a wildland fire. Frank Albini, the team's research engineer, developed the 13 fuel models that wildland firefighters are familiar with today. Using these fuel models, he developed nomograms for both high and low wind speed that

Neil Enos, left, and the author, taking a break during a wildland training session (courtesy Palm Beach County Fire-Rescue photo archive).

use data on weather, slope, and fuel moisture to predict rate of spread and flame length, critical information for fire managers. The information gained from the nomogram allows the plans chief to make recommendations to an incident commander about the number of personnel and types of resources needed to suppress fires. The next class in the fire calculation series, S-590, uses computer modeling that is still based on that early research. It was interesting for me to learn the history of the process and understand the basic calculus behind the science.[7]

The one regret I had in my fire service career was coming so late to wildland fire training. I found all of the wildland fire training classes interesting, physically demanding, and intellectually challenging. Wildland fires are akin to a three-dimensional problem, dynamic and subject to change at the whim of weather, fuel, and topography. I love structural firefighting, but the intellectual challenge associated with wildland firefighting is even more appealing.

20—Tigers and Fire

Brush fire season in South Florida runs from December through June, until spring rains bring relief from the hot, dry weather that contributes to extreme fire behavior. Fighting these fires sometimes forces us into a dangerous dance with fire; however, I never thought I would waltz with tigers!

I was the district chief on A shift in Battalion Two, an area with wildland-urban interface problems throughout. Simply said, wildland-urban interface are areas where houses or small subdivisions have been built in the middle of the woods. In South Florida these woods are typically pine forests with heavy fuel loads of palmetto scrub understory. Add narrow dirt roads, bridges that were never designed to support the weight of fire apparatus, limited water supplies, and residents who have no clue that their little patch of paradise might become their final resting place, and the potential for devastating fires increases exponentially.

Palm Beach County Fire-Rescue's normal response during dry brush season is a task force of two brush trucks, two engines, a tender, and a district chief. We routinely page the Florida Division of Forestry, and they respond with a tractor-plow and a forestry area supervisor. When the Keech-Byron drought index is in the 700s (a measurement of moisture in the topsoil that tells us the top seven inches are as dry as day-old popcorn), it's a prescription for extreme fire behavior. An index level of 700 goes hand in hand with low humidity, high winds, high temperatures, and an elevated dispersion index. A dispersion index over 60 means there will be atmospheric lifting, causing long-range spotting problems with a brush fire.

About three in the afternoon, we had those kinds of weather conditions when we received a call for a brush fire on C Road in Loxahatchee. Station 21's crew was first on scene with a brush truck, tender, and engine. Engine 28 and Brush 28 were also responding. The arrival report indicated a fast-moving fire moving from light fuels into heavier palmetto and pine overstory. I was ten miles east of the fire location when I received the page and could already see a large column of smoke moving toward the northeast. I had been monitoring the weather since early morning and knew this fire would be difficult to control. The humidity at 6 A.M. was 80 percent and the temperature around 60 degrees. For every 20-degree rise in temperature, the humidity levels drop by half. Mid-afternoon temperatures were approaching 90 degrees, so I knew without taking a weather reading that 40 percent humidity coupled with 20-knot winds would create extremely aggressive fire conditions. I radioed dispatch to page the Division of Forestry and almost at the same time heard Division of Forestry's Everglades 31 responding.

"Everglades 31" is the call sign for their D5 bulldozer, commonly termed a tractor-plow. It has a blade on the front and a plow on the back, and I always found it comforting to hear the clanking of its steel treads and the crashing of trees as it pushed through the woods, plowing a three-foot-wide furrow down to mineral soil. The plow operators work up close and personal with fire, and many times they work alone, plowing lines as close to the fire as possible. Any change in wind direction places them at risk. These guys are unsung heroes and never get the credit they deserve; we were fortunate to have them stationed in our backyard.[1]

As with most professions, there is a nomenclature that we use to describe different aspects of a wildland fire. Fires always have a point of origin, the spot where lightning, a carelessly discarded cigarette or an arsonist starts a

A Florida Division of Forestry tractor-plow operator up close and personal. This picture shows a plow pushing burning material into the black. The plow on the back of the dozer is in the raised position. The operator is probably getting ready to drop the plow and establish a line around the fire (courtesy Arthur Werkle).

fire, which then spreads in the direction of the prevailing winds. As it becomes bigger, we identify different areas of the fire as the head, right or left flank, and the heel. The head is the leading edge of the fire, the area that burns most aggressively. It's not unusual to see 10-foot flame lengths in medium fuel if the fire is being pushed by a strong wind. The heel is the back of the fire, and looking from the heel toward the head, the left flank and right flank are to the left and right, respectively. Fire can hopscotch around depending on fuel load, continuity of fuel, topography, and wind conditions, to name just a few factors, and many times there will be areas of green within the burn area that we refer to as islands. Fires can also create fingers, which are particularly dangerous areas on large fires. A finger may look like the main body of fire, with its own head and flanks, but in reality it is just an area off a flank that has grown in size with a lot of unburned fuel between it and the main fire. If a crew is not aware of their position and they are working the right flank of a finger that has formed on the left flank of the main body of fire, they are in extreme danger of being overrun if the finger and main body of fire join.

We preach safety to our crews. On large fires, when the suppression period might last days or even weeks, a formal safety briefing is conducted. During this briefing the safety officer will talk about safety zones and escape routes and one of the watchwords is LCES, which stands for *Lookouts–Communication–Escape Routes–Safety Zones*. Lookouts are experienced firefighters who are posted where they can see the fire, monitor its movement, and warn crews if the fire changes direction. Communication ensures that everyone on the fire is plugged into a chain of command, understands their assignments, and is in verbal or radio communication both up and down the chain of command. Escape routes are clearly defined avenues that lead to safety zones. If the wind shifts and starts pushing the fire in a direction that endangers crews, they need to be able to quickly move through an escape route to areas that won't support fire, usually burned-out areas. We refer to these areas as "the black," and they are designated as safety zones. Sometimes safety zones are constructed miles ahead of fires, using bulldozers to clear large areas of all flammable material.

An instructor for a division group supervisor class that I attended described a 20-acre safety zone that was dozed down to mineral soil at the 7000-foot level on the slope of a mountain in western Montana. The fire was burning up the slope toward that safety zone, incinerating 100-foot-tall ponderosa pines. A 200-foot flame front was producing hellish radiant heat, igniting trees a half-mile in front of the main flame front and forcing crews into their fire shelters, something that should not be necessary within a safety zone. A fire shelter is an aluminized personal shelter carried by each person on a wildland fire. It is deployed only as a last resort — some people refer to them as "shake and bakes." Nobody thought they would be needed in a safety zone. Some of the students thought the instructor's story was nothing more than a tall tale. They could not believe that radiant heat could be that severe, but I recalled reading *Wildfire Loose: The Week Maine Burned* by Joyce Butler. She describes a forest fire in Maine with radiant heat igniting barns and houses at that same distance.[2]

Fire can be extinguished in a lot of different ways. Depriving a fire of fuel using counter-fire techniques is one method that we use when it's too dangerous to get close enough with a brush truck to extinguish it with water. We use drip torches, canisters that dispense liquid fire, to burn out vegetation ahead of a fire. We might also burn off an anchor point such as a road or canal bank, burning out an area big enough so that when the main body of fire reaches the burned area the fire will go out because there is not enough fuel left to support combustion. Most of the time we rely on tractor-plow operators to plow lines along the flanks of the fire. A brush truck would work in tandem with the plow, catching any fire that slopped over the line. Regardless of the fire suppression strategy, it is always a choreographed event, with the incident commander calling the shots.

Upon arrival, I established C Road command and began a recon of the area. I was looking for structures that would be in the way of the fire, as well as natural barriers ahead of the fire that could be used to establish a defensive perimeter. Initiating a direct or frontal attack on a fire is an effective fire suppression technique but extremely dangerous on aggressive, fast-moving fires. It's much safer for crews to control a wildland fire through an indirect attack, either burning out ahead of the fire off barriers such as roads and canals or working the flanks. I got on the radio and started issuing orders: "Brush 21, support Everglades 31. Brush 28, catch any spot fires. Tender 21, secure a water supply. Engine 28 and Engine 21, you have structure protection. There's a house on Mandarin. See if it's defensible." Many times houses are not defensible because of heavy fuel loading too close to the house or because access roads are too narrow for fire apparatus to safely negotiate. We routinely conduct structure triage, deciding which house will be saved and which house will burn.

The area that was burning was bounded on the left flank by C Road and a canal running parallel to C Road, and on the right flank by a large orange grove. The fire was burning in a northeasterly direction, chewing through heavy palmetto scrub and pine forest. Palmetto is ubiquitous in South Florida. Even though it has bright green leaves, it burns like gasoline. It certainly wasn't disappointing us; spot fires were becoming a real problem, with the fire growing in size by the minute.

A spot fire, or spotting, occurs when the thermal column created by the fire starts to lift burning fuel and carries it downwind — sometimes hundreds of yards, sometimes much further than that — and starts another fire. Soon I noticed a column of smoke coming up from Steve Sipek's property; we all knew who he was. Steve used to be a Spanish Tarzan actor, and he was still playing that role, keeping all manner of exotic wildlife. He owned a five-acre lot with a 12-foot-high block wall surrounding the perimeter. An ornate, barred steel gate fronted C Road with a sign proclaiming that trespassers would be eaten. His property was flagged in our dispatch database so crews could get a heads-up if a 911 call came in from that address.

I drove up to the gate and rang the bell. After several minutes of standing around with no response, I was ready to get back in my truck and move on when Steve came roaring up in his truck and opened the gate. As he was telling me about the fire on his property, a large tiger came out of the woods and sat down beside his pick-up. I got back in my truck and spoke to Steve through a partially rolled-down window, informing him that we were not

This photograph is a good example of fire in a pine forest with palmetto and gallberry understory. The torching is typical in palmetto scrub fuel. The crew on the brush truck is not attempting to extinguish this fire—only to contain it (courtesy Arthur Werkle).

coming on his property with a tiger roaming around. He insisted that the tiger was more afraid of us than we were of it. I insisted that unless his tiger was secured, his place was going to burn to the ground. I gave him my cell number and told him to call me when his pet was locked up. As he reluctantly agreed to secure the tiger, another tiger came out of the woods and sat down on the other side of his truck. At this point Steve closed the gate, and I resumed my command duties.

Steve called me about 30 minutes later, informing me that all the animals were secured and the fire was getting bigger. I radioed Brush 28 to meet me at Sipek's location so that I could give them a heads-up about the property. Brush 28's crew was not as familiar with the property, or Steve's pets, as 21's crew, so I lead them in toward the fire. As we passed the house, we could see two lions and two tigers peering at us through the four barred windows facing the drive. Brush 28 quickly extinguished the fire, and we were all happy to put the 12-foot wall and the gate between Sipek's pets and us. We worked late into the evening extinguishing the fire outside the compound.

There is a sad sequel to this story. A year after the fire, Bobo, one of the tigers that belonged to Steve, escaped. Bobo was raised from birth by Mr. Sipek and was truly considered part of the family. No one is sure how he slipped through the gate, though Sipek feels someone was responsible for leaving the gate open. The first knowledge anyone had that he was loose was when he was seen happily swimming in the canal adjacent to C Road. A sheriff's officer was called to investigate. When he arrived, the tiger climbed from the canal and leaped onto the roof of the police cruiser and from there into the woods. A three-day hunt ensued before Bobo was finally located not far from the back wall of Steve's property. It was hoped that he could be tranquillized, but the tiger kept rushing the officers from the Florida Fish and Wildlife Commission. Unfortunately, Bobo was shot and killed by a fish and game officer.[3]

21—Jimmy

My folks were down from Maine for a visit, and I was giving my father the nickel tour of Battalion Two. He's a retired minister and served as a volunteer firefighter for many years in Kennebunkport. My cell phone rang and it was Jimmy Gribble, a good friend and the district chief in the neighboring battalion. I answered the phone and Jimmy, knowing full well that my dad was riding with me, asked,

"Is your dad there?"

I replied, "Yes."

And he said, "Jesus Christ, I better not swear!"

Of course, the cell phone was hands-free with a speaker, so Dad heard every word, and of course Jimmy knew he was a minister.

Jimmy is one of the funniest and most irreverent people I know. He can imitate anyone, including me, and when he's on a roll he could open as a comedian for a Las Vegas nightclub act. And like most firemen, he loves to play practical jokes. I stopped at his station one afternoon and noticed a pile of old mattresses lying on the bay floor. He wasn't in the station, so I took the opportunity to stack the mattresses on top of his bunk until they were an inch from the ceiling. Before leaving, I placed a stepladder next to his bunk — I figured that was a thoughtful touch. He got me back several shifts later by taking my pillow and placing it in the freezer, after soaking it in water (though he hinted that it might have been wet from something other than water).

Jimmy wasn't above using his considerable talents of deception on the public. He was working a house fire one afternoon when he noticed a young child watching. When there was a lull in the action, Jim knelt down in front of the boy and asked him if he knew how the fire started. The guys had figured out it was arson, and Jimmy had a sense the kid might know more than he was willing to say. He held up his portable radio in front of the kid and told him it was a portable lie detector machine, and if he didn't tell the truth, a red light would go on. Of course, Jim could key the mike and make the red light go on whenever he wanted. So Jim started grilling this kid about who set the fire, lighting up that red light whenever he knew the boy was lying. He finally got the truth when the child ratted out his older brother.

Jim Gribble is also one of the most selfless people I know, always giving back to the fire department and the community. He is famous for his barbecues, which we now term "Gribble Cues." I've lost track of the number of barbecues he has conducted, but it numbers in the hundreds, including the one for my retirement. But his most significant legacy is the Honor Guard. He broached the idea of an Honor Guard in 1985 and it was officially formed in 1986. The Honor Guard travels across the country, honoring those firefighters who have lost their lives in the line of duty. They have won numerous awards in state and international competitions and are among the busiest in the state.[1] The Pipe and Drum Corps was formed soon after, and they travel both alone and with the Honor Guard to parades and memorials honoring fallen firefighters.

Jim is one of the finest fire officers I've ever met. His dad was a lieutenant for Metro-Dade Fire Department, and when Jimmy was a child he used to

Palm Beach County Fire-Rescue Honor Guard was established in 1986 through the efforts of Chief Jim Gribble. The Honor Guard is one of the department's most visible representatives, honoring firefighters killed in the line of duty. Shown from left to right: Jim Gribble, Lenny Collins, Sean Pamplona, Ronald Macleod, Rick Gass, Steen Eriksson, Karl Hornburg, Eustacio Sanchez, Edward Moss, James Hernandez, Matt Willhite, Robert Grossbeck (courtesy Douglas Watson).

The Palm Beach County Fire-Rescue Pipes and Drums Corp travels the country representing the department. In 2012 they traveled to Ireland to march in Dublin's St. Patrick's Day parade. Left to right: Todd Fote, Doug Watson, Jim Clark, John Fischer, Lee Forshner, Ed Peek, J.T. Kavnaugh (Delray Beach Fire Department), Jon Ferguson, Khristy Osment (courtesy Douglas Watson).

follow the engines to fires on his bicycle; he's been a student of the profession for a long time, observing fire behavior since he was six years old. I like to think that a firefighter's job is to bring order out of chaos. When the world is burning down, Chief Gribble is the one you want directing operations. Many a night I have backed him up or he has backed me up on jobs that at first seemed lost.

That evening, just after I dropped off my father, I was paged to a residential structure fire that appeared to be lost. Engine 25 was first on scene and their arrival report wasn't encouraging: "Dispatch, Engine 25 arrival, single-story wood frame house. Heavy fire showing sides A and B, fire venting on side B. We have a hydrant in front of the house. We'll be defensive. Fill the alarm."

It was Friday evening, 1900 hours, and traffic was very heavy. Sometimes it's almost not worth running with lights and siren. It's not that people don't want to get out of your way; there is simply no place for them to go. As I was running through a mental checklist, prioritizing things I needed to do on arrival, my cell phone started ringing. It was Jimmy, telling me he was easing my way. We routinely backed each other up, so I wasn't at all surprised by the call.

I pulled up about 10 minutes into the incident, forever in a firefighting operation. Engine 25 was on the hydrant with a large sleeve hook-up. Radiant heat from the fire had ignited the lawn around the hydrant, forcing the driver to stamp out a smoldering grass fire as he was making the connection. Lieutenant Jeff Galloway had ordered the deck gun into operation, emptying

Engine 25's 750-gallon water tank through a one-and-three-eighths-inch tip in less than two minutes. It didn't even slow the fire down. Next, they deployed a two-and-a-half-inch handline, doing an exterior attack from side B. There was fire blowing 30 feet out of the gable end. There was certainly no need to open the roof to vent this fire, but the deuce and a half was only pushing the fire back into the attic. I ordered the line shut down as I walked around the house, evaluating what we had. It was a large house with attached garage, and the house was 50 percent involved. After a briefing from Lieutenant Galloway, I radioed dispatch that I was assuming command.

Chief Gribble arrived as I was setting up my command board, sorting out who was on scene and their current disposition, and developing a strategy that would keep my people safe and at the same time maybe save half the structure. Gribble did his own size-up and then conferred with me. I told him we were going to stay defensive, and I was assigning him Division Bravo.

We already had a partial roof collapse and I didn't think it was worth the risk to put people inside, which was the only sure way to put this fire out. He insisted that we could put a line inside the house, cut the fire off, and put it out. The incident commander has absolute authority on any emergency incident, but Jimmy and I respected each other enough to spend about a half a minute arguing the merits of defensive versus offensive. He kept insisting that he could put the fire out with a fresh crew. His plan was to enter the house through the front door and pull ceiling ahead of the fire to get water into the attic space, where the majority of fire was.

I reluctantly agreed, with the caveat that he had five minutes inside to start making a difference, or I was pulling him out. I told him he was on the clock as soon as he made entry and assigned him Engine 20's crew. Billy Gauthier was the lieutenant on Engine 20, with 18 years on the job and experienced firefighters under his command. They stretched a line to the front door and made entry.

As the incident commander, it's my job to know where everyone is and what their job is, and to develop and implement a strategy that works. It's the crew's job to break that strategy down into tactics that will mitigate the incident. The hardest part is letting the strategy develop. Most firefighters I know are aggressive, take-charge people. I'm no exception, so it was always hard for me to stand at the command post and let people do their jobs.

It was a long five minutes before I started to see white smoke slowly replacing the angry black smoke that had been pushing out of side B. After another 10 minutes Jimmy radioed me, advising, "Fire under control." Shortly after that radio transmission, he and Engine 20's crew exited the building. I sent in a fresh crew to finish mopping up and overhauling.

Jimmy saluted me with a middle finger on the way to his car and yelled, "Told you I could put it out!"

I shook my head and smiled as I radioed dispatch to advise, "Fire out."

Meanwhile, Lieutenant Gauthier was gearing down and sort of muttering to himself and shaking his head. He walked over to me, still shaking his head, and said, "He's not right."

I asked him what he meant.

Shaking his head, he said again, "He's not right."

I finally pulled the story out of him. When they entered the building, black smoke was down to the floor, dark enough that you couldn't see a gloved hand placed on your facemask, typical for interior firefighting operations. We all knew the majority of the fire was in the attic space, but when they tried to pull ceilings they realized they were in a room with vaulted ceilings and their pike poles weren't long enough to reach all the way up. Chief Gribble instructed his crew to wait, and he disappeared. He returned with a 10-foot stepladder that gave them the reach to pull ceilings, allowing them to direct their hose stream into the attic space and extinguish the fire.

Jimmy told me later that he knew there might be a stepladder in the garage. In the pitch-black darkness, he was able to find the interior door to the garage, find the ladder, make his way back to his crew, set the ladder up, and communicate the game plan to his crew. This all happened in a zero-visibility environment and under the five-minute time limit I had given him.

I called him later to praise him and to chew his ass at the same time. What he did was not something we condone. Becoming lost and separated in a burning building is bad enough; purposely separating from your crew is just what the lieutenant was saying: "He's not right." Jim laughed it off like it was no big deal and simply changed the subject by asking me to tell him a *Bert and I* story, something he's apt to do at the most inappropriate times.[2]

I grew up listening to recordings of *Bert and I*, Maine humor at its finest, and can recite them even now. When Jim and I were rookie firefighters, I would tell *Bert and I* stories late at night while lying in a bunkroom full of firemen; there would be absolute silence, except for Gribble chuckling softly. As they say in Maine, "Wicked good stories."

Jimmy is one of the few people I know who truly appreciates the humor. The problem lay in when he would ask me to tell him a story. I would be driving down a dark road at three in the morning, trying to find the address of some building that's on fire while listening to an arrival report on the radio. As I'd try to clear my sleep-fogged mind to formulate the beginnings of a coherent strategy, my cell phone would ring. It would be Jimmy, saying, "Kit, tell me a *Bert and I* story."

"Jesus, Jimmy, I'm running a call right now!"

"Yeah, I know, but you're not there yet."

22—Rookies

Over the years I gained the reputation of being a hard ass. I suppose a lot of it had to do with the nature of the profession. There aren't many second chances afforded to those who need our services, and I held my people to a very high standard. If a firefighter wasn't willing to train hard and work hard, I didn't want them on my shift. I would get this point across by handing someone transfer papers if they weren't giving me 100 percent. As far as I was concerned, they didn't have any right to be working as a firefighter, at least not under my command. More than a few decided that firefighting wasn't the right career choice. And I've lost count of the number of rookie firefighters who have come through my office for the first time, every one of them with that deer-in-the-headlights look.

I was working as a step-up district chief in Battalion Five in the mid–1990s when Lynn Fail joined our ranks. She had spent the last 12 weeks in our recruit academy and was reporting for duty as a paramedic on Rescue 55. Dave Horowitz was the station officer, and he had the shift lined up on the tarmac in front of the truck bay for morning inspection. Of course, Lynn didn't know we had done away with a morning line-up years ago, and we certainly didn't require our people to dress in class A uniform.

Every firefighter is subject to a certain amount of hazing, some more than others, depending on attitude; Lynn was about to be initiated. Captain Horowitz informed me that his crew was ready for my inspection, and I had a hard time suppressing a smile as I walked out and saw her standing proud in her brand-new uniform. Out of her line of vision, one of her fellow firefighters stood on the roof of the truck bay with a five-gallon bucket of water in his hand. I made a show of examining each person, paying particular attention to Fail, then stood back and nodded to the captain that his troops looked squared away and ready for the shift. That was the cue for the firefighter on the roof to dump the bucket of water. It scored a direct hit on Lynn's head, a really rude stunt on a bitterly cold December morning.

Lynn only stands about five foot four and can't weigh more than 120 pounds, but she makes up for her diminutive size with wiry strength and unflagging determination. Gary Sprague was standing next to her, doubled over with laughter, and was evidently the object of her desire. She jumped on Gary, wrapping her arms and legs around him, rubbing all over him until he was nearly as wet as she was. I knew she wouldn't have any trouble fitting in.

Lynn was a nurse when she joined the fire department, so the medical end of the business wasn't hard for her. In fact, she was able to forgo paramedic school by challenging and passing the state paramedic exam — not an easy feat, even for an experienced nurse. She went on to earn certification as a flight nurse and was assigned to our Sikorsky S76-C+ air rescue helicopter, Trauma Hawk.

It's gratifying to track the careers of folks who worked for me straight out of recruit school. Seven or eight years into her career, Lynn was the flight nurse on a call that demanded every bit of her medical and leadership skills. Station 21's crew on C shift received a call involving someone trapped under a front-end loader. Neil Enos was the district chief on duty, and he was at Station 21 having lunch with his crew when they received a page for an accident involving heavy equipment. They rolled out and five minutes later were on scene to find a man absolutely flailed by his machine. He had been traveling down a logging road on a front-end loader with a load of timber on pallet forks. Evidently he was traveling too fast, because the loader started to bounce. Before he could slow down, the forks dug into the ground, and the loader pitch poled.

Pulling up on a scene like this is what makes our job so interesting. The guy was pinned under a machine that weighed thousands of pounds, still alive and badly injured. The first priority was to figure out how to get the loader off him. There was plenty of readymade cribbing from the timber he had been carrying on the pallet forks, so the crew used it to crib up and support hydraulic spreaders until they could gain enough space to pull him out and begin assessing his injuries. When the loader flipped, he was thrown from the cab, with the machine trying to catch up with him as it turned over. He caught the top of his head on the roof of the cab on the way out, avulsing his scalp to the point that his scalp was draped over his face, so what they were looking at was the inside of his scalp where his face should have been and his shiny white skull where the scalp was supposed to be. Besides the obvious head injury, he had bilateral open femur fractures, a flail chest, and almost certainly internal injuries. He definitely wasn't having a good day.

The medics started to assess the extent of his injuries, and it was immediately obvious that he met the criteria for a trauma alert. One long bone fracture would have met the criteria; he had two long bone fractures, as well as other life-threatening injuries. He was also more than 20 minutes from the trauma center by ground transport, so Neil got on the radio to request Trauma Hawk.

The speed with which we treat trauma has always amazed me—from initial assessment to rapid on-scene treatment, and finally transport to the trauma center. The medics were starting IVs, flapping his scalp back to where it should be and applying multi-trauma dressings to hold it in place, giving him oxygen, and starting to splint his femurs as Trauma Hawk was coming in on final approach, getting ready to land in a field adjacent to the road where they were working. Most of the crews that I know are always happy to see the flight medics step off the helicopter. Their level of training, the medical protocols they work under, and the equipment at their disposal are all geared toward treating trauma patients—they are specialists in that area of medicine.

Lynn Fail was the first to get off Trauma Hawk, and she was all business as she walked over to confer with the medics working on the patient. Our protocols dictate no more than 10 minutes on scene for trauma-related injuries. Evidently Lynn wasn't satisfied with the speed the patient was being stabilized, and it didn't take her long to start barking orders. It looks good to have broken bones nicely splinted, but that takes time. It took Lynn about a minute to apply a long bone splint between the patient's legs and wrap them both together with cling, another minute to administer drugs to knock the patient out for rapid sequence intubation, and then a quick walk to the helicopter to load the patient. Seven minutes later Trauma Hawk was landing at the hospital.

For me, working as a firefighter was like a slideshow where you never knew what would be displayed on the screen next. A typical day might involve training with crews, working a structure fire, counseling a firefighter, or speaking with a rookie firefighter on his or her first day on shift. Shawn McCoy was fresh out of recruit school, and on his first day on shift assigned to Battalion Two, I welcomed him into my office and tried to put him at ease by starting with some small talk. I asked him about his family, his educational background, and what his interests were. Then I spoke to him about possible career paths within Palm Beach County Fire-Rescue and time frames for certain benchmarks he would have to meet during his first year on the job.

Rookie firefighters are under a probationary period for their first year and there are a number of educational challenges they must meet in order to make probation. I impressed on Shawn the importance of time-management skills so that he would be successful in passing his probation. I spoke about how important teamwork is in this business. I knew his station officer had already talked to him about expectations, but I reiterated once again his officer's expectations and mine, so that he understood how many eyes would be watching him during his probationary period. I also told him that he could bypass the chain of command and speak with me directly if he felt he wasn't getting the support he needed from his station officer and fellow firefighters. I told him that we had already invested a lot of time and money in him, and we wanted him to succeed. At the conclusion of the interview I said, "McCoy, there are a lot of perks to being a firefighter; being a rookie isn't one of them. Get back to work."

I keep track of people like Shawn, even though I'm now retired. He is working in Belle Glade and comes to work each day with the same work ethic he displayed to me the first day he was on the job. I know that when he becomes a station officer, he will instill in rookie firefighters the same pride and passion toward the job he brings to work each shift.

Some rookies stand out more than others, and I had more than my share of wayward souls when I was assigned to Station 55 as a captain. One in particular gave me fits. He was always in trouble, but he was a hard worker, a competent firefighter paramedic, and one of the funniest people I've ever met, so it was hard to stay mad at him. One day we were returning from a traffic accident and this guy was driving the rescue truck. I was in the right seat of Engine 55, and we were stopped, side by side, at a traffic light. I looked over at the rescue in time to see the front end of the vehicle jumping up and down. How he managed to do that to a vehicle that weighs 20,000 pounds while at a complete stop is something I still haven't figured out. He smiled and waved at me, then gunned the truck when the light turned green. They caught another call returning to the station, so he had an hour's reprieve before I jumped his ass. By that time I was chuckling at what he had done.

One day this guy came in with some illicit firecrackers. I'm not even sure they were firecrackers; it said they were for agricultural use on the package. I was sitting on the john after too many cups of coffee and he set one off outside the bathroom window. The whole bathroom lit up like a welder's arc. It's not hyperbole to say he scared the crap out of me. It took me longer to get over that stunt.

But what he pulled on the Fourth of July was over the top. We were getting ready to enjoy a holiday breakfast at Station 55 when we heard and felt an explosion. He had filled a latex glove full of oxygen and acetylene, stuffed the glove inside a large paper bag, and set fire to the bag. Thankfully, it had been placed out by the street a hundred feet in front of the station. The concussion almost blew all three 18-foot-high bay doors off their tracks. It wasn't long before cops arrived, lights and siren blaring. There wasn't any physical evidence, so we said to the cops, "Did you hear that?!" Sometimes people push the envelope too far; there were consequences for that stunt.

A fire officer gets one chance to influence a new firefighter. Leading by example and insisting on a work ethic that ensures a rookie will keep his or her nose in a textbook, or out on the bay floor figuring out for the hundredth time how to do a proper check of an air-pack, or learning how to buddy breathe in a zero-visibility environment, and making sure they understand it is their responsibility to get it right, every time, is the best way to start a firefighter on a successful career. Instilling in them, from the very first day, the understanding that learning never stops is the only way I know to determine who has earned the right to ride the engine. If a person is not willing to do the work necessary to become a student of the profession, they don't have the right to call themselves a professional firefighter.

23 — Unsung Heroes

I have written almost exclusively about the men and women who respond to the communities' needs, the folks in Operations who jump in their rigs, hit the lights and siren, and go to work. Before leaving this subject and talking about the other bureaus within the department, let me finish the story by discussing the other areas within Operations that also directly contribute to public and firefighter safety.[1]

Although the people in the stations are the ones the public thinks about when they dial 911, there are many people working equally hard in other areas within Operations, such as the aviation battalion, Trauma Hawk, and the training division. Training is a critical function in any fire department and has a direct bearing on the efficiency and safety of crews on emergency scenes. The training division relies on a cadre of experienced officers to deliver real-world, state-of-the-art training at the Chief Herman W. Brice Administrative Complex on Pike Road in West Palm Beach. This is a 42-acre regional training facility that is state of the art in every respect. It provides a realistic and safe learning environment for the 1,300 Operations personnel who work for Palm Beach County Fire-Rescue, as well as firefighters from other departments in the area.

The people who work in the training division are responsible for program development and delivery, assistance with the professional development of chief officers, conducting the Officer Candidate School whenever there is a promotional process for company officers, ongoing recruit training, driver operator training, aerial operator training, Special Operations training, and training of civilian staff. For each area, there is a lead instructor who has worked in the field and is an expert in that specialty.

An integral part of the training division is the video department. Palm Beach County Fire-Rescue has a television production studio that provides learning opportunities for firefighters and citizens. Medical and fire training programs are broadcast over Palm Beach County's cable channel. There is also a program designed for the public, broadcast over the same channel, which teaches fire safety and highlights all the fire department programs available to the public. However, the videographers don't spend all their time in the studio. Whenever there is an official function, such as a promotion ceremony, they are taking pictures or shooting video. They also film or take still pictures of fires and other emergency situations. Many of these pictures and films are incorporated into the video they ultimately provide as part of the training broadcast.

The aviation battalion, Station 81, is located on the grounds of Palm Beach International Airport. The crews who work at the airport are trained in aircraft rescue and fire firefighting (ARFF), and respond to aircraft accidents in crash trucks designed to pump large quantities of water and foam while on the roll. They are also responsible for structural fire protection of all the buildings on the airport grounds, as well as fuel tank farms and general aviation facilities. As with other fire rescue personnel, the crews at Station 81 provide paramedic service wherever necessary.

In November 1990, the Trauma Hawk Aero-Medical Transport Program was established, a partnership between the Health Care District and Palm Beach County Fire-Rescue. Because Palm Beach County has such a large land area, there are two trauma centers— Delray Medical Center at the south end of the county and St. Mary's Medical Center at the north end. Because they are designated trauma hospitals, there is critical care staff on duty at all times. Trauma protocol requires a ground transport time of 20 minutes or less, something that is not possible from many areas of the county, so part of the trauma system includes two Sikorsky S76-C+ helicopters capable of transporting two patients each. They are staffed with a pilot, two paramedics, and a flight nurse. The pilots work for the Health Care District, and the medical personnel work for Palm Beach County Fire-Rescue. This service is available to everyone within the county.

There is a strict protocol fire crews adhere to whenever the helicopter is called. We don't have any control over where a trauma accident occurs, so crews have to figure out the closest and safest area to set up a landing zone (LZ) for the helicopter. An engine company is assigned this duty, and they may pick a ball field or an empty parking lot, or even a roadway. The Sikorsky requires a minimum of 100 square feet to land, and the perimeter has to be absolutely secure. One person from the engine crew will stand at the center of the LZ and the other crew members take up positions to secure the perimeter. When Trauma Hawk approaches the LZ, the pilot circles to the right, allowing the pilot an unobstructed view of the landing zone. If he likes what he sees, he will announce to the engine crew that he is on final approach. At that point the man in the middle of the LZ will back off to the perimeter. Once the helicopter is on the ground, scene security is a full-time job. It doesn't matter the time of day or night; the helicopter always draws a crowd. The flight crew will exit the helicopter and assess the patient. Once the patient

Ron Lowe, left, and John Przybylek taking a well-deserved break during a training session. Training is physically demanding work, and I have tremendous respect for the guys who do it for a living. Notice the shield on JP's helmet (courtesy Craig Whitney).

is assessed by the flight nurse and the paramedic, they will approach the helicopter from the side and load the patient. This is the most dangerous part of the operation, as the rotors are turning at all times. Once the patient is loaded, the ground crew maintains security for a full two minutes after the helicopter has left the LZ. If the helicopter experiences a mechanical problem shortly after takeoff, its crew knows they have a secure LZ they can return to.

A mechanic is a firefighter's best friend, especially late at night when a truck won't crank, and Ed Erhke is one of the best. I remember one evening when Station 26's crew got banged out on a brush fire and the truck wouldn't start. I called dispatch and asked them to send a mechanic to the station, and smiled when I heard Ed come up on the radio. He was the on-call mechanic that evening and always cheerful, no matter the hour. The crew was happy to hear Ed on the radio as well. Some mechanics would have told them to swap it out with another truck without trying to fix it, but Ed knew how important that truck was to the guys at Station 26. Swapping out a truck is a long, laborious process; fixing the problem quickly, and in the middle of the night, placed the truck and crew back in service far more quickly than driving to the central repair facility 18 miles east of the station. With total land area in excess of 2,000 square miles, Palm Beach County is the largest in Florida. Station 26, directly west of the support facility on Southern Boulevard, is one of the closer stations. For stations farther north and south, driving time to the facility is measured in hours.

Support Services is the division that Ed works for, and with a fleet of 19 brush trucks, 43 rescue trucks, 43 engines, four tenders, two Special Operations trucks, four quints, four airport crash trucks, an airboat and a fire boat, as well as 25 various types of support vehicles, the mechanics will never have to worry about job security. This list of apparatus and support vehicles is not

Trauma Hawk is a Sikorsky S76-C+ helicopter configured for patient treatment and transport. Palm Beach County Fire-Rescue and the Health Care District are partners in providing trauma transport. Two helicopters and crews are available 24 hours a day. In this photograph, crews are loading a patient after extended extrication. Normally, the rotor blades are turning even while loading a patient. The pilot has shut down to save fuel because of their longer than anticipated time on scene (courtesy Arthur Werkle).

comprehensive, for there is also a reserve fleet of engines, rescues, and support vehicles for those times when the mechanics can't fix a truck at the station.

When we first consolidated, the mechanics operated out of Del-Trail's shop on Hagen Ranch Road in Delray Beach. That shop had two bays and was adequate for Del-Trail's needs, but with the expansion of the department, the shop was soon shifted to a larger and more central facility on Belvedere Road in West Palm Beach. That location was more than adequate for a number of years, but the mechanics have now shifted to an even bigger facility. As with the firefighters, the mechanics are highly trained in their profession, with certifications in all areas of automotive and heavy truck repair, plus added certification in fire pump repair.

Other areas of Support Services that keep the fire department organization running efficiently are building maintenance, warehouse services, capital projects, uniform procurement, telecommunications, and fixed assets — not very sexy, but still part of the glue that holds everything together. Operations personnel can thank these people for new fire stations, the latest in protective equipment, radios that allow unimpeded communication, and the ability to keep track of the thousands of pieces of equipment it takes to run a fire department.

The fire department's primary mission is providing fire suppression, hazardous materials mitigation, and emergency medical response, but it also is responsible for protecting lives and property through fire prevention, public education, and fire code compliance. These areas of responsibility require different skill sets from those of the firefighters, and the division that has a direct impact on public safety is the Bureau of Safety Services. This is the office of the fire marshal, and his people are responsible for reviewing building plans and carrying out periodic inspections of existing buildings to ensure compliance with local and state fire codes. Most people are unaware of the work required to ensure public safety, beyond seeing fire apparatus responding to calls. Reviewing plans and inspecting buildings is not a high-profile job like responding to fires or medical emergencies, but it is every bit as important. These folks work hard, there is never adequate staffing, and the work load is unrelenting.

Also part of the Bureau of Safety Services is community education. Community education personnel are out in the community and in the stations, providing programs for children and adults that are designed to educate people about fire and life safety. The community education folks get their message out in a variety of ways, including public service announcements, speaking engagements with civic groups, brochures in every fire station that provide information on fire safety, exhibits at the annual Palm Beach County Fair, and many classes that are free to the public, to name just a few.

A more direct method of ensuring safety in the home is providing smoke detectors and batteries, free of charge. Fire is an equal opportunity danger, and for those low-income families who place feeding their children above installing a smoke detector, this program is a life saver. Other classes include fire extinguisher use, CPR training, the proper use of the 911 system, and juvenile fire-setter programs.

I can't count the number of fires I have responded to over the years that were started by kids. Prior to the implementation of the juvenile fire-setter program, these kids found themselves in juvenile court. Most times they received a slap on the wrist and were back starting fires as soon as the judge released them to their parents. The juvenile fire-setter program is an educational tool to correct this behavior. It's a tough program that teaches kids how serious arson is and how serious the consequences can be. It is very effective; most of the kids who are caught setting fires and go through the program come out as model citizens, at least in regard to not starting fires ever again.

Another life-saving program within the Bureau of Safety Services is drowning prevention. This is a coalition of different agencies that was established in 1996 to address the escalating problem of water-related incidents. Statistics show that children, young adults, and the elderly are at the highest risk for drowning. Because South Florida has the highest unintentional drowning rate in the nation, community education and participation is critical. There are more than 30 agencies involved in the drowning coalition with a mission of supporting community education initiatives to prevent drowning and near drowning. Many firefighters are trained in a program called Whale Tails and, as part of their duties, teach drowning prevention skills to kids who live in their station's response zone.

Fire investigation is one of the most important functions of the Bureau of Safety Services. There are four investigators and a records custodian who investigate bomb calls, arson fires, and unintentional fires. They stay busy and are very good at their job. These guys have always amazed me. I know fire and arson investigation is a science, but walking into a building that is a pile of blackened rubble and being able to sift through the debris to determine the cause and origin of the fire is wizardry in my book. There is no lack of teaching moments, and the fire investigators were always willing to teach us more about their craft. Although arson investigation is something that is taught as part of basic fire curriculum, listening to these guys explain how to preserve evidence while they are pointing out burn patterns from an electrical fire or pour patterns from a flammable liquid fire is training that can't be duplicated in the classroom. That kind of impromptu training is invaluable, helping to make firefighters more aware of the dangers associated with arson fires. I especially enjoyed hearing an investigator tell me my crews made a good stop on a fire. That meant a lot coming from them. These investigators are also sworn police officers who work closely with local police and sheriff's officers. Being a sworn law enforcement officer gives them the ability to conduct criminal investigations and follow them all the way through to an arrest. Their conviction rate is one of the highest in the nation.

Some of the truly unsung heroes aren't even on the payroll for fire rescue. In 2005 the department formed the Community Assistance Team (CAT) to provide assistance to families in crisis due to a fire or medical emergency. They act as a liaison between families in crisis and the many social service agencies in the county. They are trained to provide bereavement support for families who may have lost a loved one, and they also respond with other county agencies in the event of a disaster. The CAT teams are based at strategically located fire stations and are paged to calls through our dispatch system.

Also unpaid, and equally important, is the volunteer battalion. Though Palm Beach County Fire-Rescue is an all-paid, professional fire department, there continues to be a need for volunteers. The volunteers are not initial responders, but on large incidents they may be paged to provide logistical support, especially on incidents that last for many hours or even days. The volunteers receive basic fire training, have their own equipment, and provide an invaluable service when called upon.

None of the firefighters would go to work without a dispatcher sounding the alarm. A dispatcher's job is high-tech and high stress, and they put up with a lot. Crews in the field sometimes need answers the dispatcher can't provide, not because they don't want to, but because they don't have the information. That doesn't stop some people from being a little short with a dispatcher over the radio, and I was one of them. I never won any popularity contests with the dispatchers, and I'm sure there are still dispatchers who would like to give me a piece of their mind.

The biggest conflict we had with dispatchers was when they instructed crews to switch tactical frequencies after the crews were already working. Tactical frequency 4 was used for fire ground communication, but sometimes dispatch would ask crews to use a different channel because there was too much chatter. This wasn't a problem if everyone heard the request, but it became a huge safety issue if a crew was already working and didn't hear the request. This usually happened on brush fires. Crews would already be on scene, working on Tac 4, and the dispatcher would order them to go to a different frequency without confirming that everyone had heard the request. This left crews operating without dispatch monitoring the call, a very dangerous situation if someone got into trouble.

The fire operations officer, or FOO, is the one I butted heads with the most. The FOOs are the supervisors in dispatch. As with any good supervisor, they tried to protect their people. Although I had the FOO's number on speed dial, it didn't do any good arguing with him about something that one of his dispatchers had done, but it always made me feel better. I got in more hot water over dispatch issues than anything else. I missed having a driver to keep me out of trouble.

The dispatch center is located on the corner of Military Trail and Southern Boulevard in West Palm Beach. Housed in a giant, concrete, windowless building designed to take the full force of a hurricane, this building is where all the emergency management functions take place during natural disasters or other large-scale events. A huge amphitheater down the hall from dispatch, with work stations for the county's incident management team, provides state-of-the-art communications to allow managers to run large, complex incidents by providing planning, logistical, financial, and operational support for crews in the field. Sleeping quarters, bathrooms with showers, and kitchen facilities support a large staff for the duration of any event.

Emergency management and the 911 office work for Administrative Services, which is also responsible for payroll, budget and finance, information technology, career development, strategic planning, and the wellness program. I won't belabor the obvious in regard to payroll, budget and finance, information technology, and career development, but the wellness program deserves further explanation.

The wellness program is designed to improve firefighter health and fitness through a comprehensive annual physical examination and assessment. Working as a firefighter is physically demanding and requires people to be in peak condition. Unfortunately, firefighters mirror the rest of society, with many who are out of shape and not ready for the rigors of the job. The wellness program works to improve, through individually structured programs, the health and fitness of those who are overweight or have other health issues. The program measures fitness through the use of various strength and aerobic exercises using free weights, push-ups, sit-ups, and the treadmill. I was happy to score in the top percentile throughout my career. Chief Brice, more than 20 years my senior, also scored in the top percentile. He believed in leading from the front.

There is another program within Administrative Services that is not on the organizational chart but does a lot of good in the community: the Customer Service Committee. This committee focuses on enhancing our service to the public by empowering the people who work for fire rescue to take the steps necessary to help someone in need beyond what would be a normal response to a situation. Neil Enos' crew went above and beyond when a truck plowed into two houses, doing considerable structural damage. Both homes were owned by elderly people who had no place to go. The crew responded to the 911 call and then spent the rest of the shift cleaning up the debris and boarding up the damage so the residents could remain in their homes until insurance adjusters and contractors could provide a permanent fix. Another example was my crew providing Christmas presents for a house full of foster children. Simply put, we empower our people to do the right thing without waiting for permission.

A last word about the people who work in administrative capacities has to include the secretaries who work in the different departments. As with any organization, they are the doorkeepers, and they always took the time to help me if I had a question or needed to meet with their bosses.

I'm not the first to say this, and I won't be the last: People are responsible for great organizations. Throughout, Palm Beach County Fire-Rescue is a great fire department because the people who work there are empowered. Everyone understands the importance of the mission, and everyone understands that their efforts are critical to the overall success of the department.

Adequate funding is a perennial problem and there is always the question of duplication of service in regard to many of the support functions within the fire department. I am sure there are other agencies in the county that could provide some measure of support, but providing the same high level of support would be impossible to replicate. The scope of the fire department's mission is complex and, by default, so is the fire department organization. The department is unique because it must be able to react quickly to any situation. Emergency service is just that. The fire department must have the ability to operate in any type of environment far beyond the nine-to-five routine of other agencies within the county.

24 — Reflections

I turned off the alarm before it could wake Candy and padded into the kitchen to put on a pot of coffee. It was five o'clock on a Saturday morning in early May 2007, and although I wouldn't officially retire until June, this was my last duty day.

I loved running the dogs on the golf course in the early morning, allowing me a few precious moments of solitude before the real business of the day began. The sun hadn't yet burned off the ground fog, and I could see Arctic smoke rising from the water of the canal behind our house, a view long removed from the cold Atlantic Ocean of my boyhood in Kennebunkport, Maine. I used to run on the beach with my father at this same hour, and early morning mist will always be evocative enough to make me smile each time I see the ephemeral wisps of vapor rising off a body of water.

I had been getting up at five o'clock every third day for 31 years, preparing the same way each time for a 24-hour shift away from home. In my early years I would dress in navy work pants and a blue work shirt, and pin a silver badge over my left breast denoting the rank of firefighter. Now I wore navy dress pants, patent leather dress shoes, and a white dress shirt with three bugles on each collar point and a gold badge with three bugles denoting the rank of district chief. Neatly trimmed hair and mustache and a close shave further set the example for how I wanted the people under my command to look when they reported for duty. In this regard, today wasn't any different from any other day. I had spent tours in Battalions Five, Four, Three, and Nine and was finishing my career in the battalion with the motto of "second to none." As I drove north on the Florida Turnpike, I couldn't help wondering what my last day would be like.

Shift change at a busy firehouse is the same everywhere: turn-out gear coming off trucks to be hung in lockers and more turn-out gear being placed on trucks; personal alert alarms sounding, along with the hiss of air as crews check their SCBAs; station officers giving their relief information about equipment problems and ongoing projects; rookies busy cleaning the station or checking equipment; the sound of apparatus being cranked and pulled out on the apron; the sound of chainsaws and compressors being started; the smell of diesel exhaust. It was daily life in a busy firehouse, all so familiar, and something I would never experience again.

I had spent the last two months buying and cooking steak dinners for the 65 firefighters working at the nine fire stations under my command, a small way for me to say "thank you" to the men and women I had worked with over the past seven years. For years it was the other way around: I would eat dinner at the various stations, a luxury with so many good cooks. Every Saturday I could count on a spaghetti dinner at Station 25, including chilled plates for salad. Fried venison tenderloin and chicken livers were a staple at Station 26. Each station had a specialty and it was very satisfying to end the day by eating good food with my crews. The butcher at Mario's Meat Market knew what I was doing and took extra care trimming the New York strips I would buy each week. It was a time for saying goodbye and for reflection, and also my last chance to mentor people and urge station officers to keep their people safe.

The business of a fire department doesn't vary because someone is retiring, and my day started like every other. I sat down with the off-going district chief, Neil Enos, to get a heads-up on what needed my attention. I could hear my EMS captain, John Vanek, doing the same with his counterpart. That done, Neal and John and I went to Carla's Restaurant to meet Jimmy Gribble for breakfast.

Eating breakfast with my colleagues allowed us to play fire chief for the day. We would solve all the department's problems over a cup of coffee and a plate of eggs. If only it were that simple! Jimmy and I would normally discuss what type of training we wanted to accomplish that day; since a day in our business was 24 hours, we might be pulling crews out of service at night to train. They always bitched, but we just told them they didn't have to like it, they just had to do it. I preached to my guys that if they wanted to be called professional firefighters, they had to train, every day. Today, however, would be a day to make the rounds of the stations and say goodbye to crews.

During my career I witnessed change in all aspects of the profession, but perhaps the biggest change was the pace of the training cycles. When I first started there was little formal training — it was usually left up to the station officers. Soon after I came on the job, Henry Cusell became the training officer for Del-Trail, but with no budget, it was little more than a title. Once the district fire departments consolidated, training became more focused. Now, to keep pace with new technology and the standard operating procedures that are a firefighter's Bible, training is a daily occurrence.

Regardless of the amount of training, and no matter how much time a person has been on the job, sometimes it seems like the first day. An instructor once told us that each experience is like a snapshot — it was up to us to put all those snapshots into a carousel in our heads, to be called up when we needed it. Repeated exposure to different scenarios during training is a technique called prime recognition training. This training has been adopted by the armed forces and now the fire service.[1] The more experiences you have as a firefighter, the easier it is to think back on a similar experience when faced with a difficult fire or vehicle extrication, or any of the thousands of scenarios that firefighters face over a career, and make the right decision.

A good example of this is a call that Rich Vassolotti ran when he was a new lieutenant. I was sitting at my desk plowing through a pile of training reports, half an ear tuned to the calls that were going down in the battalion, when I heard Engine and Rescue 29 roll out on a car fire. At first, I went back to my paperwork; then I heard dispatch give 29's crew an update that the car fire was actually a gasoline tank-truck on fire. That got my attention. I was out the door and heading east on Royal Palm Beach Boulevard, listening for dispatch to upgrade the assignment. After a minute with no further communication, I ordered dispatch to send a full assignment and get our Special Operations haz-mat units rolling.

Lieutenant Vassolotti reported a large column of smoke and gave an arrival report about 30 seconds later, stating that there was a gasoline tank-truck on fire, with a day care center as the primary exposure. I arrived about five minutes into the incident. The fire was out, and the day care center had been evacuated. It turned out the tanker's right rear tandem wheels were on fire, not the product. Evidently he had a hot brake that caused the fire.

Although Rich had never experienced this exact type of call, he recognized that there were two problems that had to be dealt with simultaneously: controlling the fire before the tank's integrity was compromised and evacuating the day care center. We train our folks to slow down and evaluate a situation, then take action. Life safety is always our first consideration, and Rich knew the kids in the day care center had to be moved out of harm's way; he also knew that if the fire wasn't suppressed quickly, the problem would only get worse. His training and past experiences helped him make sound decisions. This sounds like a straightforward problem, but facing that type of scenario is not simple when you have people screaming at you to do something, plus a congested parking lot that was never designed for fire apparatus, while taking the time to calmly convey a concise report over the radio and issue orders for other units responding to the scene, and at the same time trying to control the adrenaline that is our constant companion whenever we run a call. Rich had been trained well enough in the basics to make the right decisions in a stressful situation. It would be one more snapshot in his carousel of slides that he could call upon at a later date. If this type of call had occurred in the 1970s, 1980s or even the 1990s, the outcome might have been much different.

Very early in my career I would go to fires where there was little team-work and virtually no organization, referred to as freelancing. The fires would eventually go out — they all do with time — but it was by the grace of God that we didn't get people hurt or killed. Thankfully, freelancing is no longer part of our vocabulary. Now every emergency scene is a highly choreographed event with an incident commander calling the shots, but it took us a long time to get to that point, and this transformation didn't occur without a lot of false starts.

The evolution of incident management began in the early 1970s, when California experienced devastating wildfires that required thousands of per-sonnel and resources from out of state to help control the disaster. Fire man-agers with the California Division of Forestry were the first to implement incident management on those large fires, and wildland fire managers are still the experts, routinely managing hundreds (sometimes thousands) of people and diverse resources over an ever-changing landscape of fire. Fire depart-ments came late to this process, with a lot of so-called experts proclaiming that their version of incident management was the best. We would spend a year or more training in the latest version of incident management, and then someone with more pull at the federal level would think it necessary to tweak the system, confusing the hell out of us with the changes. Usually it was only the nomenclature that changed, not the process. Still, it was frustrating trying to keep pace.

September 11, 2001, changed the way we do business. The after-action reports for FDNY revealed a number of problems, including inter-operability communication difficulties and command and control issues, which precip-itated further changes in incident management. The National Incident Man-agement System (NIMS) is now the model that all emergency responders use. But even with a federal mandate for all emergency service organizations to adopt NIMS, there was still resistance and confusion — again, mostly because of changes in terminology.

I remember interminable classroom discussions about Groups and Divi-sions, the biggest area of confusion for our organization. It was straightfor-ward to me, but there were always one or two people in every class who wanted to belabor the obvious. Chief Gribble and many others spent countless hours patiently explaining how the system worked. It's not surprising to me that fire departments, especially smaller departments with inadequate training budgets, are still struggling to train their people to a level where implementing NIMS on an emergency is second nature. It took our organization several years of ongoing classroom and field training until firefighters were able to work comfortably within NIMS.

Utilizing this command system has made a huge difference in fire ground safety. Firefighters responding to an emergency are slotted into a command structure that tracks their movements from the time they arrive until they are released from the scene. Firefighters always work as part of a team, never alone, with a clearly defined assignment and a clear understanding of how they fit into the chain of command. No one works outside this framework. And there are safety officers on bigger incidents whose sole responsibility is crew safety. Although firefighting remains one of the most dangerous professions, the advance in incident management have revolutionized the way we do business in dangerous environments, a far cry from the freelancing I observed when I first started in this business.

Another noticeable area of change is the need for better educated firefighters. Despite my early reluctance to embrace higher education, finding a renewed passion for learning has been one of my biggest personal transformations. The business of providing full-service emergency service has become increasingly complicated, forcing firefighters back to the classroom to take paramedic classes, building construction classes, arson investigation classes, and so on, with local colleges and universities filling this niche. Firefighters can earn associate's, bachelor's, and master's degrees in fire science, and the National Fire Academy offers even more specialized training through advanced technical classes and the Executive Fire Officer program, the capstone training for future leaders in the fire service. These programs are in addition to the never-ending technical training that is part of every firefighter's life from the time they enter the service until they leave.

I was fortunate to be able to take advantage of many different educational and professional development opportunities. One of the most satisfying opportunities was being asked to work as a subject-matter expert during promotional examinations at different fire departments across the country. I worked as an assessor for Fort Lauderdale Fire Department; Delray Beach Fire Department; Boynton Beach Fire Department; the City of Columbus, Ohio Fire Department; and the District of Columbia Fire Department.

Working as an assessor for the D.C. Fire Department was particularly challenging. In the mid–1980s D.C. had more than 500 candidates eligible for promotion to the rank of sergeant and captain. Thirty-four fire officers from the United States and Canada worked from eight in the morning until five in the evening over a period of two weeks attempting to select the best candidates for promotion. We worked in teams of three in the front half of our hotel suites, and one of our mandates required each team of assessors to reach consensus on each candidate interviewed. Some teams were able to breeze through this process, but not my team. We had a fire officer who wanted to talk the process to death, meaning we were always the last to finish. After the third day of missing a complimentary cocktail hour, I went down to the front desk and corrected the problem. I told the staff that I was that fire officer and needed a 4 A.M. wake-up call so I could work out. I was adamant about not changing my mind, no matter how much I might protest those early morning calls. After several wake-up calls from the front desk, he was the first to reach consensus. I guess he had to get to bed early.

People ask me what I miss about the job, and I suppose part of it is the little moments that tie a good day together: a quiet chat with a lieutenant over a morning cup of coffee; seeing the satisfaction in the faces of crews following a training session they all complained about going in but after which they were all high-fiving each other; walking into a station and sitting in the dayroom before supper, talking with the crew about sports or hunting or the last job we worked; cooking breakfast for a crew on Sunday morning; meeting Jimmy for breakfast; seeing the satisfaction in rookies' eyes after their first fire; and rolling out of a station at three in the morning and seeing a glow in the sky, knowing we once again were being called upon to bring order out of chaos.

But it's the people I miss the most. Working as a firefighter is a unique calling, and the friendships formed are for life. I have a special bond with the old guard from my early days at Del-Trail. Despite the adversity we faced while trying to improve our salaries, working conditions, and benefits, we had fun. Working with those guys is something I will always cherish; the bond we formed in those early years will never be broken.

Beyond the friendships, there were many different personalities that challenged my skills as a supervisor, making me a better person and a better leader in the process. And so many that made me proud along the way. Ed O'Berry is one person who comes to mind. He was a rookie firefighter under my command and, like some others, always on the verge of trouble. He gave me fits, and I was amazed at how good he was at pushing my buttons. However, Ed was supremely competent in all aspects of the job, and it was hard to stay mad at him for long. He is now a captain and actions he took on the morning of April 8, 2009, garnered him numerous awards, not for firefighting heroics but for saving the life of a police officer.[2]

Ed was starting his shift at Station 31 when he and other firefighters observed a police officer attempting to arrest a suspect. The officer had fired a taser at the suspect, but as he prepared to handcuff the man, the suspect pulled out the barbs of the taser and overpowered the officer, fracturing an arm and his skull before grabbing the officer's gun. The officer, badly injured and barely conscious, had the presence of mind to eject the clip, but the gun still had one round in the chamber. Firefighters had been watching this scene unfold, and when they realized the officer was in trouble, several went to his aid, scaling a six-foot fence with three strands of razor wire at the top. While firefighters were yelling at the suspect, attempting to distract him, Ed retrieved his personal weapon, a Glock 40, from his vehicle and went over the fence. Ed has a license to carry a gun, and he and another police officer followed the suspect down an alley. When the suspect pointed the stolen gun at Ed and the officer, they both fired on the suspect, mortally wounding him. Ed and other firefighters then administered first aid to the suspect, who died a short while later.

Ed received Palm Beach County Fire-Rescue's Medal of Honor for bravery, as well as an award from the Office of the President of the United States. On September 22, 2010, during a ceremony in Washington, D.C., Vice President Joseph Biden presented Captain Edwin O'Berry with the Medal of Valor for Public Safety Officers. Ed also received the Combat Cross from Sheriff Ric Bradshaw of the Palm Beach Sheriff's Office, an award never before presented to a civilian. Captain O'Berry received the Combat Cross at the annual awards ceremony for law enforcement officers at the Kravis Center in West Palm Beach, Florida. Firefighters have a very good relationship with law enforcement, and Ed told me that award meant more to him than all the others. It really hit home when the entire audience of police officers gave him a standing ovation.[3]

The vice president of the United States, Joseph Biden, presenting Captain Edwin O'Berry with the Medal of Valor for Public Safety Officers. Also shown is Attorney General Eric Holder (official White House photograph).

People ask me if I have ever saved anyone's life. The answer is yes, but only once from a fire. I was working as a captain on Engine 55 when we caught a house fire in the middle of the afternoon. Heavy brown smoke was pushing out the front door as we made our way in with a hose line. I noticed there were several separate areas in the house that were on fire, indicative of arson, which was confirmed when we found a gasoline can in the kitchen. We also found a man in a back bedroom, unconscious from smoke inhalation. After removing him from the structure and providing him with medical intervention, he revived enough to let us know he had been trying to kill himself. Unbelievable — my one rescue of a fire victim, and it was someone who didn't want to be rescued.

Firefighters don't have any say about the calls they run. Some catch fires their whole career; some run a mix of calls. It's like sitting down at a poker game — you play the hand dealt. I worked in busy stations for most of my career and caught a lot of fires, but it was the car wrecks throughout my career that served as defining moments. There were many, and I have written about some of them, but a wreck on Palmetto Park Road stands as one of the grimmest. I was working out of Station 55 in an acting capacity as district chief on the evening an accident took five young lives. A Honda Civic carrying nine teenagers hit a Honda Prelude carrying three women. It was a high-speed, head-on collision, and the impact threw seven kids in the Civic out of the back windshield and the side windows. Two of the kids died immediately, three more died during transport or at the hospital emergency room, and one girl will be paralyzed for the rest of her life. I remember listening to the arrival report from Lieutenant Grady: "We have bodies everywhere. Send more help."

We have a saying in this business: "What starts bad stays bad." From a management standpoint, this started bad, with never enough resources early on. Trauma Hawk was called for transport and instructed to land to the west of the incident. Rather than landing to the west, they came in on final approach from west to east, flying low and slow 50 feet over the scene and blowing every bit of loose medical gear into a canal. They landed below the crest of a hill on Palmetto Park Road just as an engine from Boca Raton Fire was coming up the other side. The engine crested the hill and almost ran into the main rotor of the helicopter. I had requested mutual aid from Boca to assist with extrication of the women trapped in the Prelude, knowing their engine was closer than any of our engines. It seemed like an eternity before all the living were freed from the wreckage and transported to area hospitals.[4]

Back then kids carried pagers instead of cell phones, and the eeriest part of the scene was hearing pagers go off as word filtered out about the accident. Teenagers who were supposed to be home at a certain hour weren't ever coming home. There are many aspects of the job that I will miss; dealing with that kind of human tragedy is not one of them.

We all remember where we were on September 11, 2001. If you are a firefighter reading this, that date is especially poignant. My wife and I had flown to the Pacific Northwest on September 10 for a vacation, only to wake the next morning to news about the attacks on the Twin Towers, the Pentagon, and Flight 93 (which crashed in Pennsylvania). I remember going for a walk, trying to come to terms with the magnitude of this event and with my anger against those who had attacked our country. After wandering aimlessly, feeling bitter and inadequate, I began to focus on unfulfilled responsibilities and called my boss, Battalion Chief Art Miller. My first question was whether I should immediately return to Florida and report for duty. Art asked me to call him each day, but advised me to continue my vacation. At that point I didn't want to remain on vacation and felt useless knowing that firefighters, police officers, and civilians had died in this attack. If Art had asked me to return, I would have had to rent a car; it would be 10 days before commercial aircraft were allowed to fly. We did fly home on Delta Airlines the first day flights resumed, and I remember being appalled how lax security was at the airport — we weren't even asked for identification.

When I finally returned to duty, our department had already sent people to New York to assist in recovery efforts. Joe Bartlett is a long-time colleague and good friend, and a member Task Force 2, Miami-Dade's Urban Search and Rescue (USAR) Team.[5] Joe was at the clinic receiving his annual physical when his pager went off. USAR team members have six hours to assemble at their disembarkation point when they receive a page. Joe drove home, kissed his wife goodbye, grabbed his ready bag, and drove south to Homestead Air Force Base, where the team waited three days for authorization from FEMA to deploy to New York City. When they finally received the deployment order, the team loaded thousands of pounds of equipment on trucks and boarded buses to convoy to Fort Dix, New Jersey, where they staged once again. Joe was part of an advance team that immediately went to Ground Zero to coordinate with liaison personnel. Several days later the team went to work, splitting duty between an Alpha and Bravo team, each working 12-hour shifts.

Joe worked as a rigging specialist for heavy equipment, forcing him to move all over the rubble. He recounted how everyone on the pile would stop working whenever remains were discovered. If the body was identifiable as a member of FDNY, the deceased member's colleagues would retrieve the remains while everyone on the site would stand silently with helmets removed until the body was recovered. Joe helped find a member of Rescue 2 and was proud to be asked to remain and help with the recovery, an honor not usually granted to anyone but members of the fallen hero's company.[6]

Joe Bartlett, middle, with two other Task Force 2 members contemplating the enormity of the job at Ground Zero. Task Force 2's Urban Search and Rescue Team was working around the clock in two 12-hour shifts four days after the attacks on the Twin Towers (official FEMA photograph).

It has been over 10 years since that awful day, and questions of security still remain, but the larger question for me and all other firefighters is whether we, the emergency community, are prepared for another attack of that magnitude. Since 9/11, the Department of Homeland Security has taken a leading role in developing a national incident management system. Homeland Security Presidential Directive 5 mandated that federal, state, local and tribal governments establish a National Incident Management System.[7] Many fire departments view this federal directive as yet another unfunded mandate, but HSPD 5 is a good start, though more needs to be done. I doubt we will ever see enforceable emergency response standards in this country, let alone national training standards, but that is the only way to efficiently integrate different emergency services in response to large events that overwhelm local jurisdictions. Fire departments are better equipped, especially in the area of communication, to handle large events, and our training since 9/11 has utilized protocols that address the eventuality of another attack.

But is our country safer? That is not for me to answer. The National Commission on Terrorist Attacks Upon the United States, better known as the 9/11 Commission, studied the event and made many recommendations.[8]

Most of the recommendations directed toward emergency services have been implemented; however, many of the recommendations directed at federal agencies continue to languish because of inaction by Congress and turf wars between agencies. Unfortunately, Congress has a limited focus on the future — two years for representatives and six for senators. It is time for all the recommendations of the commission to be implemented because terrorism and weapons of mass destruction will forever be part of our lexicon. It would be inexcusable if another attack occurred on the United States with significant loss of life because of a failure of our government to enact measures urged by the bipartisan commission.

A career has a subtle way of nudging one toward the door. In our business, keeping up with recertification in a number of different disciplines was a constant grind, especially regarding emergency medicine. It was mandatory to earn continuing education units each year for my EMT certification — tough work for someone who hadn't treated a patient in years. I would beg the indulgence of a few kind paramedics, who would then walk me through the on-line training. Thank you to the guys at Station 27.

Keeping up with new technology was another part of the job that was becoming arduous. I had little interest in and no aptitude for computer technology, something that I had to use each day checking and writing reports. I'm forever in the debt of John Vanek, my EMS captain. He would see me struggling and guide me through the process.

The last straw for me was when they installed a Mobile Data Terminal in our command vehicle. I know there was a lot of very useful information available through the terminal, but I never used it — at least not for its intended pur-

Christopher Howes (courtesy Cindy Smith).

pose. In the morning I would place my coffee mug on the lid of the computer and place the map book on the seat. Then I would inspect my reading glasses; Gribble was known to lick Kermit Russell's glasses every once in a while before replacing them over the visor, and I knew I wasn't immune. Retirement was looking better and better.

On a more personal note, I want to thank my wife, Candy, for her support over these many years. I put on the uniform of a firefighter every third day for 31 years, kissed her goodbye and told her I loved her, and walked out the door. She always told me to be careful and stay safe, but she never knew what I was doing throughout the day; she never knew if I was truly safe. I would always call her toward the end of the day, usually a brief conversation about the day's events. I would save details about calls until I came home the next day. Sometimes it was difficult for me to leave my chief's hat at work, and she would remind me that she wasn't one of my men.

Reporting to work during hurricanes was particularly difficult for her. As a company officer and later as a chief officer, I was required to report for duty 12 hours before the storm and would remain on duty for the duration, sometimes two or three days. I would spend the day before the storm boarding up the house and laying in food and water and gasoline for the generator. I would put fresh batteries in the lanterns, stuff the cooler full of ice, and secure the outdoor furniture, all while keeping an eye on the Weather Channel. You couldn't tell whether it was day or night once the house was boarded; it was like a medieval fortress, especially with the air conditioner turned to the coldest setting possible. We would inevitably lose power, but it was nice to have the house cool for at least a day or two. After all those chores were completed, I would pack an extra jumpsuit and a cooler with bottled water, a jar of peanut butter and one of jelly, and a loaf of whole wheat bread, and then report for duty.

I am still amazed that I entered this profession simply by happenstance. And I can't imagine doing anything else for that length of time that would be so satisfying. There wasn't a day that I didn't look forward to going to work; few people can say that about their profession. I witnessed tremendous change in the way fire departments do business, transitioning from a good-old-boy system to a highly competent workforce that rivals any department in the country. I was blessed to be a part of this process, participating in and even influencing change along the way. I am proud to say that I have worked with the finest firefighters in the business.

Glossary

Aerial apparatus: Truck that has a hydraulically operated ladder, sometimes with a bucket at the end of the ladder. It may or may not have a pump.

Ambu-bag: Device that forces air into a patient's lungs by squeezing a bag that is attached to a mask.

Barway wrench: Specialized tool used to tighten couplings on booster hose.

Booster hose: Sometimes called redline — 1-inch diameter hose carried on a reel.

Brush truck: Specialized truck with a fire pump and large-capacity water tank designed for off-road use in fighting wildland fires.

Ciscoe load: Two accordian loads of hose, typically 150 feet of 1½ inch, connected to a gated wye and carried on top of the supply hose in the hose bed. This allows firefighters to pull the Ciscoe load off at the fire. The supply hose is then connected to the wye before the engine lays out to a water source.

Class A combustibles: Material such as wood or paper.

Class A pumper: Multipurpose fire truck that has a 1250-GPM pump, a 1000-gallon water tank, supply hose, and ground ladders.

Department of Homeland Security: The umbrella organization responsible for protecting states against terrorism.

Deuce and a half: Two-and-a-half-inch hose line.

Division: Geographical designation on an emergency scene. For instance, Division 2 would be the designation for the second floor of a building.

Double female: Appliance with female threads on each end that enables the male ends of fire hose to be coupled together.

Double male: Appliance with male threads on each end that enables the female ends of fire hose to be coupled together.

Draft: Method of supplying a fire pump with water from a static water supply, such as a pond or canal. Hard suction hose connected at the pump inlet to the water source allows atmospheric pressure to push water through the hose into the pump.

Drip torch: Canister that holds a mix of gasoline and diesel fuel used in wildland firefighting to ignite fires to establish control lines.

Endotracheal tube: Also called an ET tube — an airway adjunct device that is used by EMTs and paramedics to secure a patent airway.

Esophageal obturator airway: Also called an EOA — an airway adjunct device that is used by EMTs and paramedics to secure a patent airway.

Federal Emergency Management Institute: Organization responsible for assisting states in the management of natural and manmade disasters.

First due: Apparatus that is assigned to the initial alarm.

Flat-head axe: Axe with a bit and flat head.

Friction loss: Amount of pressure lost as water moves through hose, nozzles, and appliances.

Front line: Short section of pre-connected booster hose carried on the front of a brush truck — usually three-quarter-inch diameter.

Gated wye: Appliance with one inlet with female threads and two outlets with male threads. There are gate valves to control water flow to each outlet; it is used to supply water to two attack lines simultaneously.

Governor: Either a mechanical or electrical control mechanism that regulates water pressure.

Group: Crew assigned to a specific task. For instance, the vent group is responsible for ventilation of a building.

Halligan: Multipurpose tool with an adze shape on one end and a pick and fork at the other end; used for a variety of tasks on the fire ground.

Higbee-cut: Notch on fire hose coupling that is an alignment indicator.

Hot zone: Exclusion zone on an emergency incident where only those with proper training and the appropriate level of personal protective equipment are allowed to work.

International Association of Fire Fighters: The parent organization for fire department unions in the United States and Canada.

International Fire Chief Association: An organization that provides leadership opportunities for fire chiefs in the United States and Canada.

Left-hand search: Search crews entering a building begin their search by moving to the left, maintaining contact with the wall as they move through the building.

National Commission on Terrorist Attacks Upon the United States: Independent commission tasked with compiling a report on the circumstances that caused the 9/11 attacks. The report includes recommendations on what the United States needs to do to prevent future attacks.

National Emergency Training Center: The campus for the National Fire Academy and the Emergency Management Institute, based in Emmitsburg, Maryland. The mission of the NETC is to promote the professional development of firefighters and other emergency responders.

National Fire Academy: Operated and governed by the United States Fire Administration. It is the United States' preeminent training facility for fire service personnel.

National Fire Protection Administration: A trade association that administers the development of fire code standards.

Nomogram: Mathematical diagram used by wildland firefighters to figure a fire's rate of spread. This information is useful in determining number and types of resources needed to control a wildland fire.

Overhaul: A systematic search for hidden fire once a fire is extinguished.

PFD: Personal flotation device.

Pick-head axe: Axe with a bit and pointed pick.

Pike pole: Long-handled tool with a pointed end and hook used to open ceiling and walls.

Pre-connect: Hose line that is coupled to a discharge outlet and can be supplied immediately with tank water.

PTO: Power take off.

Pump panel: Area that controls all aspects of water flow on a fire engine.

Quint: A specialized apparatus that serves as both a fire engine and a ladder. It must have a fire pump with a minimum capacity of 1000 GPM, an aerial ladder with a waterway, a water tank with a minimum capacity of 300 gallons, supply hose and pre- connected attack lines, and ground ladders.

Reducer: Appliance that enables two hoses of different diameters to be coupled together.

Right-hand search: Search crews entering a building begin their search by moving to the right, maintaining contact with the wall as they move through the building.

Siamese: Appliance with two or more inlets with female threads and one outlet with male threads. Typically used to supplement water supply to a fire department connection or a fire pump.

Side A: Designation for the front of a building, typically the side facing the street.

Side B: Designation for the left side of a building.

Side C: Designation for the back of a building.

Side D: Designation for the right side of a building.

Skid load: Another name for a Ciscoe load.

Spanner wrench: Tool used to loosen or tighten hose couplings.

Supply hose: Hose carried in the hose bed that is used to supply the pump with water from either a hydrant or alternative water source. Supply hose diameter is typically two and a half, three, or five inches.

Tanker: Old terminology for tender. An airplane dropping retardant on a wildland fire is referred to as a tanker. With the advent of NIMS, some of the terminology has been updated.

Tender: Truck that carries a large amount of water.

United States Fire Administration: Part of the Federal Emergency Management Association and is responsible for fire safety in the United States. Its mission is to reduce the number of fatal fires within the United States.

Appendices

A: Palm Beach County Fire Control Districts

These 12 fire control district fire departments were the first volunteer departments to provide fire and emergency service to the predominately unincorporated areas within Palm Beach County.

Jupiter Fire Department	Fire Control District 1
Old Dixie Fire Department	Fire Control District 2
Juno Fire Department	Fire Control District 3
Military Park Fire Department	Fire Control District 4
Westward Fire Department	Fire Control District 5
Southwest Fire Department	Fire Control District 6
Trail Park Fire Department	Fire Control District 7
Tri-Community Fire Department	Fire Control District 8
Del-Trail Fire Department	Fire Control District 9
Reservation Fire Department	Fire Control District 10
Canal Point Fire Department	Fire Control District 11
Northwest Fire Department	Fire Control District 12

B: Fire District Consolidation Memo

Palm Beach County Inter-Office Communication from Commissioner Dennis Koehler to Commissioner Norman Gregory in reference to fire district consolidation.

Mr. Bailey

Inter-Office Communication
PALM BEACH COUNTY

TO Commissioner Norman R. Gregory   DATE November 14, 1979

FROM Commissioner Dennis P. Koehler   FILE

RE Fire District Consolidation

As you know, the <u>Miami Herald</u> recently completed its two-part report on the severe financial/labor paramedic service problems currently being experienced by the Del-Trail Fire District. I was pleased to see, again, your strong statements regarding the need for centralizing authority over these maverick fire districts and their often-unresponsive governing Boards.

Perhaps there's a silver lining in the clouded Del-Trail situation. It seems to me that we ought to discuss with the rest of the Commission the possibility of asking for special legislation from the 1980 Florida Legislature, giving our Board the power to create a county wide fire/paramedic authority. I believe that Commissioner Evatt might join us in requesting such legislation from our county delegation.

Clearly, residents of the unincorporated area are being short-changed in many ways by the great disparity in service, salaries, etc. between the various fire districts. Equally clearly, it seems to me, the time has come for the County Commission to seek authority to take comprehensive corrective action.

I suggest that we ask our county staff (attorney and Emergency Medical Services Director) to develop a package of information and a suggested resolution to our legislative delegation, giving the Board such sweeping fire control authority.

DPK:dhb
cc: Board of County
    Commissioners

SIGNED: *Dennis P Koehler*

C: Union Ballot

Copy of State of Florida Public Employees Relations Commission secret ballot that determined who was eligible to vote for a union and how many voted to unionize.

STATE OF FLORIDA

PUBLIC EMPLOYEES RELATIONS COMMISSION

FIRE FIGHTERS OF DEL-TRAIL, :
DISTRICT #9, LOCAL 2624, IAFF,:
                         :
      Petitioner,   :   Case No. RC-78-040
                         :
v.   : VERIFICATION OF ELECTION RESULTS
                         :   AND CERTIFICATION OF EXCLUSIVE
DEL-TRAIL FIRE DISTRICT #9, : COLLECTIVE BARGAINING REPRESENTATIVE
                         :
      Respondent.   :
                         :
                         :

Robert A. Sugarman, KAPLAN, DORSEY, SICKING & HESSEN, Miami,
attorney for petitioner.

James C. Crosland, MULLER, MINTZ, KORNREICH, CALDWELL & CASEY,
Miami, attorney for respondent.

PER CURIAM.

    A secret ballot election was conducted between November 13,
1978 and November 29, 1978 in the following unit:

          INCLUDED: Fire Fighter, Fire Fighter-Para-
              medic, Driver-Engineer, Lieuten-
              ant, and Fire Inspector.

          EXCLUDED: Fire Chief, Chief Executive Offi-
              cer, Executive Officer, Assistant
              Executive Officer, Fire Marshall,
              Chief Engineer, Training Officer,
              Rescue Officer, Captains and
              Secretary-Dispatcher.

    The election results are as follows:

1.   Approximate number of eligible voters   38

2.   Void Ballots   0

3.   Votes cast for Petitioner   32

4.   Votes cast against the participating

      organizations(s)   1

5.   Valid votes counted   33

6.   Challenged ballots   0

7.   Valid votes counted plus challenged ballots 33

8.   Challenges are not sufficient to affect the

      results of the election

    The Commission VERIFIES the results of the election
conducted between November 13, 1978 and November 29, 1978.
Petitioner received a majority of the valid votes plus

challenged ballots.

    Pursuant to Section 447.307(3)(b), Florida Statutes
(1977), the Commission CERTIFIES the Petitioner as the
exclusive bargaining representative for employees in the
unit described above. Certification number 442 is
issued to the Petitioner.

    It is so ordered.

                       PUBLIC EMPLOYEES RELATIONS COMMISSION

                       LEONARD A. CARSON, CHAIRMAN

                       MICHAEL M. PARRISH, COMMISSIONER

                       JEAN K. PARKER, COMMISSIONER

THIS IS TO CERTIFY that on
December 12, 1978, this
document was filed in the office
of the Public Employees Relations
Commission at Tallahassee, and a
copy served on each party at its
last known address.

PUBLIC EMPLOYEES RELATIONS COMMISSION
BY: _Charles F. McClamma_
         Clerk
          TITLE

D: PERC Letter, 1978

Copy of letter author wrote to PERC to document working conditions at Del-Trail Fire Department in 1978.

5/19/78

I am writing this deposition to try and describe what working conditions at Del-Trail Fire District #9 were like before the formation of Local 2624 of the I.A.F.F and what they are like now. I do not point a finger of blame at anyone but only tell what has happened and let the changes that have occured speak for themselves.

Prior to the formation of the Union we were allowed to cook breakfast in the fire house between 0700 and 0800 hrs. We were allowed to work on our personal cars after 1600hrs. We were allowed to take an extra shift day on our vacation if we worked a legal holiday prior to that vacation.

Since the formation of the Unionall of these priveliges have been revocked. The administration has also ruled that shifts working saturday will work all day and shifts working sunday will work one-half day. Prior to the Union a shift only work half a day on saturday and sunday our time was our own.

Sincerely,

Christopher T. Howes

I am giving this statement to support unfair labor practice filed by Local 2624 with P.E.R.C for use by P.E.R.C in the investigation for Local 2624. I understand this statement shall remain confidential and not to be released to anyone unless I am called to testify at an unfair labor practice hearing.

E: Contract, October 1979

This is a scan of the original contract and is accurate in all respects except for the numbers assigned to articles xxiii and xxiv. These two articles are numbered incorrectly in the body of the contract.

Copy of first contract negotiated between Local 2624 of the International Association of Fire Fighters and Del-Trail Fire Control District 9.

Oct 1979

DEVRIES

ARTICLE I

AGREEMENT

This Agreement is entered into by the DEL-TRAIL FIRE CONTROL DISTRICT NO. 9, hereinafter referred to as the "District" or the "Employer", and LOCAL 2624, INTERNATIONAL ASSOCIATION OF FIREFIGHTERS, hereinafter referred to as the "Employee Organization" or the "Union".

ARTICLE II

RECOGNITION

The District hereby recognizes the Employee Organization as the exclusive bargaining representative for all employees in the following appropriate unit:

INCLUDED: Firefighter, Firefighter-Paramedic, Driver-Engineer, Lieutenant, Fire Inspector and Assistant Fire Inspector.

EXCLUDED: Fire Chief, Chief Executive Officer, Executive Officer, Assistant Executive Officer, Fire Marshall, Chief Engineer, Training Officer, Rescue Officer, Captains and Secretary-Dispatcher.

ARTICLE III

NON-DISCRIMINATION

No employee covered by this Agreement will be discriminated against by the District or the Employee Organization with respect to any job benefits or other conditions of employment accruing from this agreement because of Union membership or non-Union membership.

ARTICLE IV

MANAGEMENT RIGHTS

1. The Employee Organization and its members recognize that the District has the exclusive right to manage and direct all of its operations. Accordingly, the District specifically, but not by way of limitation, reserves the exclusive right to:

(a) decide the scope of service to be performed and the method of service;

(b) hire, fire, demote, suspend (or otherwise discipline), promote, lay-off, and determine the qualifications of employees;

(c) transfer employees from location to location and from time to time;

(d) rehire employees;

(f) determine the starting and quitting time and the number of hours and shifts to be worked, subject to Article XIV;

(g) merge, consolidate, expand, or curtail or discontinue temporarily or permanently, in whole or in part, operations whenever in the sole discretion of the District good business judgment makes such curtailment or discontinuance advisable;

(h) contract and/or subcontract any existing or future work;

(i) expand, reduce, alter, combine, assign, or cease any job;

(j) determine whether and to what extent the
work required in its operation shall be performed by employees covered by this Agreement;

(k) control the use of equipment and property
of the District;

(l) determine the number, location, and operation
of headquarters, annexes, sub-stations and
divisions thereof;

(m) schedule and assign the work to the employees
and to determine the size and composition of the
work force;

(n) determine the services to be provided to the
public, and the maintenance procedures, materials,
facilities, and equipment to be used, and to
introduce new or improved services, maintenance
procedures, materials, facilities and equipment;

(o) formulate, amend, revise and implement policy,
rules and regulations;

(p) have complete authority to exercise those
rights and powers that are incidental to the rights
and powers enumerated above, including the right to
make unilateral changes.

2.   The above rights of the District are not all-inclusive
but indicate the type of matters or rights which belong to and
are inherent in the District in its capacity as management. Any
of the rights, powers, and authority the District had prior to
entering this collective bargaining agreement are retained by
the District, except as specifically abridged, delegated, granted
or modified by this Agreement. Those inherent common law management functions and prerogatives which the District has not

expressly modified or restricted by a specific provision of this Agreement are not in any way, directly or indirectly, subject to the grievance procedure.

3.   If the District fails to exercise any one or more of the above functions from time to time, this will not be deemed a waiver of the District's right to exercise any or all of such functions.

ARTICLE V

WORK STOPPAGES

1.   The Employee Organization agrees that, under no circumstances, shall there be any work stoppage, strike, sympathy strike, safety strike, jurisdictional dispute, walk-out, sit-down, stay-in, or any other concerted failure or refusal to perform assigned work for any reason whatsoever, or picketing in furtherance of any of the above prohibited activities, nor shall any bargaining unit personnel refuse to cross any picket line at any location, whether the picketing is being done by the Employee Organization or any other employee organization or union.

2.   The Employee Organization agrees that the District shall retain the right to discharge or otherwise discipline some or all of the employees participating in or promoting any of the activities enumerated in paragraph 1 above, and the exercise of such rights by the District will not be subject to recourse under the grievance/arbitration procedure.

3.   It is recognized by the parties that the activities enumerated in paragraphs 1 and 2 above are contrary to the ideals of professionalism and to the District's community responsibility. Accordingly, it is understood and agreed that in the event of any violation of this Article, the District shall be entitled to seek and obtain legal and/or equitable relief in any court of competent jurisdiction.

4.   For the purpose of this Article, it is agreed that the Employee Organization shall be responsible and liable for any act committed by its officers, agent, and/or representatives,

which act constitutes a violation of State law or the provisions
herein. In addition to all other rights and remedies available
to the District under State law, in the event of a breach of
the provisions herein, the District shall have the right to uni-
laterally and without further notice terminate this collective
bargaining agreement, withdraw recognition from the Employee
Organization, and cease dues deductions.

ARTICLE VI

GRIEVANCE AND ARBITRATION PROCEDURE

1. In a mutual effort to provide a harmonious working relationship between the parties to this Agreement, it is agreed and understood that there shall be a procedure for the resolution of grievances between the parties and that such procedure shall cover grievances involving the application or interpretation of this Agreement (subject to the provisions of paragraph 5, below).

2. Time is considered to be of the essence for purposes of this Article. Accordingly, any grievance not submitted or processed by the grieving party in accordance with the time limits provided below shall be considered conclusively abandoned and shall be barred, forfeited and foreclosed for all contractual or legal purposes and shall result in the forfeiture of all rights to arbitration. Any grievance not answered by management within the time limits provided below will automatically advance to the next higher step of the grievance procedure.

3. Grievances shall be presented in the following manner:

    Step 1: The employee shall first take up his grievance with the Training Officer within five (5) calendar days of the occurrence of the event(s) which gave rise to the grievance. Such grievance shall be presented to the Training Officer in writing, shall be signed by the employee, and shall specify: (a) the date of the alleged grievance; (b) the specific article or articles

of this Agreement allegedly violated; (c) all
facts pertaining to or giving rise to the
alleged grievance; and (d) the relief requested.
The Training Officer shall, within five (5)
calendar days after the presentation of the
grievance (or such longer period of time as is
mutually agreed upon), render his decision on
the grievance in writing;

Step 2: In the event that the employee is not
satisfied with the disposition of the grievance
in Step 1, he shall have the right to appeal
the Training Officer's decision to the Chief
Executive Officer within five (5) calendar days
of the date of issuance of the Training
Officer's decision. Such appeal must be accompanied by the filing of a copy of the original
written grievance together with a letter signed
by the employee requesting that the Training
Officer's decision be reversed or modified.
The Chief Executive Officer shall, within five
(5) calendar days of the appeal (or such longer
period of time as is mutually agreed upon),
render his decision in writing.

Step 3: In the event that the employee is not
satisfied with the disposition of the grievance
in Step 2, he shall have the right to appeal
the Chief Executive Officer's decision to the
Fire Chief within five (5) calendar days of the
date of issuance of the Chief Executive Officer's
decision. Such appeal must be accompanied by
the filing of a copy of the original written

grievance together with a letter signed by
the employee requesting that the Chief Executive Officer's decision be reversed or
modified. The Fire Chief, or his designee,
shall, within five (5) calendar days of the
appeal (or such longer period of time as is
mutually agreed upon), render his decision
in writing.

4.   Grievances under this collective bargaining agreement
shall be processed separately and individually. Only one
grievance shall be submitted to an arbitrator for decision in
any given case.

5.   It is recognized that the District has a Code or Regulations Governing Employment, which provides a procedure for
the resolution of grievances involving discharge, demotion, suspension or other disciplinary action. Accordingly, the parties
agree that any employee covered by this Agreement may, at his
option, pursue a grievance over discharge, suspension, demotion
or other disciplinary action through the procedures provided in
the aforesaid Code of Regulations Governing Employment or through
the grievance-arbitration procedure outlined herein. The selection
of one of the two available procedures (i.e., the grievance-arbitration procedure or the procedures provided in the Code of Regulations Governing Employment) for pursuing a grievance over discharge, suspension, demotion or other disciplinary action shall
effectively foreclose the employee (or the Employee Organization)
from pursuing the same grievance through the other available procedure.

6. In the event a grievance processed through the grievance procedure has not been resolved at Step 3 above, either party may request that the grievance be submitted to arbitration within seven (7) calendar days after the Fire Chief, or his designee, renders a written decision on the grievance. The arbitrator may be any impartial person mutually agreed upon by and between the parties. However, in the event the parties are unable to agree upon said impartial arbitrator, the parties shall jointly request the American Arbitration Association to furnish a panel of five (5) names from which each party shall have the option of striking two (2) names in alternating fashion, thus leaving the fifth (5th), which will give a neutral or impartial arbitrator.

7. The District and the employee shall mutually agree in writing as to the statement of the grievance to be arbitrated prior to the arbitration hearing, and the arbitrator, thereafter, shall confine his decision to the particular grievance thus specified. In the event the parties fail to agree on the statement of the grievance to be submitted to the arbitrator, the arbitrator will confine his consideration and determination to the written statement of the grievance presented in Step 1 of the grievance procedure. The arbitrator shall have no authority to change, amend, add to, subtract from, or otherwise alter or supplement this Agreement or any part thereof or amendment thereto. The arbitrator shall have no authority to consider or rule upon any matter which is stated in this Agreement not to be subject to arbitration or which is not a grievance as defined in this Agreement, except to the extent as specifically provided herein.

8. The arbitrator may not issue declaratory opinions and shall confine himself exclusively to the question which is presented to him, which question must be actual and existing.

9. Consistent with the provisions of the Florida Public Employees Relations Act, Chapter 447, et seq., it is mutually acknowledged and agreed that this collective bargaining agreement shall be administered within the amounts appropriated by the District for funding of the collective bargaining agreement. Accordingly, and notwithstanding any other provision of this collective bargaining agreement, the arbitrator shall have no authority, power, or jurisdiction to construe any provision of law, statute, ordinance, resolution, rule or regulation or provision of this collective bargaining agreement to result in, obligate, or cause the District to have or bear any expense, debt, cost, or liability which would result, directly or indirectly, in the District exceeding the amounts initially appropriated and approved by the District for funding of this collective bargaining agreement as agreed upon by the parties. Any such award which contravenes or is not in compliance with the provisions of this paragraph shall be null and void.

10. Each party shall bear the expense of its own witnesses and of its own representative or representatives for purposes of the arbitration hearing. The impartial arbitrator's fee and related expenses and expenses of obtaining a hearing room, if any, shall be equally divided between the parties. Any person desiring a transcript of the hearing shall bear the cost of such transcript unless both parties mutually agree to share such cost.

11. The arbitrator's award shall be final and binding on the parties.

12. Probationary employees shall have no right to utilize this grievance procedure for any matter concerning discharge, suspension or other discipline.

13. The Employee Organization shall not be required to process grievances for employees covered by this Agreement who are not members of the Employee Organization.

ARTICLE VII

DEPARTMENTAL RULES AND REGULATIONS

It is agreed and understood that each employee will be provided with a copy of any departmental manual which replaces, updates, and/or supersedes the present manual containing the department's rules and regulations. Any such new departmental manual shall be posted on the Department Bulletin Board at each station upon adoption, and shall be distributed to the employees as soon thereafter as practicable. The new departmental manual shall become effective upon posting on the Department Bulletin Board.

ARTICLE VIII

BULLETIN BOARDS

The District shall furnish at each station space for a bulletin board for the purpose of posting Employee Organization notices, which shall be strictly of an informational nature. Any notice or item placed on the bulletin board shall bear on its face the legible designation of the person responsible for placing such item or notice on the bulletin board. The Employee Organization will supply the bulletin board at each station. A copy of each notice or item to be posted shall be transmitted to the Fire Chief, prior to posting, for his approval or rejection. Such approval or rejection shall be within the sole discretion of the Fire Chief.

ARTICLE IX

LICENSES AND REGISTRATION FEES

The District agrees to maintain its present policy with regard to the payment of licenses and registration fees for the duration of this Agreement.

ARTICLE X

SHIFT EXCHANGES

Employees may exchange their working shifts with other employees of equal rank or comparable qualifications, with the approval of the fire chief or his designee. The determination of what constitutes "comparable qualifications" shall also be within the sole discretion of the fire chief or his designee.

ARTICLE XI

TUITION REIMBURSEMENT

The District agrees to maintain its current policy with respect to its Tuition Reimbursement for the duration of this Agreement.

ARTICLE XII

HOLIDAYS

1. The below listed holidays shall be granted for
both shift and non-shift personnel covered by this Agreement:

> New Year's Day
>
> Memorial Day
>
> Thanksgiving Day
>
> Labor Day
>
> Independence Day
>
> Christmas Day

2. Non-shift personnel will get the holiday off with
pay, at the employee's regular straight time rate of pay.

3. Shift personnel will receive one shift compensation
at the employee's regular straight time rate of pay. For
each holiday worked, the compensation day will be added to
the vacation time of the employee.

ARTICLE XIII

UNIFORMS

The District agrees to maintain its present policy
with regard to uniforms.

ARTICLE XIV

DUTY HOURS

1. Non-Shift Personnel: The normal work week for the
Fire Inspector shall consist of five (5) working days from
Monday through Friday, and shall normally be of forty (40)
hours' duration. A normal day shall begin at 8:00 A.M. and
continue through until 5:00 P.M.

2. Shift Personnel: The normal work week for the Fire
Department shall be an average of fifty-six (56) hours based
on a three shift system of twenty-four (24) hours of duty and
forty-eight (48) hours off duty. A normal shift shall begin
and end at 0700 hours. Nothing herein shall guarantee any
employee payment for a fifty-six (56) hour work week unless
the employee actually works fifty-six (56) hours or his
actual hours worked and his authorized compensated leave
total fifty-six (56) hours. For the purpose of this Agreement, authorized compensated leave shall mean leave compensated
under District policy.

3. Hours worked in excess of the regular fifty-six (56)
hour week as defined in Section 2 shall be compensated at
the rate of time-and-one-half of the employee's regular
straight time rate. However, no employee shall receive
straight time or time-and-one-half for time spent in correcting
work performed by the employee, which had been assigned and
was improperly performed during the employee's normal work
day. Further, nothing herein shall require the payment of
straight time or time-and-one-half when an insubstantial amount
of time is worked in excess of the normal workday. For the
purpose of this Article, an insubstantial amount of time shall
be considered any period of time less than one-half (1/2)
hours.

4. If an employee covered by this Agreement is called
out to work at a time outside his normal working hours, as

defined in paragraph 2, he shall receive a minimum of two
(2) hours' pay at the rate of time and one-half (1/2) his
regular straight time. However, an employee who has not
worked a fifty-six (56) hour work week as defined in paragraph 2, will be compensated for the call-out at his regular
straight time rate.

ARTICLE XV

FUNERAL LEAVE

1. Employees covered by this Agreement may be entitled
to funeral leave with pay for one (1) twenty-four (24) hour
shift in the event of a death in the employee's immediate
family which occurs within the State of Florida. Employees
covered by this Agreement may be entitled to funeral leave
with pay for two (2) twenty-four (24) hour shifts in the
event of a death in the employee's immediate family occurring
outside the State of Florida.

2. The immediate family shall be defined as wife, husband, son, daughter, brother, sister, father or mother of the
employee, or of the employee's spouse.

3. Proof of death in the immediate family as defined above
may be requested by the Fire Chief or his designee before compensation is approved.

4. The Fire Chief, in his sole discretion, may approve
additional time off.

5. It is agreed and understood that all funeral leave
shall be charged against sick leave.

ARTICLE XVI

INSURANCE

The District shall provide, within its sole discretion, hospitalization and liability insurance during the term of this Agreement. Further, this Article shall not be subject to the Grievance/Arbitration procedures (Article VI) contained in this Agreement.

ARTICLE XVII

PROMOTIONAL EXAMINATIONS

When notification of a promotional examination is posted, the District will make available one (1) copy of any reference material from which the test is derived and which is in its possession. The aforesaid reference material shall be available in the main Fire Station. Employees assigned to sub-stations may check out the aforesaid reference material from the main Fire Station for utilization at the sub-stations, provided that the District shall not in any manner be responsible for any reference material checked out of the main Fire Station, and shall be under no obligation to replace same. The procedures for checkout and return of said reference material shall be established by the District. All employees shall have the right to examine their examinations and test scores in the presence of the examining officer(s).

All promotional vacancies shall be filled in accordance with criteria established by the Fire Chief or his designee.

ARTICLE XVIII

SICK LEAVE

The District agrees to maintain its present policy regarding sick leave for the duration of this Agreement. However, the parties recognize that sick leave is a privilege -- not a benefit -- and that, from time to time, employees abuse this privilege. Accordingly, the parties further agree that the District may take any steps it deems appropriate to strictly administer and enforce the District's current sick leave policy in such a manner as to eliminate abuse of the sick leave privilege.

ARTICLE XIX

SENIORITY

Seniority shall consist of continuous accumulated paid
service with the District. Seniority shall be computed from
the date of hire, as recorded on the personnel action form.
Wherever applicable, seniority in rank shall have preference.
Seniority shall be utilized for the following purposes:

    A.   Vacations for each calendar year shall be drawn
        by employees on a basis of seniority preference;
        provided, however, that the District shall retain
        the right to disregard seniority preference in the
        event that it becomes necessary to do so in order
        to provide adequate coverage in any given vacation
        period. Nothing contained herein shall be inter-
        preted as restricting the District's right to
        cancel all vacations during any given period in
        the event of disaster or emergency;

    B.   In the event of personnel reduction, employees shall
        be laid off in the inverse order of their seniority
        in their classification; provided, however, that
        where two (2) or more employees have seniority
        standing within sixty (60) days of each other,
        the fire chief shall determine the order of layoff
        based on education and performance evaluation. If
        more than one classification is affected, an
        employee laid off from a higher classification
        shall be given an opportunity to revert to the
        next lower classification, provided that he is
        fully qualified to perform the work in that lower

classification. Upon reverting to a lower
classification, an employee's seniority shall
be determined by the date of his permanent
appointment to that classification.

Employees shall be recalled from layoff in accordance with
their seniority in the classification from which they were laid
off. No new employee shall be hired in any classification until
all employees on layoff status in that classification have had
an opportunity to return to work; provided, however, that in
the discretion of the Fire Chief, such employees are physically
and mentally capable of performing the work available at the
time of recall. No laid off employees shall retain recall
rights beyond twelve (12) months from date of layoff.

ARTICLE XX

CHECKOFF

Any member of the Employee Organization, who has submitted a properly executed dues deduction card or statement
to the Fire Chief or his designee in accordance with a format
prescribed or approved by the District may, by request in
writing, have his membership dues and uniform assessments
in the Employee Organization deducted from his wages. Dues
shall be deducted monthly and shall be transmitted to the
Employee Organization within thirty (30) days. However,
the District shall have no responsibility or any liability
for any monies once sent to the Employee Organization, nor
shall the District have any responsibility or any liability
for the improper deduction of dues. Further, the Employee
Organization shall hold the District harmless for non-intentional
errors in the administration of the dues deduction system.

It shall be the responsibility of the Employee Organization
to notify the Fire Chief or his designee of any change in the
amount of dues to be deducted at least sixty (60) days in advance
of said change. Under no circumstances shall the District be
required to deduct Employee Organization fines, penalties, or
assessments from the wages of any member.

Any member of the Employee Organization may, on thirty
(30) days' written notice to the District and the Employees
Organization, request that the District cease deducting dues
from his wages.

The Employee Organization agrees to pay the District $.30
(thirty cents) per member per deduction as a fee for the District's
deduction of membership dues and uniform assessments.

ARTICLE XXI

VACATIONS

The District agrees to maintain its present policy with regard to vacations.

ARTICLE XXII

WAGES

1. Employees covered by this Agreement shall receive a
five percent (5%) across-the-board wage adjustment effective
October 1, 1979, provided that said employees are still employed
by the District as of the date this Agreement is ratified by the
District; a five percent (5%) across-the-board wage adjustment
effective January 1, 1980; a five percent (5%) across-the-board
wage adjustment effective April 1, 1980; and a five percent (5%)
across-the-board wage adjustment effective July 1, 1980.

2. In addition to the above wage adjustments, a Paramedic
who is certified by the State of Florida shall receive a ten
percent (10%) wage adjustment effective October 1, 1979, provided that said Paramedic is still employed by the District
as of the date this Agreement is ratified by the District. However, should the Paramedic lose his State certification, for any
reason, he shall no longer receive the above ten percent (10%)
wage adjustment, but shall immediately return to Firefighter pay
status.

3. In addition to the wage adjustments provided in paragraph
1 of this Article, a Paramedic Lieutenant who is certified by the
State of Florida shall receive a fifteen percent (15%) wage adjustment effective October 1, 1979, provided that said Paramedic Lieutenant is still employed by the District as of the date this Agreement is ratified by the District. However, should the Paramedic
Lieutenant lose his State certification, for any reason, he shall
no longer receive the above fifteen percent (15%) wage adjustment,
but shall immediately return to Firefighter pay status.

ARTICLE XXIV

SEVERABILITY CLAUSE

Should any provision of this Collective Bargaining Agreement, or any part thereof, be rendered or declared invalid by reason of any existing or subsequently enacted legislation, or by any decree of a court of competent jurisdiction, all other Articles and Sections of this Agreement shall remain in full force and effect for the duration of this Agreement.

ARTICLE XXV

PROHIBITION AGAINST RE-OPENING OF NEGOTIATIONS

Except as specifically provided herein, neither party hereto shall be permitted to re-open or re-negotiate this Agreement or any part of this Agreement. This Agreement contains the entire agreement of the parties on all matters relative to wages, hours, working conditions, and all other matters which have been, or could have been negotiated by and between the parties prior to the execution of this Agreement.

The District, in its sole discretion, may re-open this Agreement for the sole purpose of negotiating additional provisions, or modification of existing provisions thereto where new federal or state legislation (or regulation) has created a hardship upon the City in implementing any of the terms of this Agreement. In that case, the parties, at the District's request, shall promptly meet to negotiate such new provisions, or revisions of existing provisions, as would alleviate the hardship upon the District.

ARTICLE XXV

TERM OF AGREEMENT

This Agreement shall be effective October 1, 1979 [with the exception of those provisions in Article XXII (Wages) requiring employees to be employed as of the date of ratification of this Agreement by the District] and shall remain in full force and effect until and including September 30, 1980.

DATED this __3rd__ day of __December__, 1979.

LOCAL 2624, INTERNATIONAL
ASSOCIATION OF FIREFIGHTERS

DEL-TRAIL FIRE CONTROL
DISTRICT NO. 9

F: *First Country Jam Flyer*

Flyer advertising the first Country Jam. Layout and artwork were created by Bill Rogers.

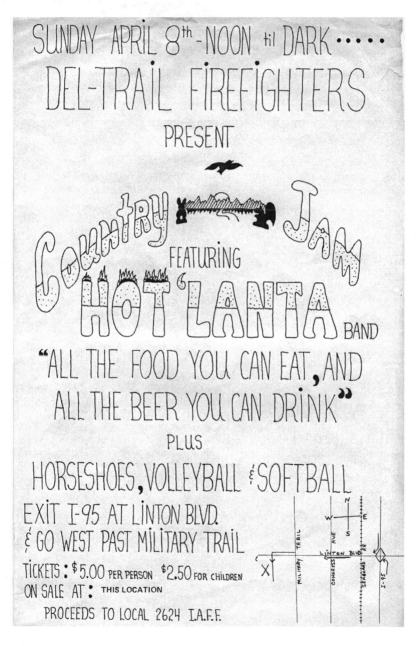

G: *Florida Firefighter Bill of Rights*

State of Florida Firefighter Bill of Rights. This is a legal document that protects the rights of firefighters whenever there is disciplinary action.

Firefighter Bill of Rights

Florida Statute 112.82 Rights of firefighters.--Whenever a firefighter is subjected to an interrogation, such interrogation shall be conducted pursuant to the terms of this section.

(1) The interrogation shall take place at the facility where the investigating officer is assigned, or at the facility which has jurisdiction over the place where the incident under investigation allegedly occurred, as designated by the investigating officer.

(2) No firefighter shall be subjected to interrogation without first receiving written notice of sufficient detail of the investigation in order to reasonably apprise the firefighter of the nature of the investigation. The firefighter shall be informed beforehand of the names of all complainants.

(3) All interrogations shall be conducted at a reasonable time of day, preferably when the firefighter is on duty, unless the importance of the interrogation or investigation is of such a nature that immediate action is required.

(4) The firefighter under investigation shall be informed of the name, rank, and unit or command of the officer in charge of the investigation, the interrogators, and all persons present during any interrogation.

(5) Interrogation sessions shall be of reasonable duration and the firefighter shall be permitted reasonable periods for rest and personal necessities.

(6) The firefighter being interrogated shall not be subjected to offensive language or offered any incentive as an inducement to answer any questions.

(7) A complete record of any interrogation shall be made, and if a transcript of such interrogation is made, the firefighter under investigation shall be entitled to a copy without charge. Such record may be electronically recorded.

(8) An employee or officer of an employing agency may represent the agency, and an employee organization may represent any member of a bargaining unit desiring such representation in any proceeding to which this part applies. If a collective bargaining agreement provides for the presence of a representative of the collective bargaining unit during investigations or interrogations, such representative shall be allowed to be present.

(9) No firefighter shall be discharged, disciplined, demoted, denied promotion or seniority, transferred, reassigned, or otherwise disciplined or discriminated against in regard to his or her employment, or be threatened with any such treatment as retaliation for or by reason solely of his or her exercise of any of the rights granted or protected by this part.

H: NIMS Management Model

This is the model developed by the National Incident Management System to manage personnel and resources. It is designed as an all-risk model capable of expanding or contracting as the incident dictates. This model has been adopted by all emergency services to better coordinate diverse resources and different agencies that may be called upon to work together on a single incident.

NIMS Model Incident Command System

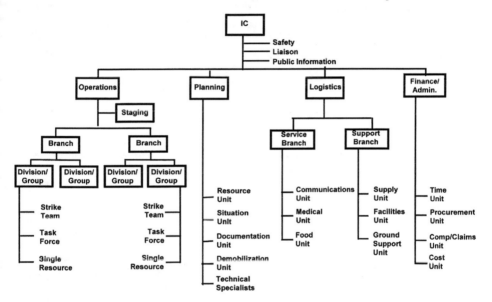

I: Graduation Speech

These are my remarks to the officer candidates of Class 1 after they received their lieutenant's badges.

Good evening, gentlemen:

The fire service has a long history of overcoming obstacles to get the job done. We've been taught that if a strategy is not working, we make adjustments. We've been taught to think ahead, to anticipate needs, and to manage our resources to ensure the best possible outcome during an emergency situation. This is a history and a tradition that we can be proud of.

Another part of the fire service history that we don't talk about as much is our reluctance to accept or effect change when it comes to managing our most precious resource, the people we work with and the people that you, as newly promoted lieutenants, are now responsible for. This part of our history is not one we are proud of, and it is a tradition that we must change.

The training that you received during the past two weeks didn't answer all of your questions and it won't make you seasoned fire officers. Only time and experience on the job will make you truly comfortable and capable in your new positions. The training that you received has, however, forced you to think about your own strengths and weaknesses, and hopefully it has provided you with a mechanism for developing those strengths and overcoming those weaknesses. The training that you received has given you the opportunity to effect change in this fire department. And the training that you received has given you the skills necessary to help other people accept this change.

With this promotion you have been given much more than a responsibility. You have also been given a trust. Be honest with the people you will be working with, and be honest with yourself. I wish you success, gentlemen. I applaud each of you.

Chapter Notes

Chapter 1

1. *10th* Anniversary Yearbook, Palm Beach County Fire-Rescue (1984–1994), 36.

Chapter 2

1. *10th Anniversary Yearbook*, Palm Beach County Fire-Rescue (1984–1994), 30.
2. Ibid., 4.
3. Florida minimum fire training standards require 398 hours of training (see http://www.myfloridacfo.com/sfm/bfst/bfst _index.htm).
4. *10th Anniversary Yearbook*, Palm Beach County Fire-Rescue (1984–1994), 32.
5. Ibid., 38.
6. S. Anderson, "Fire District Consolidation Plan Will Go to Legislature," *Sun-Sentinel*, February 23, 1983.
7. S. Nichols, "County Seeks to Alleviate Worries Stemming from Fire Consolidation," *Sun-Sentinel*, February 11, 1983.
8. *10th Anniversary Yearbook*, Palm Beach County Fire-Rescue (1984–1994), 39.
9. Ibid.
10. The Commission on Fire Accreditation International falls under the umbrella of the Center for Public Safety Excellence, a nonprofit agency that provides accreditation services for emergency organizations worldwide (see http://www.publicsafetyexcellence. org). For information specific to the process for Palm Beach County Fire-Rescue, see http://www.pbcfr.org.
11. *10th Anniversary Yearbook*, Palm Beach County Fire-Rescue (1984–1994), 3.

Chapter 3

1. A training video depicting a church raise can be viewed at http://www.youtube. com/watch?v=1h1BZKXRZFY.
2. Video footage demonstrating the use of a Pompier ladder can be viewed at http://

www.fireserviceinfo.com/pompierladders.h tml.
3. C. McCabe and B. Brown, "Esophageal Obturator Airway, ET Tube, and Pharyngeal-Tracheal Lumen Airway," *American Journal of Emergency Medicine* 4, no. 1 (1986): 64–71.

Chapter 4

1. P. Brodeur, "Migrant Farm Workers Today and Tomorrow" (PDF), Voice of the Poor (2006), http://www.voiceofthepoor.org/ Presentations/MIGRANT%20FARM%20W ORKERS.pdf.

Chapter 5

1. R. Hodges, personal communication, August 25, 2011.
2. Additional information on lung disease in firefighters and the complete text of this article can be found at the IAFF website (http://www.iaff.org/hs/resi/lung_disease_i n_fire_fighters.htm).

Chapter 6

1. Original record of signed union cards and photocopy of bank draft.
2. S. Brown, "Hydrants Are Off; Cold War Goes On," *Boca Raton News*, July 7, 1977.
3. M. Robinson, "Judge Tells City to Turn Water On," *Boca Raton News*, July 24, 1977.
4. B. Berlow, "Fire Inspector Wants Out, Says He's Not Qualified," *Boca Raton News*, February 21, 1979, 1A, 8B.
5. Ibid.
6. P. Gordon, "Chief Frye May Face Charges Over Reservist," *Sun-Sentinel*, March 20, 1979.
7. C. Cioe, "Pickets Take to the Road to 'Fire' Up Citizens," *Boca Raton News*, August 12, 1979, 5A, 2C.

8. B. Berlow, "Two Del-Trail Firemen Resign; More Expected," *Boca Raton News*, January 12, 1979, 1A.

9. Editorial, "Work Slowdown Can Hurt Cause of Firefighters," *Sun-Sentinel*, August 14, 1979, 18A.

10. Editorial, "Del-Trail Firemen Deserve Fair Wages," *Miami Herald*, November 11, 1979, 2B.

11. B. Berlow, "Del-Trail Firemen Play 'Wait-See' Game," *Boca Raton News*, May 21, 1979.

12. T. Kastanotis, "Del-Trail Fire Talks Suffer Breakdown," *Boca Raton News*, July 20, 1979, 1A.

13. M. Robinson, "Del-Trail Budget Receives Tentative Approval," *Boca Raton News*, August 22, 1979.

14. T. Kastanotis, "Del-Trail Officials Study Union's Proposal," *Boca Raton News*, August 28, 1979.

15. R. Hodges, personal communication, August 25, 2011.

16. C. Lawrence, personal communication, August 24, 2011.

17. T. Kastanotis, "Struggling Del-Trail Negotiators Resume Talks," *Boca Raton News*, August 28, 1979.

18. S. Nichols, "Impasse Declared in Del-Trail's Fire Talks," *Sun-Sentinel*, September 10, 1981.

19. J. Harris, "Single Fire District Decision Due," *Sun-Sentinel*, February 14, 1983.

Chapter 7

1. J. Brier, personal communication, August 12, 2011.

2. This voluntary reporting system is affiliated with the International Association of Fire Fighters and the International Fire Chiefs Association (see http://www.firefighter nearmiss.com).

3. This program is administered through FEMA (see http://www.fema.gov/firegrants/safer/index.shtm).

Chapter 8

1. The United States Department of Labor Occupational Safety and Health Administration established rules addressing respiratory-protection requirements for firefighters. This standard is supported by the International Association of Fire Fighters and the International Fire Chiefs Association (see http://www.iaff.org/hs/PDF/2in2out.pdf).

Chapter 9

1. Author's personnel file.

2. Official correspondence from Palm Beach County personnel file.

3. R. Pausch, *Really Achieving Your Childhood Dreams* (DVD) (Pittsburgh: Network Media Group, Carnegie Mellon University, 2007), www.cmu.edu/randyslecture.

4. M. McCutcheon, *The Final Theory: Rethinking Our Scientific Legacy* (Boca Raton, FL: Universal Publishers, 2002).

Chapter 11

1. R. Shmitz, "Extrication Tips: The Evolution of the Air Chisel," *Canadian Firefighter and EMS Quarterly (2011), http://www.fire fightingincanada.com/content/view/2928/213.*

2. M. Turnbell and D. Williams, "Canal Deaths Defy Easy Solution," *Sun-Sentinel*, November 18, 2001.

Chapter 12

1. C. Howes, "A Quicker Compass," *Fire Chief* 39, no. 5 (1995): 82–84.

Chapter 13

1. For more information on Critical Incident Stress Management, see http://www.drjeffmitchell.com.

2. J. Mitchell and G. Everly, *Critical Incident Stress Debriefing: An Operations Manual for the Prevention of Traumatic Stress among Emergency Services and Disaster Workers, revised edition* (Ellicott City, MD: Chevron, 1996).

3. C. Jung, *Memories, Dreams, Reflections,* edited by Aniela Jaffé and translated by Richard and Clara Winston (New York: Vintage Books, 1989).

Chapter 14

1. Palm Beach County no longer conducts water rescue with helicopters; however, Miami-Dade Fire Department continues to provide that service. Additional information on helicopter water rescue can be found on Miami-Dade Fire Department's website (http://www.miamidade.gov/mdfr/emergency_special_air.asp).

2. Additional information about rescue diver training can be found on Dive International's website (http://www.diverescue intl.com).

3. G. Haupt, *Drowning Investigations*, FBI law enforcement bulletin (2006), *Law enforcement bulletin*. Retrieved from http://www.findarticles.com/p/articles/mi_m2194/is_2_75/ai_n16111608/pg_2/?tag=content;coll.

4. C. Howes, "Hazmat Case Study: The Call to the Mall," *Fire Chief* 38, no. 7 (1994): 50–53.

5. For a chronology of the 2001 anthrax events, see http://www.Sun-Sentinel.com/news/local/palmbeach/sfl-1013anthraxchronology,0,4805314.story.

Chapter 16

1. K. Austin, personal communication, August 29, 2011.

2. J. Rogers, personal communication, August 29, 2011.

3. K. Austin, personal communication, August 29, 2011.

4. U.S. National Library of Medicine, "Cardiac Tamponade," *PubMed Health* (May 2010), http://www.ncbi.nlm.nih.gov/pubmedhealth/PMH0001245.

5. Reprinted with kind permission from Bill's wife, Roseanne Rogers.

Chapter 17

1. J. Brier, personal communication, August 12, 2011.

Chapter 18

1. *ICS-300: Intermediate ICS for Expanding Incidents* (student manual), Emergency Management Institute course number: G300. Additional information about NIMS can be found through the FEMA website (http://www.fema.gov/NIMS).

2. In 1970 California experienced devastating wildfires that claimed 16 lives and destroyed 700 structures. Congress mandated that the state of California and the California Division of Forestry develop a plan to integrate diverse resources to mitigate future incidents of that magnitude. This led to the first formal incident management plan: Firefighting Resources of California Organized for Potential Emergencies (FIRESCOPE) (see http://www.fema.gov/txt/nims/nims_ics_position_paper.txt).

3. *ICS-300: Intermediate ICS for Expanding Incidents* (student manual), Emergency Management Institute course number: G300. See FEMA website for additional information on the use of plain language (http://www.fema.gov.NIMS).

4. Palm Beach County Fire-Rescue dispatch protocols (protocols are subject to change). Visit PBCFR's website for up-to-date and additional information on the latest protocols (http://www.pbcfr.org).

5. C. Howes, "Worthy of a PAT on the Back," *Fire Chief* 41, no. 11 (November 1997): 50–55.

Chapter 19

1. "Smoke Diver's School Isn't For the Fainthearted," *Sarasota Journal*, November 20, 1978, http://www.news.google.com/newspapers?nid=1798&dat=19781121&id=3hQhAAAAIBAJ&sjid=gI4EAAAAIBAJ&pg=6487,3393802.

2. Taken from the author's Del-Trail Fire Department personnel file.

3. C. Howes, "Management Skills for Fire Service Officers" (bachelor's thesis, Palm Beach Atlantic College, West Palm Beach, Florida, 1993).

4. For additional information on the certification criteria for Florida Burn Boss, visit the Florida Division of Forestry website (http://www.fl-dof.com).

5. For more information, see "The Yellowstone Fires of 1988" (PDF), National Park Service (2008), http://www.nps.gov/yell/planyourvisit/upload/firesupplement.pdf.

6. C. Howes, "Wildland Fire," *Forum for Applied Research and Public Policy* 14, no. 1 (1999): 30–34.

7. Joint Fire Science Program, "The Rothermel Fire-Spread Model: Still Running Like a Champ," *Fire Science Digest* 2 (March 2008), http://www.firescience.gov/Digest/FSdigest2.pdf.

Chapter 20

1. For additional information on suppression of wildland fires and tractor-plows, see the Florida Department of Agriculture and Consumer Services website (http://www.fl-dof.com).

2. J. Butler, *Wildfire Loose: The Week Maine Burned* (Kennebunkport, ME: Durrell, 1978).

3. See M. Schwed, "The Nine Lives of Bobo," *Palm Beach Post*, July 13, 2005, http://www.palmbeachpost.com/accent/content/accent/epaper/2005/07/13/a1E_bobo_0713.html.

Chapter 21

1. J. Gribble, personal communication, September 15, 2011.

2. Yale University students Marshall Dodge and Robert Bryan recorded the first *Bert and I* album in 1958. *Bert and I* is synonymous with Down East Maine humor. For more information, see http://www.islandportpress.com.

Chapter 23

1. The information about the department is both from my own knowledge gained over a 31-year career and from the official department website. Because Palm Beach County Fire-Rescue is a dynamic and ever-changing organization, information cited in this chapter will change over time. For the latest information, visit PBCFR's website (http://www.pbcfr.org).

Chapter 24

1. R. Ditch, "Applying the Principles of Command and Control to the Employment of Emergency Services in the Air Force" (applied research project for the Executive Development Program, National Fire Academy, 1999).

2. For official White House press release, see http://www.medalofvalor.gov/awardees_09.html. For official White House photographs, see http://www.whitehouse.gov/the-press-office/2010/09/22/background-todays-medal-valor-ceremony.

3. E. O'Berry, personal communication, September 19, 2011.

4. C. Howes, "A Two-Way Street: Communication Lessons Learned On the Highway," *Fire Rescue Magazine* 15, no. 7 (September 1997): 37–40.

5. Additional information about Task Force 2 can be found on Miami-Dade Fire Department's website (http://www.miamidade.gov/mdfr/usar/asp).

6. J. Bartlett, personal communication, September 16, 2011.

7. *ICS-300: Intermediate ICS for Expanding Incidents* (student manual), Emergency Management Institute course number: G300 (2–8).

8. For more information on the conclusions and recommendations of the National Commission on Terrorist Attacks Upon the United States, see http://www.9–11commission.gov/report/index.htm.

Bibliography

Aehlert, B. *Paramedic Practice Today*. Volume 2. St. Louis: Mosby, 2009.

Anderson, S. "Fire District Consolidation Plan Will Go to Legislature." *Sun-Sentinel*. February 23, 1983.

Berlow, B. "Del-Trail Firemen Play 'Wait-See' Game." *Boca Raton News*. May 21, 1979.

_____. "Fire Inspector Wants Out, Says He's Not Qualified." *Boca Raton News*. February 21, 1979.

_____. "Two Del-Trail Firemen Resign; More Expected." *Boca Raton News*. January 12, 1979.

Brodeur, P. "Migrant Farm Workers Today and Tomorrow" (PDF). Voice of the Poor (2006). http://www.voiceofthepoor.org/Presentations/MIGRANT%20FARM%20WORKERS.pdf.

Brown, S. "Hydrants Are Off; Cold War Goes On." *Boca Raton News*. July 7, 1977.

Butler, J. *Wildfire Loose: The Week Maine Burned*. Kennebunkport: Durrell, 1978.

Cioe, C. "Pickets Take to the Road to 'Fire' Up Citizens." *Boca Raton News*. August 12, 1979.

Ditch, R. "Applying the Principles of Command and Control to the Employment of the Emergency Services in the Air Force." Applied research project for the Executive Development Program, National Fire Academy, 1999.

Editorial. "Del-Trail Firemen Deserve Fair Wages." *Miami Herald*. November 11, 1979.

_____. "Work Slowdown Can Hurt Cause of Firefighters." *Sun-Sentinel*. August 14, 1979.

Gordon, P. "Chief Frye May Face Charges Over Reservist." *Sun-Sentinel*. March 20, 1979.

Harris, J. "Single Fire District Decision Due." *Sun-Sentinel*. February 14, 1983.

Haupt, G. Drowning Investigations. FBI law enforcement bulletin, 2006.

Howes, C. "Hazmat Case Study: The Call to the Mall." *Fire Chief* 38, no. 7 (1994): 50–53.

_____. "Management Skills for Fire Service Officers." Bachelor's thesis, Palm Beach Atlantic College, West Palm Beach, Florida, 1993.

_____. "A Quicker Compass." *Fire Chief* 39, no. 5 (1995): 82–84.

_____. "A Two-Way Street: Communication Lessons Learned on the Highway." *Fire Rescue Magazine* 15, no. 7 (1997): 37–40.

_____. "Wildland Fire." *Forum for Applied Research and Public Policy* 14, no. 1 (1999): 30–34.

_____. "Worthy of a PAT on the Back." *Fire Chief* 41, no. 11 (1997): 50–55.

ICS-300: Intermediate ICS for Expanding Incidents (student manual). Emergency Management Institute. September 2005.

Joint Fire Science Program. "The Rothermel Fire-Spread Model: Still Running Like a Champ." *Fire Science Digest* 2 (March 2008). http://www.firescience.gov/Digest/FSdigest2.pdf.

Jung, C. *Memories, Dreams, Reflections*. Edited by Aniela Jaffé. Translated by Richard and Clara Winston. New York: Vintage, 1989.

Kastanotis, T. "Del-Trail Fire Talks Suffer

Breakdown." *Boca Raton News*. July 20, 1979.

_____. "Del-Trail Officials Study Union's Proposal." *Boca Raton News*. August 28, 1979.

_____. "Struggling Del-Trail Negotiators Resume Talks." *Boca Raton News*. August 28, 1979.

McCabe, C., and B. Brown. "Esophageal Obturator Airway, ET Tube, and Pharyngeal-Tracheal Lumen Airway." *American Journal of Emergency Medicine* 4, no. 1 (1986): 64–71.

McCutcheon, M. *The Final Theory: Rethinking Our Scientific Legacy*. Boca Raton: Universal, 2002.

Mitchell, J., and G. Everly. *Critical Incident Stress Debriefing: An Operations Manual for the Prevention of Traumatic Stress among Emergency Services and Disaster Workers*. Revised edition. Ellicott City, MD: Chevron, 1996.

Nichols, S. "County Seeks to Alleviate Worries Stemming from Fire Consolidation." *Sun-Sentinel*. February 11, 1983.

_____. "Impasse Declared in Del-Trail's Fire Talks." *Sun-Sentinel*. September 10, 1981.

Pausch, R. "Really Achieving Your Childhood Dreams" (DVD). Pittsburgh: Network Media Group, Carnegie Mellon University, 2007. www.cmu.edu/randyslecture.

Robinson, M. "Del-Trail Budget Receives Tentative Approval." *Boca Raton News*. August 22, 1979.

_____. "Judge Tells City to Turn Water On." *Boca Raton News*. July 24, 1977.

Schwed, M. "The Nine Lives of Bobo." *Palm Beach Post*. July 13, 2005. http://www.palmbeachpost.com/accent/content/accent/epaper/2005/07/13/a1E_bobo_0713.html.

Shmitz, R. "Extrication Tips: The Evolution of the Air Chisel." *Canadian Firefighter and EMS Quarterly* (2011). http://www.firefightingincanada.com/content/view/2928/213.

"Smoke Diver's School Isn't for the Fainthearted." *Sarasota Journal*. November 20, 1978. http://www.news.google.com/newspapers?nid=1798&dat=19781121&id=3hQhAAAAIBAJ&sjid=gI4EAAAAIBAJ&pg=6487,3393802.

10th Anniversary Yearbook. Palm Beach County Fire-Rescue, 1984–1994.

Turnbell, M., and D. Williams. "Canal Deaths Defy Easy Solution." *Sun-Sentinel*. November 18, 2001.

U.S. National Library of Medicine. "Cardiac Tamponade." *PubMed Health* (May 2010). http://www.ncbi.nlm.nih.gov/pubmedhealth/PMH0001245.

"The Yellowstone Fires of 1988" (PDF). National Park Service (2008). http://www.nps.gov/yell/planyourvisit/upload/firesupplement.pdf.

Index

Numbers in **bold italics** indicate pages with photographs.